# Cambridgeshire Kitcheners

# Cambridgeshire
# Kitcheners

## A History of the 11th (Service) Battalion (Cambs) Suffolk Regiment

Joanna Costin

Pen & Sword
**MILITARY**

First published in Great Britain in 2016 by
Pen & Sword Military
an imprint of
Pen & Sword Books Ltd
47 Church Street
Barnsley
South Yorkshire
S70 2AS

ISBN 978 1 47386 900 4

A CIP catalogue record for this book is available from the British
Library

Typeset in Ehrhardt by
Mac Style Ltd, Bridlington, East Yorkshire
Printed and bound in the UK by CPI Group (UK) Ltd,
Croydon, CRO 4YY

Pen & Sword Books Ltd incorporates the imprints of Pen & Sword
Archaeology, Atlas, Aviation, Battleground, Discovery, Family
History, History, Maritime, Military, Naval, Politics, Railways, Select,
Transport, True Crime, and Fiction, Frontline Books, Leo Cooper,
Praetorian Press, Seaforth Publishing and Wharncliffe.

For a complete list of Pen & Sword titles please contact
PEN & SWORD BOOKS LIMITED
47 Church Street, Barnsley, South Yorkshire, S70 2AS, England
E-mail: enquiries@pen-and-sword.co.uk
Website: www.pen-and-sword.co.uk

# Contents

# Introduction

The Cambridgeshire Kitcheners, or 11th (Service) Battalion (Cambs) Suffolk Regiment, to give it its official title, was one of a multitude of 'Pals' or 'Chums' battalions formed across the UK during the First World War. Raised in Cambridgeshire and the Isle of Ely, officered in large part by university men who had been part of the Officer Training Corps, the Kitcheners went to France in 1916 and saw their first major action on 1 July 1916, the first day of the Battle of the Somme. Despite suffering staggering casualties – 188 men killed on that one day, with the casualty total reaching 205 when those who died of wounds soon after are included – the battalion continued to fight throughout the remainder of the war, seeing action during the Battle of Arras, the German Spring Offensive and the Allies' Hundred Days campaign at the close of the war.

During the war the Kitcheners suffered around 970 men killed and numerous others wounded and taken prisoner (exact figures are hard to come by, as those logged in the war diary as 'missing' might be prisoners, dead, wounded, or simply men separated from the rest but who returned unharmed). About 4,500 men passed through the battalion, including those who were transferred out for reasons other than wounds. With the exception of one website and a mention on another First World War commemorative website, however, the battalion is largely unknown, even in Cambridge. Other Pals battalions have become famous (most notably the Accrington Pals, thanks in large measure to Peter Whelan's play) and the Sheffield City Battalion was immediately commemorated and had an old pals association in the years following the war. Perhaps because Cambridge also had a Territorial Regiment, one battalion of which went abroad on active service, with three others remaining at home as training battalions, perhaps because of high casualties and the fact that men were drawn from all areas of the county and Isle, the battalion seems almost to have been forgotten.

Much of the information behind this book is drawn from battalion, brigade and division war diaries and local newspapers. Thanks are due to the staff at the Cambridgeshire Collection, who have been very helpful both in suggesting materials and in assisting, without laughing, when the microfilm machine (used to read the local newspapers) ran away with me. There were a small number of interviews recorded with veterans in the 1970s and 80s, held at the Imperial War Museum, and a small number of documents survive at the Bury St Edmund's branch of the Suffolk Record Office. The Shire Hill office of the Cambridgeshire Record Office holds the records of the Territorial Association (which raised the battalion) and more general records relating to the First World War (particularly training documents) have been consulted at the Imperial War Museum and at the National Archives.

Valuable help has been given by Phil Curme, who maintains the sole website devoted to the battalion. This can be found at www.curme.co.uk. Tony Beeton has shared his research into Sidney Beeton and Arthur Josiah Elbourne and kindly allowed me to use his family letters, photos and memories. Paul Hammond of Perth has also shared his family history with me. Thanks also to Janice Ellam for assistance with some of the Balsham soldiers. Professor David Reynolds first directed my attention towards the Pals battalions and supervised my initial research into the Accrington Pals. It was while researching them that I first came across mention of a Cambridgeshire equivalent. Thanks are also due to Nicola, who supplied countless cups of tea and somewhere to work while this was being written. Any typos I will blame on the cat!

I would also like to thank Irene Moore for editing the book and the team at Pen & Sword.

Finally, without the website Lives of the First World War, created and maintained by the Imperial War Museum, much of the research into the personal details of members of the battalion could not have been carried out. The site platform has enabled research using medal records, census returns, BMD data and other military records.

*Chapter 1*

# Recruitment

The Cambridgeshire Kitcheners were formed less from a sense of local pride, which inspired the formation of many of the other Pals battalions, nor from a social class (as in the Public Schools Brigade or the Sportsmen's battalions), than because of an overflow of recruits for general service. In September, the Bury St Edmunds depot of the Suffolk Regiment – the nearest Regular unit and the one to which most Cambridge men who attested for general service were being sent – was full to overflowing. They requested that no more men be sent, so the men who joined up were gathered into the Corn Exchange in Cambridge and began taking over various local schools for barracks, as well as erecting tents. Preliminary training began to be conducted on Parker's Piece, and it was decided to apply to the War Office for permission to keep these men all together and to form a 'Pals' or 'Chums' or 'Kitchener' battalion (the local papers never quite appear to have agreed on what the battalion should be called, but the most common references are to the 'Kitcheners' and the 'Cambs Suffolks').

That said, once the Cambridgeshire Kitcheners were formed, the local newspapers were keen to emphasise what an honour it was to the county to have been given this task. The *Cambridge Daily News* exhorted readers:

> *'It was from East Anglia that Cromwell drew his Ironsides, those famous soldiers by whose aid he banished from England the doctrine of the divine right of kings. Let the successors of the Ironsides come forward in increasing numbers and help our modern Cromwell to smash the equally blasphemous pretensions of the homicidal maniac who is ravaging Europe.'*

This comparison with Cromwell's Ironsides was frequently made, and the intention was that the battalion would be (according to the *Cambridge Weekly*

*News)* '*the envy of the neighbourhood, and if it had the chance to fight it would be the terror of their opponents.*'

It was very much a county, not a Cambridge, battalion, as emphasised by the *Wisbech Standard*'s editor in response to a letter from 'Citizen' who suggested towards the end of October 1914 that the Isle and county was behind in recruiting and patriotic fervour. With a Cambridge Regular battalion in the offing, '*why not an Ely Battalion of the Suffolk Regiment or Wisbech Battalion of the Suffolk Regiment? Let not the Isle allow this Borough Battalion to be raised alone.*' The editor, unsurprisingly upset at seeing his area disparaged in this way, replied:

> '*Our correspondent appears to be under quite a wrong impression. The new Battalion of the Suffolk Regiment is not associated exclusively with Cambridge; it represents the whole of the county, including the Isle of Ely, and as the requisite number of recruits has not been obtained to complete the*

Market Place, Wisbech. Postcard sent in 1910. At least 27 members of the battalion came from this town. Wisbech had its own recruiting station, and so many members of the battalion who joined from nearby villages would have enlisted there rather than at Cambridge. (*Author's collection*)

*strength of the County Battalion, we cannot expect to have other battalions formed until that has been accomplished. The Isle has contributed largely to the Forces --ED.'*

Unlike in most other areas of the country where municipal authorities or local worthies took charge of raising a Pals battalion, in Cambridgeshire the task fell to the Cambridgeshire and Isle of Ely Territorial Force Association. This body was also responsible for the Cambridgeshire Regiment – a Territorial Regiment which sent one battalion overseas in February 1915 and raised a reserve battalion for home service into which those men who were unable or unwilling to volunteer for service abroad were combined with new recruits to form a second line battalion. By the end of the war, the Cambridgeshire Regiment had expanded to include the front line battalion overseas and three home battalions. The head of the Territorial Force Association was Charles Robert Whorwood Adeane, whose seat was at Babraham Hall. He was much involved with agricultural improvement, both during and after the war and at one stage visited France to suggest to local farmers how they might rebuild and make good war damage.

In 1915, Charles Adeane was selected as the Lord Lieutenant of Cambridgeshire, when the previous Lord Lieutenant, Viscount Clifden, resigned his post. He was well liked and respected by most in the county, though not by all. In February 1916, the Chairman of the County Council, Sir George Fordham, got rather uppity about the fact that Charles Adeane had sent a letter to the King George V wishing him a speedy recovery after an accident in France. He had signed it on his own behalf and of the people of Cambridgeshire. A rather nasty letter, with little actual sense behind it, was sent to Charles Adeane from Sir George, and when he didn't reply, Sir George sent it to the press.

The *Cambridge Chronicle*, a conservative leaning paper anyway, took severe umbrage at both the letter and the fact that Sir George intended to put it before the County Council for them to censure Charles Adeane. The editor commented that *'Sir George's action would be regrettable at any time, but it is particularly so now when national interests claim sole attention. Petty distinctions are not vital just now, and unless Sir George thinks fit to ask leave to withdraw the report it would be a charity to him if some member moved to proceed with the next business.'*

That weekend, the letter was duly brought to the County Council, who were less impressed with Sir George's sense of self-importance and rather more inclined to accept that Charles Adeane had acted in the right:

> *'Sir George started badly and finished worse, and the round of applause that met his ears, when Mr Redfern's motion "that the letter be not entered on the minutes" was carried, must have been extremely mortifying to him. It was to all intents a vote of thanks to the Lord Lieutenant, who has acted throughout with great dignity and has declined to be drawn into a controversy which never ought to have been begun.'*

The Territorial Force Association in Cambridgeshire took on a huge variety of tasks in raising and training not only their own Territorial Force battalions, both for overseas service and home service, but a number of additional bodies of troops. After the Military Service Act introduced conscription in 1916, they organised the Volunteers (the battalions into which men who had temporary exemptions were put, to prepare them for service overseas once they were called up). They raised the Cambridgeshire Kitcheners (11th Suffolks), a Reserve battalion for the Suffolks (13th Suffolks), an engineering company (203rd Company Royal Engineers), a Sanitary Section, additional troops for guarding vulnerable points in England (a sort of precursor to the Home Guard) and they maintained responsibility for the First Great Eastern Hospital and its staff throughout the war. This hospital was erected on a temporary basis on the site where the University Library now sits, progressing from being a tented encampment (originally in a court of Trinity College), through to hutments.

This was a truly spectacular amount of work, in which they were greatly assisted by the Ladies' Recruiting Committee. These prominent women did a great deal to encourage enlistment and, later in the war, to provide comforts for the troops and relief for prisoners of war. Pressure from women and on behalf of women was seen in some of the posters of the Parliamentary Recruiting Committee. 'Women of Britain Say Go', or 'To the women of Britain. Some of your men folk are holding back on your account. Won't you prove your love for your Country by persuading them to go?'

First Eastern General Hospital. (*Author's collection*)

A ward in the First Eastern General Hospital. (*Author's collection*)

Wounded soldiers relaxing outside the First Eastern General Hospital. (*Author's collection*)

Partial picture of 203 Company Royal Engineers in 1915 – the whole panoramic photograph can be seen in the Cambridgeshire Collection, Cambridge Central Library. (*T.G.K15 54189*)

National Reservists leaving Cambridge in 1914. These were men recalled to the Colours on the outbreak of hostilities. Cambridgeshire Collection, Cambridge Central Library. (*T.G.K14 2360*)

Market Square Cambridge during mobilisation. Cambridgeshire Collection, Cambridge Central Library. (*S.1914 53050*)

Social pressure did not come from women alone. According to the *Newmarket Journal*, the Newmarket Board of Guardians met and agreed that '*each Guardian should do his utmost to induce every young man in his parish who is eligible for service to enlist. Such an effort on the part of gentlemen who have great local influence, and who are, most of them, large employers of labour, should at the present time, when harvest operations are rapidly approaching their conclusion, prove invaluable.*'

Charles Adeane was himself a prominent local landowner, and the journal of postmaster William Brand suggests that the attitude of the local gentry could have a big impact. He notes with indignation the difference between Adeane's treatment of his villagers who had joined the Army with that of his own local gentry. He said that Private Day came home on leave and met Mr Adeane who enquired how he was doing and gave him half a sovereign, with two more for two other Abington men in the same regiment who were not on leave. That same day, William Brand's son Jack, who was also on leave, took a telegram up to Pampisford Hall. Mr Binney, the local worthy, was seen in the grounds. Jack greeted him and all he received in response was a 'good morning'.

In Balsham, the local squire, Hanslip Long, encouraged the villagers to enlist. Amongst them was Sidney Beeton, who travelled to Linton where he and his pals were among the first members of the battalion. The men were promised an acre of land and two cows when they returned, a promise that was never fulfilled and about which Sidney's younger brother Eric confronted the squire.

Reasons for enlisting in the Army varied widely. Common to many, however, was a sense of outrage at German atrocities, particularly the execution of Nurse Edith Cavell. Coupled with atrocity stories and an influx of Belgian refugees, many of whom settled in Cambridge and formed a target for charity, hatred of Germany played a large part in recruitment. These atrocities were used by speakers at recruitment meetings and in the press to suggest what would happen if the Germans got to Britain and East Anglia was invaded. Atrocity stories reported in the press were not entirely made up and newspapers did their best to ensure they had reliable sources. The official report by the Belgian government supplied much of the evidence, though of course things could and did grow in rumours. Patriotism was also

The first Balsham men to volunteer. First on the left is Sidney Beeton, fourth from the left is Ernest Samworth. (*With thanks to Tony Beeton*)

Balsham c. 1910. (*Cambridgeshire Collection, Cambridge Central Library. Y.BAL.K1 16909*)

Belgian refugees outside Matson's House, Littleport. (*Cambridgeshire Collection, Cambridge Central Library. Y.LIT.K16 21868*)

important – either a triumphal determination to support the nation, or as a sense of duty. Either way, it was a vital component of recruitment.

Later in the war, it was claimed that thinking of 'the women and kids' back home was one of the greatest motivations for men to carry on fighting. The men of the battalion, many of whom were married, were concerned about the food situation at home. Well they might be, as food queues became a common sight in Cambridge. And, it was claimed by the *Cambridge Independent Press* in 1918 that:

> '*No man has looked upon the ruin that has been wrought in the fair land of France and in beautiful Belgium without picturing the possibility of similar scenes in his native land. The actual sight of the ruins of Ypres or the shattered Cathedral of Arras is more convincing than a thousand newspaper articles. Even greater, perhaps, is the effect of a tour through one of those areas devastated by the German in his retreat. The wanton destruction of once-lovely villages with their little homesteads and orchards makes one's blood tingle. No wonder the soldiers of East Anglia have made*

*up their minds that not in Norfolk, Suffolk, or Cambridgeshire shall such scenes be witnessed. Rather are they prepared to fight on until the Bosche cries "Hold! Enough!"'*

These comparisons of England with Belgium were not uncommon when the war began, and an interest in the Belgian refugees who had fled to England was maintained throughout the war.

The vast majority of men in the battalion were agricultural workers – whether general labourers on farms, grooms, ploughmen or stock-keepers. In industrial areas such as Accrington local unemployment played a large part in recruiting; similarly in Cambridgeshire harvest and agricultural work patterns had a big impact upon when recruiting occurred. It seems likely that the rhythms of harvest had as much of an impact on the rate of recruitment as did the exhortations in the newspapers, recruitment meetings and the general condition of the British Expeditionary Force (BEF) in the fighting. The *Newmarket Journal* on 29 August recorded that *'there is every reason to*

Soldiers working on the land – these would have replaced the young men who left their villages to fight. Special agricultural companies were formed to make up for the loss of manpower caused by the war, of those who were unfit for service overseas or who had particular skills (especially ploughing). (*Cambridgeshire Collection, Cambridge Central Library. W22.K1 9401*)

*expect that the number of recruits sent in by the rural parishes in the district will be largely augmented, now that the harvest operations are nearing their close.'*

Over 200 recruitment meetings occurred in Cambridgeshire and the Isle of Ely in the first year of the war alone. The reliance on recruitment meetings was encouraged by the Parliamentary Recruiting Committee, which sent speakers around the country in conjunction with its more often remembered poster campaign. By the end of March 1915 they had distributed twenty million leaflets and two million posters. However, not everyone was so enamoured with the mass distribution of posters that took place during the opening months of the Great War.

In September 1914 Henry Pendle was prosecuted under the Malicious Damage Act 1861 for washing three posters off the Soham Parish notice board. He was the parish's official bill poster and was given 6d for each poster he put up. As there were so many notices, Serjeant Heylock (who had received the posters to put up) put them up himself and claimed that this was common practice for non-parish notices. When Serjeant Heylock went back a few days later to paste an amendment onto one of the posters, he discovered that all three posters had been washed off. Going to confront Henry Pendle, he was told *'I shall tear every b--- notice off that you put on the board, unless you pay me sixpence.'* He was fined £3 10s, including costs, and was told *'this is a time when everybody ought to act loyally, and not think too much of his own personal interests.'* This story was reported with anger in the *Newmarket Journal*, with the reporter expressing amazement at how unpatriotic Henry Pendle had been.

The Parliamentary Recruiting Committee also encouraged people to make use of politicians in cross-party efforts to spur men to enlist. This non-partisanship was not always well received. A correspondent calling himself 'Poor Old Marine' accused Fred W. Saunders, the Honourable Secretary of the Unionist Party, of *'being a traitor to [his] party in organising a semi-Radical patriotic recruiting meeting'*. Saunders took to the *Cambridge Weekly News* to refute this charge, saying that the Histon recruiting meeting referred to had been organised by the Cambridgeshire and Isle of Ely Territorial Recruiting Committee and was non-partisan. Most were happy to accept this state of affairs. The editor of the *Ely Standard*, in praising the Cambridgeshire branch of the Parliamentary Recruiting Committee, said *'it*

High Street, Soham. At least 29 members of the battalion came from this town. (*Author's collection*)

Advertisement for International Stores, Cambridge, showing the store's patriotism in how many of its pre-war employees had enlisted. (Cambridge Weekly News *18 August 1916*)

*will be to the lasting credit of the rival political parties that they have put aside their differences and have united in pursuing a campaign by which a valuable service is rendered to the country.'* The party organisations were later called upon to canvas houses as part of the Lord Derby scheme, by which every man in the country of military age was asked to supply his particulars, and if he was willing to serve his country.

The format of a recruitment meeting generally consisted of a few patriotic songs, followed by several speeches, an appeal for men to come forward, rousing cheers if anyone did so, and perhaps a few more patriotic songs at the end. Sometimes the songs were written for the occasion, such as this one, apparently popular in Wisbech:

> 'In the midst of war's alarms,
> When we heard the call, "to Arms!"
> Then we knew it was our duty to recruit;
> So we changed the fountain-pen,
> For a bayonet, and we then
> Got a gun to learn the proper way to shoot,
> You can bet when we rehearsed
> We'd a "gruelling" at first,
> For a City man is not a Soldier-made
> Still, we did our little best,
> And the Sergeant did the Rest,
> And we learned to march to music on Parade.
>
> We're all plain Civilians,
> Taken from the Warehouse and the Banks;
> Raw recruits are we,
> Still, we mean to be,
> Ready to fill the gaps up in the ranks.
> We're just plain Civilians,
> But comrades staunch and true;
> Show your heart's not in your boots,
> Come and join the new recruits,
> For England wants you!

All the cricket stumps are drawn,
And the football is in pawn,
And the racket to the lumber-room has gone;
While the golf balls we'll exchange,
For some balls of longer range,
That will reach the German greens and "hole in one"
For the game the Kaiser plays,
Isn't "cricket" nowadays;
He has sold his country's honour and good name;
But we'll fight him, fair and square,
And the world will yet declare,
That, win or lose, at least we "played the game."'

Written by Foden Williams, with the music composed by Ernest Hastings, it was performed at a series of recruiting meetings before being printed in the *Wisbech Standard* in October 1914.

This song shows how ideas about sport and 'playing the game' were prevalent in the language used of war. That men used these metaphors doesn't mean that they necessarily thought war would be easy or bloodless. Indeed, local papers were not shy about reporting the horrors of war, and the description in *The Times* of the British at Mons, describing how close a call it was, was a great spur to recruiting. The use of sport continued throughout the war in training and in recreation. From 1917 and 1918, instructions on how to properly train troops – either fresh ones or those who were receiving further instructions having already spent time in the lines – emphasised the importance of team sports and especially football.

During recruiting meetings, the public (not necessarily just, or even primarily, young men of the appropriate age and fitness) were encouraged to 'do their bit' and a wide range of reasons to support the country and join the war effort were given. Local papers printed many of the speeches and details of the events, so it's possible to get a good idea of what they were like. Sometimes wounded soldiers who had come home from the fight were asked to speak, though not usually for the whole meeting. The bulk of the speech making was done by local worthies and by senior army officers. It might dwell on the plight of Belgium, the possibility of the Hun coming to England and repeating atrocities there, or on notions of duty and honour.

However, they did not always follow this format. One recruitment meeting was not really a meeting at all, but rather a speech during half time at a football match played between the First and Reserve Battalions of the Cambridgeshires. Dr Chapple MP, spoke to the crowds, saying that he had good news: they would win the war. However, they still needed more men to join the Army. He declared: *'We want you to help them, not so much to win, but to win now, and, if so, you will save the lives of your brothers here and of your brothers at the front, and crush, and crush for ever, the military despotism of one of the most savage races history has known.'* Dr Chapple also carefully distinguished between the evils of the German leadership, and the ordinary German people who had been forced into war. Thus, he portrayed the Great War as a fight against tyranny. It is unclear how successful this meeting was, despite having the right crowd. Interestingly the report in the *Cambridge Weekly News* makes no mention whatsoever of men coming forward specifically because of this meeting.

Recruitment meetings, although well organised and a more visible part of the recruiting process, may not have had such a great impact as their organisers had hoped. On one occasion in October, the *Cambridge Independent Press* went into some detail about the meeting, the speeches, the exhortations to join and the patriotic song singing, but could only add, in a rather painfully optimistic tone, that some of the young men had surely gone home and thought about it and might be expected to join later in the week. Other meetings could list only two or three names at most who came forward as a direct result of the meeting.

It must also be remembered that not everyone who signed up was able to join, despite enthusiasm. At one recruiting meeting in Oakington, seven men gave their names for service, but only three were successful in reaching the required standard. Likewise in Gamlingay, two men put their names down for service, but only one was accepted. Private Joseph Utteridge made it through the recruiting centre, but was discharged after forty-three days' service as *'not likely to become an efficient soldier'*. He had been well over the minimum height at 5 feet 9½ inches, but the precise details of why he was unlikely to make a good soldier are not recorded.

More informal meetings could sometimes be quite successful. At a fair in Ely in October, a number of men from the Cambridgeshire Kitcheners were present in uniform. According to the *Cambridge Independent Press* they took the opportunity *'of speaking to their "pals" on the desirability of serving King and country'*. While the fête was affected by the war through the presence of local men in uniform and through the raising of money for Belgian refugees, supporting the war was not its primary aim. Instead, it was a local fair which was used as an informal venue for recruitment.

Although the local papers trumpeted the importance of Cambridgeshire and the Isle of Ely getting its own Regular battalion, not everyone was as aware of the significance of this. To W.J. Senescall, an apprentice coach-maker who joined up in the first week of September, the battalion was rather less special. *'Went to Cambridge and joined the Cambridge – Suffolk regiment. Actually it was the Suffolk regiment. It was Kitchener's New Army so I suppose they put the Cambridge on for that reason.'* His account of the battalion, written out as a series of answers to questions put by the local library and archives where he lived in Suffolk, gives much-needed insight into some of the early days of the battalion and the first part of its war service, before he was wounded and moved to another battalion.

For others though, the chance to serve together with mates clearly played a part in their choice of battalion, and the peer pressure seems to have played a part in enlistment. A number of brothers bear consecutive regimental numbers and a similar pattern can be seen in recruits from a village, who had evidently gone to sign up together. A good example of this is the Wilburton men, William Alsop (15885), Sidney Alsop (15887), Sidney Sharp (15879) and Fred Sulman (15880). All four men went to the recruitment office together on Monday, 2 November and enlisted. The *Cambridge Independent Press*, in recording their enlistment as part of the local roll of honour, states that it was in response to *'several strong appeals from the Vicar, who had two sons at the front'*.

Sometimes, the reason for several men joining together was because a member of the village with a car took them all together. William Brand wrote in his journal of one such occasion – a Mr Byrne took two batches of men from Cheveley at the request of Sir Ernest Cassell. On another occasion, Mr Godfrey of Ickleton drove the local recruits to the doctor at

Wilburton Church in 1910. (*Cambridgeshire Collection, Cambridge Central Library. Y.WILB. K1 5844*)

Cambridge. Again William Brand contrasted the attitude of the worthies in his village: *'Our few (four) from Pampisford quietly walked out the village – a few women and myself being the only ones to see them off – no one of importance troubled.'*

It's quite possible something like this happened in Elsworth too. Nine Elsworth men enlisted on the same day, in the week ending 18 September, and have almost consecutive regimental numbers. They were: 14423 Edwin Alfred Lyon, 14425 Herbert Webster Driver, 14427 Thomas Edwin Circus, 14429 Harold Allgood, 14430 Arthur Samuel Dawson, 14431 George Day, 14432 George Percy Driver, 14434 William Henry Braybrooke and 14436 Herbert Desborough. The risks of having so many from such a small village (Elsworth's total population in 1911 was around 550) serving together were significant. By the end of 1917 all nine men who enlisted together on that day had become casualties, and by the end of the war two of them had been wounded twice. One was killed and six wounded on 1 July 1916. One died on 3 August 1916 and the final soldier, who up until that point had escaped unwounded, was killed in action on 28 April 1917.

14427 Lance Corporal Thomas Edwin Circus of Elsworth. Killed in action 28 April 1917. (*Cambridge Weekly News 29 June 1917*)

As the war continued, voluntary enlistment alone proved insufficient. In January 1916 conscription was introduced and casualties, once the battalion was overseas and engaged in heavy fighting, were often replaced by conscripts. After July 1916 the army largely ended its policy of sending men from the same place to fight together, although most men still seem to have been sent to local regiments, at least for training. The men who were brought into the battalion afterwards could be from anywhere in the country, but it seems likely that the core of the battalion remained fairly strong, despite the approximately 4,500 men who passed

Elsworth Cricketers in 1912. It's not certain, but several members of the battalion did later return to Elsworth in 1915 for a cricket match, so it's likely that several members of the battalion are pictured here. (*Cambridgeshire Collection, Cambridge Central Library. Y.ELS.K12 42746*)

through it. With a war establishment of 1,500 (on paper – at times the numbers of men in the battalion available for duty were significantly below this level, dropping to as low as 300–400 men) this suggests that each man was replaced three times over, however there was a high rate of movement between battalions so this statistic is less alarming than it first seems.

Later in the war, it was claimed by the *Cambridge Independent Press*:

*'One of the secrets of the success of the New Army was that it was founded on a territorial basis. Each unit was composed of men from the same county – whole platoons were frequently formed from a single district – and the officers were for the most part drawn from the local landed and professional classes. County patriotism was thus allied with national patriotism. The resultant esprit de corps was of immense value both in the training of the new units and in their behaviour on the battlefield. The wastage of war, and the necessity of filling up vacancies with whatever drafts were available, have to some extent weakened, though they have not destroyed, this territorial characteristic, the value of which was emphasised by every officer with whom I discussed it while in France…. Particularly does this apply to Norfolk, Suffolk and Cambridgeshire units, for the East Anglian is a type unto himself, and needs to be known to be appreciated. In clannishness he is second only to the Scot. He is slow to trust, but once he has made up his mind, he is faithful even unto death.'*

One of the officers in the Cambs Kitcheners, Isaac Alexander (Alec) Mack, made a similar observation of his men, stating that: *'I am very glad I am not in a town battalion like the Northumberlands and such regiments. They are not nearly so easy to control or so well disciplined, and I am pleased to discern to-day that our men seem much quicker in picking up new ideas, despite the fact that they are not so educated.'*

The Cambs Kitcheners were in the same division as those Northumberlands that he mentioned, and officers had wider horizons than their men, dining with those in other units regularly, so Alec Mack was in a good position to compare them.

Conscripts cannot be taken out of the consideration of even Pals units. They made up around fifty per cent of British soldiers and were placed into existing battalions once trained and sent overseas from training battalions in England. Conscripts were not necessarily men unwilling to fight; of those who protested their enlistment in a military tribunal, the majority seem to have done so on family or business grounds. This was particularly true for farm hands – arguably all those who could be spared had already enlisted by the time conscription was brought in.

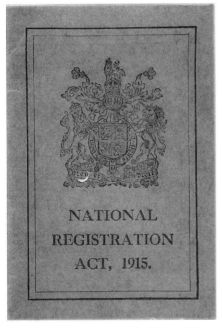

National Registration Card of Theophilus Percy Gallyon, a Gunsmith who lived in Cambridge. He is likely to have been exempt from the Military Service Act because of his profession. (*Author's collection*)

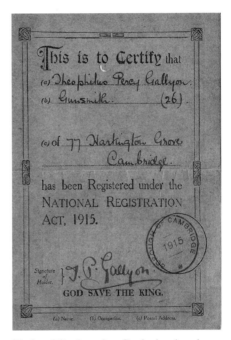

National Registration Card, showing the details inside. He might have hoped this would enable him to prove to those who thought he was 'shirking' by not going overseas that he was engaged on work of national importance. (*Author's collection*)

*Chapter 2*

# The Ladies' Recruiting Committee

The Ladies' Recruiting Committee was reformed at a meeting on 29 August 1914. These formidable women, headed by Mrs Adeane, surely deserve a good deal of the credit for the formation of the various additional battalions raised in Cambridge, as well as for their concerns to do all they could for the welfare of the troops they helped to raise. At the first meeting of the Territorial Force Association in 1915 a resolution was passed: *'That the best thanks of the Association be given to the Ladies' Recruiting Commander-in-chief for the very valuable work they have done in connection with recruits for the Regular and Territorial Forces in the County and Isle.'* The committee had first been formed in January 1914, for the Territorial Recruiting Week, at which the Cambridgeshire Regiment (Territorials) was brought up to strength, putting the Cambridgeshires in a stronger position at the start of the war than many other Territorial battalions which were under strength.

Their first meeting was at the request of Mr Adeane, who sent a letter read out by his wife, saying:

> *'If the whole population is to be aroused to a proper sense of the importance of the crisis, the assistance of the women of the county must be invoked. It is desirable, therefore, that the Women's Recruiting Committee, which did such excellent service last winter in obtaining recruits for the Territorial Force, should be called together and asked to work on the same lines: (1) By personal calls try to arouse the young men of the district and explain to them the situation, and urge them to come forward; (2) when meetings are held, induce the man to attend.'*

The ladies were then addressed by General Keir, General Paget, and Mr Almeric Paget MP. The first remarked:

'In no other nation in the world did women hold a more honourable or powerful position than in England. That position had been gained by centuries of noble work, and by their influence on the formation of that greatest of all assets in national life – national character. We were now asking them to help us to waken and save the nation from the lethargy into which it had unfortunately fallen, and awaken in the manhood of the nation that sense of duty which existed in every man worthy of the name. If the men who claimed superior qualities over women really possessed them, now was the time for them to show it.'

This meeting was reported in full in every local newspaper, so that those women who did not attend the meeting would have become aware of it too and, perhaps, so that men might have been shamed into action by the fact that women were making such efforts to organize for the war.

The chairman, Madeline Adeane, was from the influential Wyndham family, her father being an MP, her brother, George Wyndham the Irish Secretary. Mrs Adeane was selected as an Alderman on Cambridge County Council in August 1917, becoming the first woman to sit as such in Cambridge. When she was elected it was noted in the *Cambridge Independent Press*:

'A great deal of the work now being placed upon the Council is of a kind where the sympathy and judgement of women would be a most important asset. Much of it is connected with the public health, the care of children and of the sick, and the mentally and physically disabled, matters where the help of women must obviously be very useful... Mrs Adeane will fill the position well. For many years she has taken a prominent part in such organisations as the County Nursing Association, and since the war began, she has ably supported the Lord Lieutenant in all kinds of war work – recruiting, Red Cross societies, prisoners of war funds, and the provision of comforts for troops. The experience of public work thus gained will stand her in good stead when she comes to her new duties on the County Council.'

As the wife of Charles Adeane, she would have been aware of many of the wider developments of the war; she may also have been privy to information that seems to have been received about the various battalions later on in the war but was neither published nor minuted for security reasons.

Postmaster William John Brand was (possibly) paranoid about the importance of the information that passed through Babraham Hall, and feared a German spy might be at work there. He wrote in his journal:

'Fraulein has been for this last fifteen years, on and off, German governess at Babraham Hall ... Babraham Hall is closely connected with military matters. Mr Adeane is chairman of the Cambs Territorial Association, has a dozen or so relatives in the Army, is frequently at the War Office and has a private wire between there and Babraham Hall. And Mrs Adeane is very prominent in Red Cross work ... Ah! Fraulein no wonder you returned to Babraham when trouble was ahead – things will leak out and Babraham Hall was the place to hear them!'

A family of soldiers was right; Madeline Adeane's nephew Percy Wyndham died on 14 September, and within ten months of the outbreak of the war two of her daughters (Sibell and Madeline) had married soldiers. Pamela Adeane went to work at Queen's Hospital in North London, having been dissuaded from going overseas to France to nurse there. Queen's specialised in heads and jaws, difficult and often gruesome work. Meanwhile Lettice Adeane was spotted by a coachman, who took the collection of eggs to Whittlesford Hospital, scrubbing the floor. William Brand observed that 'it seems funny to see the daughter of the Lord Lieutenant doing that work.' Anxious about members of her extended family, Mrs Adeane nevertheless threw herself into war work, perhaps as a distraction from her own fears.

Also serving on the Ladies' Recruitment Committee was Lillian Mellish Clark, the chairman of the executive committee, who became the first woman to chair a county outside London when she was elected to Cambridgeshire County Council in 1947. One of Anglia-Ruskin University's buildings is named after her, for she was a governor and chair of governors there for thirty-five years.

The honourable secretary, Rosamond Philpott, was of a more artistic persuasion, being a bookbinder and much involved in art projects and displays. Another member of the committee was Mrs Harding-Newman, whose husband was appointed honourable organiser (of recruiting) for the borough and county of Chippenham.

Many of the other women on the committee were wives of Cambridgeshire Regiment officers. These included Mrs Twelftree Saint, whose husband, Lieutenant Colonel Edward Twelftree Saint died of wounds on 29 August 1918 aged 33. Although he is buried at Daours Communal Cemetery Extension on the Somme, he is also commemorated on his family grave at Mill Road Cemetery. Over 125 soldiers, sailors, and airmen are either buried or commemorated in the cemetery on family graves, so that relatives had a more local focus for remembrance. Mrs Littledale's husband was, in early 1914, the captain and adjutant of the Cambridgeshire Regiment.

Another was Mrs Tebbutt, wife of Lieutenant Colonel Louis Tebbutt, the commander of the 1st Battalion, The Cambridgeshire Regiment. All three of their sons were in the Army. Captain Oswald M. Tebbutt was killed in action in March 1915 and at the same time his younger brother Captain Roger Joseph Tebbutt was severely wounded. Both were in the 1st Cambridgeshires, serving under their father. Roger went back to the front after his recovery, having been transferred to the Essex Regiment, and was killed in action on 23 August 1918. Their youngest son, Charles, was in the Royal Engineers and was also wounded, returning to France in late 1918. In the early part of the war, Lieutenant Colonel Tebbutt had resigned as commander of the 1st Cambridgeshires, citing ill-health, and became instead the commander of the reserve battalion. However, he does later seem to have gone overseas to take up command of them. Doubtless Mrs Tebbutt, with three sons and a husband overseas, was just as anxious as Mrs Adeane about the fate of her family.

Almost immediately they had been formed, the Ladies' Recruiting Committee published its first appeal in the local press.

*'Within the last three weeks the nation has had so strong a warning of the madness of refusing to face facts, and continue to dwell in a fool's paradise, that now, when every heart is stirred to the depths by reading of deeds of heroics, and scanning the lists of the killed and wounded, it may be that the moment has come for women seriously to consider their position and responsibilities, and to see what they can do to help to rouse those who are*

*still sunk in lethargy, sleepily oblivious of their danger, comfortably sure that "Somebody else will do something."*

*Let us just consider what may happen if the present "Call to Arms" is not responded to by every man who is eligible. We break faith with our countrymen who are heroically upholding the honour and traditions of this great Empire and who have a right to adequate support from it. If we leave our army to its fate in this critical moment by failing to send reinforcement (not only reinforcements, but efficient reinforcements), the destroying blight of dishonour will for ever rest on this nation. The Navy and our small Army have in the past secured for us the blessing of peace, and therefore the advancement of civilisation all over the world. Shall not we in return spend every sinew of our strength, use every means in our power to repay them now?*

*We are fighting an ambitious, cruel, implacable enemy, and if he ever reaches our shores he will spread desolation and want over our fair land, and inflict upon us indignities which every man and woman must dread. We call upon the men of Cambridge to consider the possibilities of the future, to remember what defeat would mean to their women and children, and homes and to do their duty by enlisting at once.*

*We who have to stay at home have duties bereft of the glories and excitements of battle, duties full of sadness and responsibility, but our first and most urgent duty at this moment is to do all in our power to swell the number of recruits.*

*'Wake up, Cambridge!'*

A pamphlet from the Mother's Union, 'To British Mothers: How they can help enlistment' distributed in 1914, emphasises the sacrifices that were needed of mothers and that they were a shared sacrifice. Thus, when the Ladies' Recruiting Committee went out to speak to women across Cambridgeshire to get them to encourage their sons and sweethearts to enlist, they would have drawn upon an idea of shared sacrifice. The mother, wife, or sweetheart of a soldier was that first, minimising the social gulf between the members of the Ladies' Recruiting Committee and the ordinary women of Cambridgeshire.

The mother who wrote the pamphlet called on her readers to do two things. The first was to pray, regardless of whether that was through the Church of England or in their own homes, '*that the pitying Father may pity you and yours, forgive us all our shameful sins which have deserved this stern chastisement of war, and teach us to hate and repent them.*' The second thing was '*hard for me to say and hard for me to hear. Remember it is a mother who says it. GIVE YOUR SONS.*' She wrote of those soldiers out there already that '*English Mothers gave them, English Mothers from the Queen to the cottager, sending*

Sweetheart broach with Suffolk Regiment cap badge. Probably given by an officer to his wife or girlfriend. Hallmarked Birmingham 1916. (*Author's collection*)

*their sailor boys and soldier lads ungrudgingly to live or die for the Country. But they may give in vain, so far as success goes because NOT ENOUGH MEN ARE SENT OUT, AND THIS LARGELY BECAUSE NOT ENOUGH MOTHERS SAY TO THEIR BOYS AS ONE DID LATELY "My boy, I don't want you to go but if I were you I should go."'* [Emphasis in original] She also spoke of men who did not go to fight because their mothers forbade them to go. This, she claimed, was not the fault of the men being tied to their mother's apron strings, but the fault of the mothers, who ought to do all they could to encourage their sons to fight and to stand firm at home without showing the sorrow they doubtless felt.

When he had called upon the nation to do its duty, Kitchener had addressed not only the young men of fighting age and fitness, but those who could not fight, for reasons of gender, age or ill-health. For them, the *London Standard* offered a booklet on 'How to help Lord Kitchener', the focus of which was that those who were not able to be recruits should be recruiters. They should inform themselves completely of the terms of service, where the nearest recruiting station was, and if necessary provide the means of getting to the recruiting station. Members of the public were also advised that *'If you can catch a local recruiting officer in a moment of leisure, seek his advice'* –something that seems highly unlikely given that most local recruiting offices were swamped in the first month of the war, and even afterwards were experiencing a much higher stream of recruits than they would have been accustomed to in peace time.

The huge numbers coming forward, and the unpreparedness of the Army for the influx of men, led to an almost complete reliance on civilians and, as necessity overcame Kitchener's prejudices, the Territorial County Associations. Citizen recruiters were, however, prone to using 'short-cuts', which led to lost paperwork and the recruitment of medically unfit men who subsequently had to be discharged.

The ideal in personal recruiting was to meet with young men who might be considered shirking and encourage them to join, by persuasive words, by promising that if they were capable they would go themselves. Or, for those who were a little less convinced of their own persuasive powers, to get an idea of who they thought ought to be joining the army and to pass those details on to the nearest recruiting serjeant. One wonders what the overworked recruiting serjeants thought of these busy bodies informing on 'shirkers'. Spotting shirkers was a popular pastime. Much of William Brand's diary was taken up with comments on the manhood of his village and the fact that they hadn't enlisted and were lazing around the pub.

When women took on the role of recruiting serjeant, this could lead to resentment in the press. There does not seem to have been much of a white feather campaign in Cambridge itself, if any – it's not mentioned in the Cambridge local newspapers – but the campaign was reported in the national press and was the subject of a question in the Commons. Mr Cathcart Watson complained that some of those employed by the State were *subjected to insolence and provocation at the hands of some advertising young women presenting them with white feathers.* He requested that they be arrested, though the Home Secretary replied that that might be an overreaction. Stories are often told of these women giving feathers to wounded soldiers who were at home recovering and were out of uniform, or to those who were ineligible to fight for health reasons. Although this practice was started by a man, Admiral Charles Penrose Fitzgerald, the support for women who sought to encourage men to enlist by the suffragettes might have helped lead to popular resentment. It also seems that as the war drew on and casualties mounted, the presentation of white feathers became more problematic – and was made unnecessary by conscription.

There does seem to have been a white feather campaign in Newmarket, where some of the Cambs Kitcheners came from. An editorial in the *Newmarket Journal* made mention of the campaign. The topic was 'Work for Women', and it read:

*'The young ladies who have formed themselves into the White Feather Leagues, and go about presenting the badge of cowardice to the men they think ought to be wearing khaki, would be a great deal more profitably employed in doing something for the wives and children of soldiers and sailors who are fighting their battles for them. We have never been too generous as a nation in this respect, but there is much ground for hope that we are going to do better now. It would be a lasting disgrace to us, an indelible stain upon our national honour, if any woman or child dependent on our brave fellows at the front is allowed to suffer in any way by the absence of the*

*breadwinner … It is for the nation to see that allowance is supplemented, and to regard the well-being of the wives and children of soldiers and sailors as a sacred charge. There, young ladies, is a chance for you. If you accept it, and if you are the right sort of young ladies, you will get a great deal more solid satisfaction from it than from presenting white feathers to men of whose circumstances you know nothing at all.'*

A few weeks later, the Ladies' Column of the newspaper suggested that *'It would surely be well for some of us to take up some special work, seeking and finding one, two or more families left lonely and desolate, and keeping them until the trouble has cleared.'*

Women in recruiting were thus less acceptable than women in other war work, particularly charitable work. Perhaps the secret to the success of the Ladies' Recruiting Committee was that they were involved in both, at a personal level with a great deal of overlap between the various Red Cross committees and the Ladies' Recruiting Committee, and at a committee level with concern for the men they had raised continuing past getting them to the recruiting serjeant.

The Ladies' Recruiting Committee helped the authorities in putting up posters and doing other organisational tasks. An appeal poster drawn up by the Territorial Force Association in September was circulated largely by the Ladies' Recruiting Committee.

They also organised recruiting meetings, though they did not speak at them. One was held at the Guild Hall on 29 October. It was described as *'an enjoyable entertainment'*, with *'intervals being allowed for appeals for more men for the colours'*. By October it was felt that although Cambridge had done well so far, *'there are still a large number of young men in the town, whom the call of duty ought to place shoulder to shoulder with those already drilling on Parker's Piece.'* Unfortunately, although there were plenty of women present at the meeting, there were not that many men, and in particular not that many men of the right age. Alderman Stace presided, supported by the Mayor and Alderman A.S. Campkin.

The appeal was altered to take account of the wrong audience being present. Alderman Campkin said that *'he was afraid the sentiments and sympathies of their meeting and its purposes would have to be conveyed in a somewhat vicarious manner. All those present would have to use their influence with a number of those absent. If ever there was a justifiable war in regard to which there was a unity of feeling of all classes it was this terrible war which was now being waged, and their sympathies went out to those brave men who were waging it on their behalf.'* Like other recruiting meetings, this one was reported in detail in the *Cambridge Independent Press*.

Another meeting was held in the Romsey Council Schools, where the school hall was well filled. There was a musical programme and a series of lantern slides, which included *'some capital photographs of the 6th Division at Cambridge.'* Appealing to the young men of Romsey Town, Alderman Campkin said:

*'Lord Kitchener wanted a million men. He saw that the Kaiser and the Germans had expressed doubts as to the existence of Kitchener's Army, and that it was quite impossible to get the million men. But already there were something like 700,000 of them, and it was up to the young men of the country to show the Kaiser and the Germans that they were wrong in their surmise... Mr Fay, of the Cambridge University Officers' Training Corps, in the course of a spirited appeal for recruits, said it was very nice to know that one Englishman was a match for two or three Germans, but it was not fair on the Englishman to let him do all the work whilst there were plenty more men at home able to help him. Emphasising the importance of enlisting at once, Mr Fay pointed out that although the recruits might not be fit to go for the front for some time, yet on joining the Army they at once released some men who were sufficiently advanced in training to do so.'*

The Ladies' Recruiting Committee did not confine themselves solely to questions of recruiting. They arranged comforts for the troops, both while they were in training and once they moved overseas. And, unlike many, instead of simply requesting random articles to pass on to the troops, they spoke first to Colonel Somerset to determine what was really needed by the men, and provided patterns and advice to knitters to enable them to make things that were actually useful and the right size. Colonel Somerset told them that *'the most useful gifts will be mufflers, mittens and socks. The mufflers should be 12 inches wide and 2½ yards long, single or double knitting, and the*

Waterbeach Ladies Working Party. During winter 1915 they made 92 shirts, 130 pairs of socks, 66 pairs of mittens and 28 mufflers. Top row: Miss Rayner, Mrs Wallace, Mrs Lambert, Mrs Waddelow, Mrs Saunders, Mrs Brown, Miss Burgess, Mrs Todd, Miss Adams, Miss Simpkin, Mrs Craft. Second row: Miss Buttress, Miss Clay, Miss Sanders, Mrs Webb, Mrs Chapman, Mrs Hazel, Mrs Dimock, Mrs Collins, Miss Swann, Miss Lewis, Miss Asplin. Third row: The Misses Mason, Hill, Bouling, Mullocks and Barton. (Cambridge Weekly News *12 May 1916*)

*mitten should have a thumb but no fingers.'* An appeal in the local newspapers was duly published in November and Cambridge's knitters got busy.

By early 1915, Ladies' Recruiting Committee was able to report that they had collected over £1,000, distributed *'12,800 garments and woollen comforts to Cambridgeshire men now serving in the forces of the Crown at home or abroad'*, organised meetings for women in large shops, factories and laundries, and in villages across the county, to teach them how best to help with recruitment.

In October 1915 a fresh appeal was made, largely for similar items to the previous year. However, it added:

'*The 11th (Cambs.) Battalion of the Suffolks is going out to the front shortly, and will want the following things: ten pairs of field glasses, fifty-two periscopes, sixteen telescopes, sixteen telescopic sights, spare telephone parts and wire, and various things required by the medical officer which are not provided by the Government. The cost of the whole will be about £260.*

*This sum, expended in the manner indicated, will, we are assured by those who have studied the matter on the spot, make a great difference to the safety of our county battalion, and we confidently rely on those who have its welfare at heart to send us as much as thy can spare and without delay.'*

Around the same time, the committee gained an additional function, that of being a Prisoners of War Help Fund.

With the combination of local importance and prominent work in helping the troops they raised, it's not surprising that the Ladies' Recruiting Committee apparently came in for none of the criticism that dogged other efforts by women to recruit men to the Army. Perhaps, in part, it was because a lot of these women were well known and it would be known that they weren't requesting anything of other families that they hadn't already done themselves. Their own husbands and sons were either already enlisted in the Territorials, or enlisted shortly after the outbreak of war.

*Chapter 3*

# Training in Cambridge

While recruitment was still ongoing, training of those who had already joined began. In common with most of Kitchener's New Armies, there was a distinct lack of equipment – uniforms were slow to arrive, being temporarily replaced with civilian clothes, and then with blue serge uniforms that looked distinctly unsoldierly, despite attempts in the press to pretend otherwise. More worryingly, rifles and other equipment were not available for training until late in the programme, and when the Cambridgeshire Kitcheners joined their division, the divisional artillery did not receive a full complement of guns until a few weeks before going overseas.

One of the non-commissioned officers spoke to the *Cambridge Independent Press* in October 1914 and said that in twelve years of soldiering he had never had better rations issued to troops and that the troops were very comfortable. This was not entirely typical of the New Armies in general – one battalion of the East Lancashire Regiment, based at barracks in Preston, was close to mutiny at the lack of food, and reports of cramped conditions in training camps put many people off enlisting – but the Pals battalions tended to fair better. In large part, this was because they were not reliant on the Army for everything, but could instead have many things supplied by the local authorities, raisers, or, in this case, the Territorial Force Association. While that didn't help with rifles, it certainly helped with food and basic equipment. Arrangements were made to lodge the soldiers in Melbourne Place Schools and on Parker's Piece for the time being.

For these first few months, the battalion's training was more a weekday routine and the men would obtain passes to cycle home at the weekends. Sidney Beeton would send a postcard back to his mother each week to reassure her that he had arrived safely back in Cambridge, a distance of some ten miles. He would take his washing home with him – apparently the army

15766 Private Sidney Edward Beeton in khaki uniform. (*With thanks to Tony Beeton*)

15766 Private Sidney Edward Beeton in blue Kitchener uniform. (*With thanks to Tony Beeton*)

did not do such a good job at washing it as his mother. On 21 October he wrote that he had no address, presumably being encamped on Parker's Piece or Midsummer Common at this time; by his next letter he was, however, barracked at Melbourne Place Schools.

Initial training consisted primarily of route marches and drill, the latter being somewhat tricky to achieve. Most of the officers and non-commissioned officers who would normally have drilled the new soldiers had gone overseas. The battalion was fortunate in receiving Colonel Charles Wyndham Somerset as their first commanding officer. Colonel Somerset had been brought over from the Indian Army, rather than being a 'dug out' – a former officer who had retired long ago, but was brought back in desperation. Many of the 'dug outs' would not proceed abroad with their battalions, their health being too poor for active service, but Colonel Somerset remained with the battalion until he was invalided home in July 1916. He was from a soldiering family, his father also having been a colonel, and his first commission is recorded in the Indian Army List in January 1884. He seems to have spent much of his service in India where he married and where his son Alan was born.

Some of the non commissioned officers were old soldiers (some of them really were old and might lie about their age to get into the Army, much as many younger men did, though in the opposite direction). Most of the officers initially came from the Cambridge University Officer Training Corps (CUOTC). Both of these sources of men would bring in valuable experience, as most of the men in the battalion had no experience whatsoever of military life. A few had been in the Scouts, like Gadsby Dring of Chatteris, who was killed by a shell in June 1916. After his death, a memorial service was held in the parish church for the Scouts, and was well attended, with the Scout Headquarters flag being flown at half-mast and current scouts wearing black armbands.

Lord Haldane had set up the Officer Training Corps in 1907 as part of the army reforms, and his idea was that they would provide officers not only to go straight into the Army, but also to be prepared should mass mobilisation be needed. Lord Esher remarked that *'If ever it should be the misfortune of this country to mobilise all the military forces of the Crown, it would be impossible for them to take the field without the assistance of the Officers' Training Corps.'* So it would prove.

Amongst the officers of the CUOTC were Captain Osbert Harold Brown, who would die in 1916 after surviving the first day of the Somme, and Gerald Tuck who ultimately commanded the battalion, beginning in 1914 as its adjutant. These men almost certainly knew each other, as, most likely, would many of the other officers who had come from the university. Of the officers in the battalion, over twenty had attended Cambridge University, many of them matriculating at around the same time. Nicholas Beauchamp Bagenal (matriculated 1910), Ian Drummond Claughton (1909), Desmond John Darley (1914), Paul Vychan Emrys-Evans (1912), William Moulton Fiddian (1908), C.O.F. Jenkin (1909), Arthur E. Seddon (1910) and Gerald Louis Johnson Tuck (1910) were all members of King's College and though they might not all have known one another, they probably all knew at least some of their fellow officers and would have significant shared experiences and shared friends.

The CUOTC in 1913 ran several field days, giving those involved valuable experience that would serve them well during the war. The Lent Term 1913 was particularly busy for them, with a programme of field work and lectures that included two field days for all arms (the CUOTC included not only infantry, but also cavalry, artillery, engineers and an ambulance section) in conjunction with contingents of the Junior Division of the OTC (from public schools), regimental tours, lectures, night marching and other competitions, and night operations, and was to end with a trip to Paris. There they would study the operations round Paris during the siege by the Prussians – and probably have a good time too!

The night operations were carried out in late January, in conjunction with various regular troops, the Cambridgeshires and Junior Officer Training Corps in the area. The experience gained here probably helped some of the officers during the war – in particular Captain Tuck who commanded a night raid and, when conditions proved unfavourable, made the decision to stop it going ahead when the night was too bright and enemy sentries too alert, to cut the wire safely by hand. Perhaps that night he recalled the difficulties faced by both sides in the practice night operations before the war. During 1913 he was the honourable secretary of the CUOTC, so it is almost certain that he played a leading role in the operations. With the moon shining brightly, rather than the threatened rain, *'it was possible throughout the whole evening to see a single man, let alone a force, more than half-way across the largest field the invaders had to cross, and this fact, combined with the scanty cover afforded by bare hedges at this season of the year, illustrates the tremendous task imposed upon a force which was attacking such a position as that occupied on the hills between Shelford Station and Hills Road.'*

Later that same term, the 'Battle of Histon' took place around the village of Histon. Part of the CUOTC encamped in a field just off the main road to Cambridge, with trenches as well as tents, and the area was visited by locals, especially younger ones. The manoeuvres drew a good deal of attention from the whole village, as manoeuvres by the Cambs Kitcheners would do the following year.

Cambridge University Officer's Training Corps at camp at Mytchett 1913. (*Author's collection*)

Cambridge University Officers Training Corps Group Photo 1912. (*Cambridgeshire Collection, Cambridge Central Library. T.G.K12 41820*)

Cambridge University Officers Training Corps at Farnborough Common for training in 1912. (*Cambridgeshire Collection, Cambridge Central Library. T.G.K12 41817*)

Cambridge University Officers Training Corps at Farborough Common for training in 1912. (*Cambridgeshire Collection, Cambridge Central Library. T.G.K12 41819*)

In early 1918 the lives and contribution of these young officers was reflected upon by a journalist who found himself in The Leicester Lounge, the officer's mess of the Cambs Kitcheners, 'somewhere in France' [probably near Arras]. He wrote:

'Substituting wooden benches for easy chairs... it would have been easy to imagine oneself in an undergraduate's den. Perhaps it was the somewhat bizarre decorations, and the youth and accent of the occupants, for it may be remembered that while the ranks were filled almost exclusively from the County, the Battalion was officered, with few exceptions, from the University. Four of the original officers – all ex-undergraduates – are still with the Battalion. They are splendid examples of the type, and after a few hours in their company one realises what an asset the young life of Oxford and Cambridge must have proved in the formation of the new Armies. Trained in mind and body; keen, alert, and fearless: steeped in the best traditions of public school and University life, they made ideal leaders.'

Before the Cambs Kitcheners was even fully formed, training had begun on Parker's Piece, and Captain Gerald Tuck had been appointed captain and adjutant to the body of men that was, at that time, part of an overflow of recruits for which no room could be found anywhere in Suffolk, where they had previously been sent. Colonel C.T. Heycock of the CUOTC was appointed to command; he would later become the commanding officer of the 1st Cambridgeshires.

Training operations commenced on Parker's Piece with the men divided up into three bodies being put through preliminary drill, in their shirt sleeves due to the hot weather. A report on this initial training in September, which aimed to pull in more recruits as well as reassure families about the progress of loved ones, stated that: 'at present there is a great need of non-commissioned officers for the drilling of the men, and if there are any former non-commissioned officers in the town not eligible for active service who could give assistance in this respect their services would be very welcome.'

For those who lacked any background in the Army, but still found themselves in the position of having to train green soldiers, there were plenty of books and pamphlets offering to explain everything simply and to give the proper words of command.

Amongst these books was *A Short Course of Physical Training for the New Armies* by Allan Broman. This explained that physical training was vital, and after numerous enquiries this book had been produced for instructors '*without the advantage of the training given at the Headquarters Gymnasia, but who nevertheless have to undertake the training of Territorial and other units.*' Helpful illustrations and the words of command were given. For the more advanced, there was *What Every Private Soldier Ought to Know on Active Service* which assumed that drill was well known, containing only information '*he would be expected to know when acting on his own responsibility without the guidance of any officer or non-commissioned officer.*' This book was reviewed in the *Cambridge Independent Press* in October 1914 and was praised as being one '*which should be in the hands of every recruit in Lord Kitchener's Army*'.

The Cambs Kitcheners were quite fortunate in having Bob Sitton, a boxer amongst their number. He had previously served in the Army before becoming a boxer. His wife, Harriet, was the mistress of Reach Elementary School; they had married in 1895. On the outbreak of war, Bob Sitton rejoined the Suffolks and served as an instructor, though it must be remembered that one man would struggle to adequately train 1,500 men on his own!

Other books were aimed at junior officers, telling them how to live, and later in the war the Army's Stationery Service would produce similar pamphlets, on '*questions a platoon commander should ask himself*'. The emphasis was on quickly training recruits, but with the huge problems of equipping them there was no chance of the battalion going overseas any time soon, especially as it took until December for the battalion to be filled. And even when that had been accomplished, the War Office requested an additional company of men, bringing the establishment of the battalion up to 1,350 men. This was completed in January.

The *Cambridge Independent Press* used reports of the progress of the battalion to aid further recruiting, not just of former non-commissioned officers who might be able to help the training, but for the numbers needed to finally fill the battalion. They reported in October that although an excellent start had been made and '*no pains will be spared to make the battalion one of which the county may well be proud*', more men were still needed, urgently:

'*It remains for the men of the county to justify the confidence which the County Association reposed in them when they offered to raise the battalion*

*... The sooner the battalion is complete the sooner it will become efficient. It is quite clear that the battalions that will go first to the front will be those that get on the quickest and are the best trained ... Therefore recruits are wanted at once, and it behoves all who have the reputation of the county at heart to do all they can to bring the battalion up to full strength.'*

By mid-October the newspaper was able to report that the Cambs Kitcheners were making good progress, helped by the excellent weather and by the fact that men had *'joined with a definite and high object, that of making themselves as quickly as possible efficient soldiers and able to take their share in the great fight which is being waged against barbarous militarism and oppression'*. The newspaper also recorded what happened each day, as follows:

## 'A DAY AT MELBOURNE-PLACE

*At Melbourne-place "Reveille" is sounded at 6am, and the men, after some hot coffee and bread and butter, have a spell of Swedish exercises – splendid training for the body. Then they have breakfast, after which from 9 to 10 they have a lecture on judging distances, outposts, musketry, the duties of orderlies, guard-mounting, or some such subject by the non-commissioned officers, who are all old soldiers, and rare good ones too. From 10 to 10.30, 11 to 11.45 and 12 to 12.45 they are drilled, the intervals being allowed for resting. Dinner is served at one o'clock, and each man can obtain up to a pint of beer at the canteen. After dinner a short spell is allowed for a rest and a smoke and a look at the daily papers which are supplied. Afternoon parade begins at 2.30 and drill lasts an hour. Then comes half an hour's lecture and from 4.15 to 5.30 the men go for a short route march, during which they are allowed to smoke and exercise their vocal abilities in "Tipperary" and other popular ditties of the day. Tea is served at 5.30, after which the men are free to go out until 9pm, when they must return to headquarters for the night. For those who prefer to remain in at night newspapers are provided, various games have been kindly given by generous donors, in the town and county, and Colonel C.T. Heycock has lent a large gramophone. Entertainments are also given in the evening twice a week. Mr Bedwell has kindly given a couple of concerts on Thursday evenings, and other concerts are being arranged by various friends.'*

Until the battalion went overseas, there was no war diary kept (or, if there was, it does not survive), and so this newspaper report is almost all that remains of the battalion's day-to-day training activities. The Swedish exercises mentioned were stretches and strength moves, performed largely without need for any equipment. Anything that could be done without equipment was seized upon – note that there is no mention of actual musketry, with real guns and bullets, although there might be lectures on the subject. Later in training they would have access to a miniature rifle range, but for the first few months the men were drilled and lectured, had sham fights (Sidney Beeton was captured during one), and practised digging trenches.

The schools at Melbourne Place were a good intermediate solution to the problem of housing the battalion, but not a permanent one. As the war continued, and the soldiers remained in the classrooms, Cambridgeshire schools were increasingly concerned about the amount of schooling that was being missed. And, at the same time, the conditions in the schools were not ideal for the men living in them. W.J. Senescall recalled that at the schools:

*'We had to sleep on some gallery steps. The chap above me kept rolling on to me. What a night! However one can get used to anything. I had a lot worse later. The next morning – breakfast – went to the Melbourne Place again – two slices of bread and some baloney sausage. No good I just could not face it. I sat and looked at it and the chap next to me said "Can't manage it?" and promptly stuck his fork in it and it was gone.'*

Hut barracks, therefore, were decided upon as a solution. They were designed by a local architect, Mr C.F. Skipper, of St Andrew's Street, Cambridge, and built by Messrs. W. Sindall, of Mill Lane. There was some debate about putting up hutments on Parker's Piece – various people complained, while others pointed out that it was the town's patriotic duty to do all it could to support their soldiers. Eventually it was decided not to use Parker's Piece, though it was frequently used for training, and a tented encampment may have been put up briefly. The hutments were instead built in fields just off Cherry Hinton Road, and provided a semi-permanent home for the battalion. Much thought seems to have been put into these hut barracks, and they included a Regimental Institute, shower blocks, cookhouses, stores, and a miniature rifle range.

However, the construction, which does seem to have been remarkably quick, was not all that it could be. Sidney Beeton described them in a letter to his mother dated 7 December, before the battalion had quite moved in, saying that *'I don't think we are moving now as the huts are condemned for letting in the wind and water and they have to match board them inside.'*

Training continued apace, with a parade in November, before they moved to the hut barracks, being inspected by Lieutenant General C.L. Woollcombe, the General Officer Commander-in-Chief, Eastern Command. Many locals turned up to watch, as they would do for all anticipated parades (and for rumoured parades, too!) Parker's Piece was used for much of the drilling, and after the war it was one of the sites considered for a war memorial, though eventually this was placed on Hills Road, marching away from the railway station, to show a soldier coming home, victorious.

While at the Melbourne Place Schools, a private in the battalion wrote a rousing song for enjoyment on long marches:

## THE MARCH OF THE MEN OF CAMBRIDGE

Tune: *Men of Harlech*

From Belgian shores we hear them calling;
Shrieks and clamour, loud, appalling,
homes uprooted, churches falling,
Vengeance, Cambridge men!

Leave your shops and benches
For the camp and trenches
A need so dire should inspire,
A coward he who blenches.

Men of Cambridge, see our neighbour
Weltering 'neath the tyrant's sabre,
Cease your useful peace-time labour,
Arm! ye Cambridge men!

Many are there gone before ye,
Mons and Cambrai know their story;
Let us share their death or glory!
Let us do our part!

Nobly have they striven,
Odds before them driven;
And surely, then, we Cambridge men,
Can give what they have given.

Well we know how just the cause is;
'Tis no time to count the losses,
Think of this each one who pauses:
God defends the right.

Shall the future generation
Live enslaved, a conquered nation,
And beneath a vile taxation
Sweat to pay the price?

Loudly answer 'Never!'
Each makes his endeavour
Till that last fight, when German might
Be crushed and slain for ever.

Freedom in the balance wavers,
Freedom that our forebears gave us;
Numbered with that freedom's saviours,
Be there, Cambridge men.

The song would have served as a call to further recruits to come forward as well as for keeping the men already in the battalion in time. With their presence in the centre of the city, the Cambs Kitcheners were very visible to the local community, particularly those who lived in Cambridge. On route marches, though, they would have travelled much of the local countryside, and while Kitchener Blue might not have been so attractive as khaki, the local character of the battalion and the fact that people could see those like them in the battalion already probably countered the poor uniform.

In December, Sidney Beeton wrote home that Billy Daniels had returned a day late from camp, and so received seven days confined to barracks. In these early days discipline was reasonably loose. Sidney wrote home one week in December:

'Dear Mother,

*Just a few lines hoping you are quite well as it leaves me now. We arrived here quite safe with one flat tyre in my hind wheel of my byke. I hit a stone at the bottom of the turnpike hill there is a lot of stones in the road and I forgot about them and turned right on to them and before I got a hundred yards it was flat, so I pumped it up and it carried me to Shadloes Farm and H.O. [Harold Orly?] caught me up and he stopped and helped to mend it. We started away from there about three minutes to nine and we got in about quarter past nine but we were not the last, there was a lot more came in behind us. But nothing was said about the pass not being late so everything was alright. But we are moved again today in another hut ? two higher we have moved in as we are in sections, two lots in a room so put No. 8 room on the address and they know where to send it. I don't suppose you know I forgot to bring my towel and button stick so will you send them by post as soon as you can as we expect having to show our kit this week so I shall want it. So I think this is all this time.*

*With best of love from your son. S Beeton xxx.'*

The battalion moved to the hut barracks on 18 December, spending Christmas there. Leave for Christmas was rotated in such a way that three of the four companies were in the huts over Christmas. A competition was held for the best-decorated hut in C Company, with No 6 Hut of 11 Platoon taking the prize. Before Christmas arrived, the Ladies' Recruiting Committee was busy securing a gift for every soldier in Cambridgeshire who was at home or abroad. On Christmas Day, there was a church parade at 9.30, followed by a visit round all the huts by Colonel Somerset who was warmly greeted by his troops. The officers arranged Christmas fare for their men, and in the afternoon there were to be sports. However, the weather did not co-operate and so only the boxing, arranged by Bob Sitton, was able to go ahead.

In early February, the battalion was confined to barracks for two weeks, suffering from measles. It is likely that this is what led to the death of Private Harry Hopkins. According to the *Cambridge Independent Press* he passed away in the First Eastern General Hospital after a short illness.

One of the highlights of the battalion's early existence came on 11 February 1915. The king came to Cambridge, in truth this time rather than mere rumour, and inspected not only the Cambs Kitcheners, but also all battalions training in Cambridge at the time. The king sent a special order to the Welsh Division, printed in the newspapers, that *'His Majesty was much pleased with the smart appearance on parade of the men of the Welsh Division and the 11th Suffolks and B Company National Reserve local guard, and with the soldierly manner in which they marched past.'* The king inspected the troops, drawn up on Parker's Piece, among whom the Cambridgeshire Kitcheners were conspicuous in their blue, rather than khaki, greatcoats. All troops were on foot, though cavalry were present, for there was no space for horses and vehicles on the Piece.

*'The King drove along the diagonal path leading to the centre of the Piece in a grey motor car, which pulled up opposite a flagstaff which had been erected about midway between the central lamp and Regent-terrace. As he alighted here the Royal Standard was hoisted at the flagstaff. Meanwhile, the troops, who had been standing "at ease", with bayonets fixed, came to "Attention" and then to the "Slope'. This evolution was executed with excellent precision and unison. At the word of command the various units moved almost as one man, a forest of rifles topped by the "cold steel", swung up to a sloping position upon the men's left shoulders, and the sun's ·rays glinted upon thousands of shining blades. It was an impressive and wonderfully pretty sight. A moment before nothing could be seen but rows on rows of ruddy, healthy faces surmounted by flat-topped caps.*

*Then, across the whole width of the Piece, the great billow of shimmering steel reared its shining crest, flickered a moment, and came to rest. Somewhere in the centre of the Piece a bugle note rang out – a solitary "G". A myriad of flashes of steel replied as the troops brought their rifles to the "Present" for the Royal Salute, and the band struck up the National Anthem. While the band was playing the vertical lines of steel remained steadfast and immovable, whilst the spectators bared their heads. Then back went the rifles to the "Slope". The cold glint of the steel hovered above the silent ranks for a moment and then suddenly it was gone. The rifles sank, like some great machine, to the "Order", and the ranks stood "At ease" once more.'*

The troops then marched past the king, with the reporter again waxing lyrical about their fine physique and observing that the Cambs Kitcheners looked ready to take the line overseas. The commanders of the battalions were presented to the king, and then he went home. No doubt this day would live on in the memory of all who were present, a welcome contrast to the disorder and mud that would be found in the trenches.

King George V talking to the Mayor W.L. Raynes, near Parker's Piece, during visit of 1915. (*Cambridgeshire Collection, Cambridge Central Library. S.1915 45706*)

In May the Cambs Kitcheners hosted a boxing tournament in Cambridge, inviting other troops billeted in the town for training to compete against them. Sport was an important part of all training, and the presence of Bob Sitton in the battalion, along with a number of other soldiers who seem to have been equally enthusiastic about boxing, made it particularly popular. The quiet period in Cambridge was soon to be over, however, and with it a more urgent focus upon war training and, in less than a year, active service overseas in France.

15766 Private Sidney Edward Beeton (seated) and 15474 Private Percy Dawson (standing). (*With thanks to Tony Beeton*)

Private Stanley Jacobs of Balsham. Wounded five times during the war, on 1 July 1916, 24 March 1917, 21 October 1917, 23 April 1918 and 30 August 1918. (*With thanks to Tony Beeton*)

Shoulder badge, unique to the Cambs Kitcheners. (*Author's collection*)

Cap badge of the Suffolk Regiment. (*Author's collection*)

Cambridgeshire Kitcheners in training in Cambridge, 1914. (*Cambridgeshire Collection, Cambridge Central Library. T.G.K14 29838*)

Buglers and drummers of the Cambridgeshire Kitcheners on Midsummer Common during training. (*Cambridgeshire Collection, Cambridge Central Library. T.G.K14 29840*)

Cambridgeshire Kitcheners Band during training. (*Cambridgeshire Collection, Cambridge Central Library. T.G.K14 29839*)

Cambs Kitcheners in training in Cambridge. (*Cambridgeshire Collection, Cambridge Central Library. T.G.K14 13348*)

Cambridgeshire Kitcheners in training in Cambridge. (*Cambridgeshire Collection, Cambridge Central Library. T.G.K14 29842*)

Soldiers of the Suffolk Regiment, billeted in Cambridgeshire in the early part of the war – most likely Cambridgeshire Kitcheners, but definite information not available. (*Cambridgeshire Collection, Cambridge Central Library. T.G.K16 36076*)

Soldiers on Parker's Piece in 1914, most likely the Cambridgeshire Kitcheners. (*Cambridgeshire Collection, Cambridge Central Library. T.G.K14 21580*)

# Chapter 4

# The 34th Division

On 18 June 1915 the battalion left Cambridge to join the rest of their division. They were now part of the Army, authority over them having been given over entirely to the Army Council. The Territorial Force Association which had raised them no longer had any responsibility for them, though the minutes of the meetings show that they still took an active interest in the battalion which they had put so much work into raising. From this point on, therefore, it seems fair to refer to them as the 11th Suffolks, though in the local newspapers they continued being called, variously, the Cambs Kitcheners and the Cambs Suffolks, as well as the 11th Suffolks, until the Army forbade the publishing of any more identifiable information than regiment.

The battalion left early in the morning, too early for families in the outlying districts to come to the town to see them off at the station, but townsmen turned out to wave them away. The battalion would eventually return to acclaim in 1919, at cadre strength, having seen active service from January 1916 to the end of the war and beyond it. They left in two parties, the first marching out at 6.15, with a good crowd from Cherry Hinton and there was a small crowd in Tennison Road, where they were boarding the trains. By the time the second party left, the whole area was lined with well wishers, and Charles Adeane came to see them off too. *As the train moved off the men raised a cheer and waved their hands and caps, the crowd outside responding with a cheer and the waving of handkerchiefs and hands.*

They reached Ripon where they joined the rest of 101 Brigade, which had already arrived. A brigade at this time was made up of four infantry battalions; later they would join two other brigades, along with engineer and artillery companies, to make up a division. For now, 101 Brigade consisted of the 15th Battalion The Royal Scots, partially raised in Edinburgh, partially in Manchester; the 16th Battalion The Royal Scots, raised in Edinburgh

Great Eastern Railway Station Cambridge. (*Cambridgeshire Collection, Cambridge Central Library. C.1914.1N.K14 4913*)

and, known as McCrae's Battalion, containing a number of footballers and football fans and the 10th Battalion The Lincolnshire Regiment, or Grimsby Chums. In the hilly moors, the pace of training increased, and the Cambridgeshire Kitcheners, accustomed to the flat land around Cambridge, were not impressed with the slopes. Months later in France, according to the divisional historian, steep inclines were greeted with *'cries of "Ripon!" in mocking disapproval'*.

Sidney Beeton wrote home to his mother: *'God knows when we are going to get some food, they say we shall not get any until Sunday dinner and the beer is sixpence a pint if you sit down and five pence if you stand up. We arrived about half past three and then got three miles to walk to camp. They are going to put the town out of bounds tomorrow, I expect we shall save money.'*

Their brigade was under the command of Brigadier General Hugh Gregory Fitton. Born in 1864 into a military family, he was gazetted lieutenant in the Royal Berkshire Regiment in 1884. He saw service in the Sudan, Egyptian Frontier Force, Dongola Expeditionary Force and the Nile Expedition. During the Dongola Expedition in 1896 he was awarded the

Cambs Kitcheners on a route march while at High Lindrick Camp, Ripon. In the centre with a moustache is 17360 Private Arthur Elbourne. (*With thanks to Tony Beeton*)

Distinguished Service Order. Later, in the Boer War, he served in a Staff position, while from 1913 he was the Director General of Recruiting. Given that he had also seen service in the same battle of Khartoum for which Kitchener was famous, this brigadier, with command of some of Kitchener's New Army, probably knew Kitchener personally.

Before being given command of 101 Brigade, he had been in charge of a portion of the coastal defences, being based in Tynemouth. He and his wife, May Fitton (née Hickman), who he had married in 1910, became well known in the area for their support of the Priory Army and Navy Institute, the YMCA movement and local relief funds. He would have been a man deeply interested in the lives of his subordinates, and his Staff experience meant that he would have a good background for starting a new division from scratch. Personally brave, he was the brigade's first battle casualty while he was inspecting the trenches that his men were shortly to move into.

Although training has been criticised as failing to embody the principles of trench warfare, and a failure to adapt to the realities of modern warfare, letters show that trench digging and defending was a common part of the routine. Various military-minded men wrote training schemes and gave advice which emphasised teaching the men to dig trenches, post sentries and relieve one another in exercises. Captain B.C. Lake wrote *Knowledge for War: Every Officer's Handbooks For the Front: Based on the War Office Syllabus of Training* based on his own experiences overseas. It wasn't just the public that sought and printed the advice of soldiers who had served overseas. One pamphlet printed by the War Office and distributed to troops was *CDS 383: Extract from Notes on the minor tactics of trench warfare*. This had been written by 'a casualty', and detailed not only the ideal way of capturing a trench or a small trench system, but also some of the common problems that might be encountered.

And Edgar Wallace, writing of the training process in 1915 or 1916, claimed that *'from start to finish... "war conditions" was the keynote of all the "Kitchener's Army" training. It was a training, first, last, and all the time, in the essentials of war. It could hardly be otherwise.'* He continued: *'tricks of trench war especially appealed to the Kitchener soldier, since the great war had developed so largely into a vast conflict of entrenchments.'* Others did not think it had gone so well. Captain Basil Williams, writing in 1918 admitted that up till the end of 1915 *'owing to the stress of circumstances during this first period, the training of the new armies was necessarily not so organised and systematised as it has become in the second period.'*

The time training in Ripon was not without incident – Sidney Beeton wrote home that a man in one of the Scottish battalions was killed in early July after being struck by lightning during a tremendous thunderstorm. There was a story going round that a second soldier, in the town, had also been killed while with his wife.

Unfortunately the *Cambridge Independent Press* makes no real mention of the training at Ripon, other than to say that it happened. However, the *Edinburgh Evening News* in July 1915 carried an account of the camps around Ripon from one of their staff who visited the area. Their correspondent wrote:

*'The lovely countryside was submerged in floods of khaki and the woods echoed to the din of war preparations. Troops of soldiers, in battalions, companies, and platoons, and in single spies, tramped past as gaily and gallantly as British troops are wont to do the world over. Then a battery of artillery would*

SERGT. T. HARD.    SERGT. C. HARD.    SERGT. A. HARD.

Brothers Theodore, Claude Reginald and Alec Hard, all of whom were serjeants in the battalion. They enlisted together on 7 September 1914. Alec was discharged on 26 July 1917 due to wounds. Theodore was commissioned into the Royal Warwickshire Regiment. All three survived the war and returned to Long Stanton. (Cambridge Weekly News *21 July 1916*)

> *go thundering by, despatch riders on motorcycles would flash past. The men in the area were those of the 'world-famed Kitcheners armies. It was a fashion among German writers to dismiss these armies as mere bluff... It is true, a mere assemblage of men does not constitute an army, and it has taken a longer time to fashion them into one than some supposed at first. But what I was now witnessing was the finished manufactured article, only awaiting the final polishing process before being put to use.'*

The 16th Royal Scots, which included most of the Hearts of Midlothian football team, were able to thrash their fellow battalions in various football tournaments organised during training. In the brigade championships, they triumphed, beating the 10th Lincolns 8-0, the 11th Suffolks 7-2 and the 15th Royal Scots 6-1.

The 11th Suffolks then embarked on a two-week musketry course. This was Sidney Beeton's favourite part of the training. He wrote to his brother Albert to say *'we are starting our firing tomorrow, Monday and I am on the butts marking Sunday afternoon just under the targets, this is the place to hear the bullets wiss [sic] and sing. I have got some in my pocket would you like one or two, I will bring some home when I come if you would like them. Well I hope you will get on with your jobs you are taking in hand. Well dear Albert I hope to see you all before long with love to all xxxxxx.'*

At the end of August, 101 Brigade moved to Salisbury Plain. Here they joined the rest of the 34th Division – the 102 (Tyneside Scottish) and 103 (Tyneside Irish) Brigades. First outnumbered by Scots, the 11th Suffolks were now thoroughly outnumbered by Geordies. This was their first chance to train together under their Divisional Commander, Major General Edward Charles Ingouville-Williams, known to his men as 'Inky Bill'.

Major General Ingouville-Williams was a Regular officer, and had commanded 16 Brigade of 6th Division from mobilisation until he was sent to take command of the 34th Division on 15 July 1915. In this time he was twice mentioned in despatches and often led patrols himself – a 'brass hat' who was prepared to expose himself to danger. He was a highly experienced officer from a military family. Born in 1861, he was the son of General Sir John William Collman Williams and joined the Army when he turned 20. He was commissioned in the East Kent Regiment, being promoted to captain in 1892 and serving as an adjutant between 1894 and 1898. He first saw active service during the Sudan Expedition in 1884-5, followed by the Nile Expedition in 1898-9. In 1903, after he had become a major, he was transferred to the Worcestershire Regiment, and the following year was promoted to lieutenant colonel, and full colonel in 1908. In 1910 he became the commander of the School of Mounted Infantry in Longmoor.

Here he was to face one of the major challenges of his pre-war career, when what was initially reported as a mutiny broke out in the camp. Initial reports claimed that Scottish soldiers, angry at not being given leave for New Year's Day, rioted and trashed the camp. Supposedly an officer then challenged one of the rioters to a boxing match and, having seen their champion thrashed in a fair fight, the men sullenly retreated to their huts. There were wild rumours too of bayonet attacks on each other and shots fired. However, Ingouville-Williams refuted these rumours and issued a statement that what had really happened was that some of the soldiers from the East Yorkshire Regiment grew angry at the result of a match between themselves and the Scottish contingent. A fight broke out and, with bricks, stone and rubble lying about, the fight became a general battle for around twenty minutes, with no fewer than 170 panes of glass in the huts being smashed. Some of the Scotsmen may have fixed bayonets to defend their quarters, but by this point officers were arriving with a contingent of men who had not become involved in the argument or subsequent fight and the matter was quickly quietened down.

Two men were injured; Ingouville-Williams insisted no one had been shot, and added that the Scotsmen were far from discontent as they had come to his quarters on New Year's Day and serenaded him (and presumably his family) with bagpipe music. Sadly for the sake of a good story, the boxing match probably never took place. He had not only averted a crisis amongst the men who were at least riotous in behaviour, if not in intent, but also did an admirable job of persuading the public nothing had really happened, and certainly nothing they needed to be concerned about.

Unfortunately, before divisional training was much advanced, Ingouville-Williams crashed his car into a traction engine in September and was unconscious for a week. Anxious not to lose his command, he was back a fortnight later and eventually made a full recovery, but it put the larger-scale divisional training somewhat on hold. Though unit training continued and much hard work was done, it meant a high pressure on training when he returned.

Alec Mack, one of the officers of the 11th Suffolks, would later write of him: '*He says he is going to save every life he can in his division. He is going to improve any trenches we go into, to make them absolutely safe, and so on. He is a fine man. He was in command of a brigade at the beginning of the war, and saved his own brigade by his calmness and bravery.*' The combination of active service experience and determination to look after his own men, meant that 'Inky Bill' was generally well thought of, at least by the junior officers like Alec Mack.

Training on Salisbury Plain was similar to that already carried out, but larger formations now had to work together. If putting four infantry battalions together was hard, there were now twelve, plus gunners and engineers, transport and sanitary sections and myriad other specialties. For this period of training, unusually, some brigade orders survive, though these are for 102 Brigade and not 101 Brigade. Much of their training would have been the same and a number of the orders recorded are divisional orders.

Amongst the men in the sanitary section was Corporal Wilfred Hipwell, of the 11th Suffolks, son of Mr Solden Hipwell (surveyor to the Chatteris Urban District Council). After his death in July 1916, his parents received a letter from a captain in the Royal Army Medical Corps, printed in the *Ely Standard*, describing some of the work he had done, as well as giving an account of his death. The captain wrote:

> *'I fear I can only confirm the sad news the rumours of which have already reached you. Today we heard officially from the Divisional Authorities that your son Wilfred had been buried. I daresay the official news has reached you by now, but I feel that I would like to take an opportunity of telling you what a high opinion I had of him. He was my sanitary corporal, as you know – a most important position for the health of the troops, but one that gave him ample opportunities of shirking danger if he had wished to. But he was never that sort, and I often had to restrain him when he would have exposed himself willingly to danger to do something I wanted doing but which could quite well wait till darkness lent more safety. He was known among us to be as brave as a lion, and he had great talent also. He was frequently complimented on his arrangements for the sanitation of the camp, and I think we were ahead of any other battalion in the division in this respect. I feel sure he would have won a decoration of some sort had he lived. As it was he died fighting. He was wounded once, I am informed, but refused to go back, and only when he got his second and mortal wound would he admit defeat and return to the ambulance. He died, I believe, just after admission to a casualty clearing station. And so perished a gallant soldier. It was a source of great regret to me that I did not see him during the fight, and was therefore not able to dress his wounds myself.'*

Signallers, too, would continue with their training. Rudyard Kipling described seeing: *'A platoon – or whatever they call it – was giving the whole of its attention to its signalling instructors, with the air of men resolved on getting the last flicker of the last cinema-film for their money.'* Signallers got out of some of the route marches and other exercises that the rest of the battalion and division had to do, but theirs was not a cushy job once the men went overseas. Signalling equipment was often heavy and difficult to manoeuvre and maintain, particularly when it had to be dragged forward during an advance, set up and then the wires kept free from breaks.

Second Lieutenant D.B. Johnson was a good example of this, receiving the Military Cross for his work as battalion signal officer on 22 and 23 March 1918. The citation read: *'as signal officer he helped, under very heavy fire, to maintain an exposed wire connecting battalion headquarters with a buried cable. Also he led a reconnoitring patrol, and under very heavy shell fire brought back valuable information.'*

At least two other signallers received Military Medals in June 1918. They were Serjeant Percy Albert Dowe and Corporal William Ernest Buck. Unfortunately the citations for the Military Medal were not given in the *London Gazette* or in any other official source of information. It is thus impossible to know for sure, but it seems likely they were awarded for the same or similar actions to those which led to the award of a Military Cross to their officer.

On 12 October there was a special machine-gun class, for the non-commissioned officers of machine-gun sections, by Captain Bruce Bairnsfather. Captain Bairnsfather had served in a machine-gun section in France, came close to being court-martialled for his participation in the Christmas truce and, after being wounded, had been given training responsibilities rather than returning to the front. It was while in a training role that he created the famous cartoon character 'Old Bill'.

The grenade-throwers, or bombers, also came in for special training. Major General Ingouville-Williams wrote in divisional orders that *'Too much importance cannot be attached to the training of Bombing Patrols for night work.'* He gave orders for the training of patrols, consisting of one officer and six other ranks, at night. Battalion scout officers were to be consulted for help in preliminary training and, once the basics were in place, night exercises were to be regularly carried out. Eight selected parties from each battalion were to do an hour's training every evening, some to represent the 'enemy' and some to be a 'patrol'. The enemy were to leave camp first, take up position in a particular section of the practice trenches and prepare for the bombing party to arrive. Everything possible was to be done to develop initiative in dealing with situations as they arose, but *'the work must not be allowed to degenerate into a "rag".'*

Bernard Hammond's Mentioned in Despatches certificate. (*With thanks to Paul Hammond*)

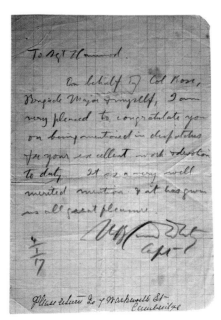

Notification to Bernard Hammond that he had been Mentioned in Despatches. (*With thanks to Paul Hammond*)

Another important section was that of the headquarters staff, men selected for their clerical skills. Amongst them was Bernard Hammond. Prior to the war, Bernard had been working as a clerk in Mülheim an der Ruhr, Germany, probably for S.G. Kaufmann GmbH, a Jewish leather-working firm. Bernard returned to England in 1914 because of the outbreak of war. A family story tells of Bernard's employer looking forward to re-employing him once hostilities had ceased, suggesting both that he was a good employee and that his employers had not been prejudiced against the British by propaganda. Perhaps too they expected a short war, more of a brief spat to decide a few matters of international policy before people got back to work. Upon his return from Germany in the late summer of 1914, Bernard found himself living in Cambridge with his family, just around the corner from Parker's Piece where the Cambs Kitcheners were being formed. Perhaps peer pressure was a factor in Bernard's decision to sign up to fight against the countrymen of his recent work colleagues. This predicament must have caused him some mixed feelings.

Bernard enlisted on 26 September 1914. His clerical skills were put to use as a quartermaster serjeant. Those skills may have spared him from going over the top on the first day of the Somme. Bernard served throughout the war, first at both brigade and battalion level. However, his work was not entirely without risk. He was mentioned in a despatch from General Sir Douglas Haig dated 13 November 1916, and later awarded the Meritorious Service Medal. He served throughout the war, though he sustained a leg injury that left him with a limp.

In June 1919 Colonel G.L.J. Tuck, wrote a reference for Bernard, stating that he *'showed himself to be an exceedingly hard working and competent NCO and made a great difference to the welfare of the battalion. I can very strongly recommend RQMS Hammond'*. After the war, Bernard returned to the continent, working in the leather business in Rotterdam, for N.V. Kaufmann Huidenhandel, where he met his future wife and established a family home. His son Peter wrote in his memoir that, after the birth of Bernard's second son Robert, ten years after the Armistice, that Bernard *'kept bursting into song with renderings of war-time evergreens like "It's a long way to Tipperary", "Madamoiselle from Armentières" and "John Brown's Body" and his version of the well known Verdi operatic aria "La Donna É Mobile", to which, in moments*

15578 Regimental Quartermaster Serjeant Bernard Hammond and tall corporal, c. 1918, photograph label R. Guilleminot, Boespflug et Co. (*With thanks to Paul Hammond*)

15578 Regimental Quartermaster Serjeant Bernard Hammond, c. 1918, photograph label R. Guilleminot, Boespflug et Co. (*With thanks to Paul Hammond*)

15578 Regimental Quartermaster Serjeant Bernard Hammond's cap badge and medals. (*With thanks to Paul Hammond*)

*of elation, he was given to singing the words "Ta-ra-ra boomdeeyay, where's Mrs Rossier?"'*

Another group of specialists were those in the transport section. Lance Corporal Arthur Josiah Elbourne had been in the Duke of York's Own Loyal Suffolk Hussars as a young man, but when he returned to the Colours on 12 December 1914 he re-enlisted, initially in 1st Cambridgeshires but then was either transferred or volunteered for transfer to the 11th Suffolks. His whole family walked part way with him from their home in Stapleford, going as far as the youngest child could walk, while his wife Elizabeth pushed baby Kathleen in the pram. As a man who could handle horses, his skills were much in demand; during the war he was awarded a Card of Honour on 26 June 1916 for galloping out an ammunition wagon that had caught fire.

The weather at Salisbury Plain *'showed pro-Boche tendencies'*, and a special demonstration for some Japanese generals, according to the 34th Division

Three horsemen of the 11th Suffolks transport section in France. On the left is 17360 Lance Corporal Arthur Elbourne. (*With thanks to Tony Beeton*)

history, became a *'distinctly amphibian performance'*. This was acknowledged in the subsequent congratulatory message from Ingouville-Williams, who sent all troops a message saying that he *'wishes to express his satisfaction of the good work put in by the troops today. He regrets the terrible weather experienced, but is extremely gratified at the cheerfulness in spite of it shown by all ranks.'*

The military authorities had a constant battle with *'hawkers of the gipsy class'*, who seem to have got onto the training ground and gone where they wanted, until chased off by officers who were under strict orders to prevent the men buying food or goods from anyone other than the authorised traders.

In September an urgent order was put out that stretcher-bearers were to be trained by battalion medical officers. These were to be all drummers, pipers and buglers in the battalions, and *'when a Battalion is being exercised in the trenches the removal of wounded men to the rear by means of the communication trenches will be practised.'*

Much mention is made of these practice trenches; in mid-September an order went out to commanding officers, reminding them that *'on all occasions when trenches at Bedlam Buildings (or elsewhere) are occupied by their units for instructional purposes the trenches must be left clean whether the trenches were found to be in a dirty condition or otherwise on occupation. Entrenching tools will invariably be taken into trenches and utilized after dark for repair purposes.'*

Despite the weather – which flooded out their first camp on Salisbury Plain and necessitated a move from Windmill Hill to Sutton Veny at the end of September – and hard work, high spirits continued. The 16th Royal Scots unsurprisingly won the football Divisional Championship on 23 October, defeating the 18th Northumberland Fusiliers. There were also cross-country races and other sports. Some of these were of a more military nature. Over the Christmas period, a bomb-throwing competition was held across the whole division, with brigade, battalion and company heats. The £3 prize was won by the 21st Northumberland Fusiliers. And, at the same time, someone in the division came up with an ingenious and labour-saving idea. Why lay your own wire when you could steal the German's by sending rocket-propelled grapnels across no man's land and simply tugging it across to lie in front of the British trenches? Unfortunately, the rockets were not particularly reliable and in early trials one nearly set a portion of the camp in the rear of the experiment on fire. Perhaps not the best idea.

The town of Sutton Veny. (*Author's collection*)

From October, some parts of the division began to feel that 'staleness' was setting in. They had been training hard, some of them for over a year, and they were keen to get to the front to make a difference. This eagerness to go abroad was not as naive as it has been portrayed – local newspapers in particular did not hide horrific truths. Men wanted to do their bit, weighed duty above fear, and were spurred on by the sacrifice of others. When they finally did get to France, Alec Mack commented: *'The men are extremely smart at present; the easy time and change of circumstances seems to have returned to them all the original keenness we had rather lost during our rather boring time during the last few months.'*

An anonymous officer of one of the New Armies, writing in mid-late 1915 made a similar point. He expected that *'It must soon be very near the time when training will cease and we of the New Army will be called upon somewhere to follow in the steps of the professional soldiers'*; his main concern was upholding the traditions of the British Army and to kill enough Germans *'to bring the great war to a triumphant conclusion.'* He concluded:

*'When those who stay behind read the story of its achievements... I for one should wish them always to base their criticism or their approval on the rock-bottom fact that it is a "civilian" army of men who have left their homes to defend them, and have taken up military studies under stress of dire national peril.... Many men have not felt the call; very likely they will be brought in under compulsion.'*

Though the infantry was ready (or thought it was), the artillery wasn't. All New Army divisions suffered from a severe shortage of guns and instruments to practise with. Most of these resorted to drilling with tree trunks in place of guns, with a handful of horses that they pretended were a full team. Parts of the 34th Division artillery had only three days training with actual guns before they went overseas. This was common across the whole of the New Armies. Many divisional gunners had to try and learn their trade without seeing, never mind firing, the guns they were being trained to use:

*'Some attempt was made to remedy the defect by various substitutes for the service gun. Dummy wooden guns were made or purchased by enthusiastic officers with which to teach their men the positions and notions of loading and firing; obsolete 15-pounders, 12-pounders and antiquated French 90-mm were utilised for the purpose; but even when some such guns as these were available, there were no artillery instruments such as dial sights, range finders, directors, and so on, without which a modern battery is almost helpless, except such as could be improvised by an ingenious limber-gunner.'*

Horses, harness and the proper wagons were also lacking and the horses that they did have were almost invariably as green as the men who were riding and manoeuvring them. Because of the massive importance of artillery and its more technical nature, problems in artillery training were probably more significant than any shortcomings in infantry training. Unsilenced machine guns would cause casualties regardless of how the infantry tried to advance across no man's land – only accurate artillery fire, either as covering fire or to destroy targets before an advance, could cut that completely.

On 13 December the division was ordered to mobilise for Egypt. Because they were now going on active service, the various battalions began to keep war diaries and these are valuable (if sometimes dry) accounts of the doings of the battalion. Sun hats and other stores were issued. Meanwhile, the generals were discussing strategy for the year ahead. On 6–8 December, the Second Inter-Allied Military Conference took place, deciding strategy for Britain, France and Russia to collectively defeat Germany. Chief of the Imperial General Staff, Archibald Murray, wrote this up into 'A paper by the General Staff on the Future Conduct of War', submitting it three days after the 11th Suffolks had been ordered to mobilise for Egypt. In this paper he argued that *'the General Staff see no sufficient prospects of success at the Dardanelles, with the means now at our disposal, and in view of the lateness of the season, to justify any further offensive efforts there at present.'* The whole tone of the paper was that offensive operations had best be conducted on the Western Front, as it was not advisable to withdraw troops from there, and that decisive operations were unlikely anywhere else. It is unsurprising, then, that the division was ordered on 26 December to go to France and the sun hats collected back up.

According to Murray: *'The General Staff find that our responsible officers in France, who are in close touch with the situation and with the relative "morale" of the opposing armies, are entirely confident in the possibility of defeating the enemy there, if we set about it in the right way.'* The 'right way' was, as it would turn out, more difficult to find than the paper would imply.

# Chapter 5

# To France, At Last!

The *Cambridge Independent Press* on 14 January was able to report that the 11th Suffolks had gone overseas.

*'In the darkness of a wet and cheerless January morning the platoon serjeants splashed their way through the mud to their different huts, passing the command, "Fall in – Company." … The Cambridge Boys drowsily rubbed their eyes, and, in a moment or two, when the real nature of the occasion dawned upon their sleepy senses (it was 3 am) they at once sprang from their not-too-luxurious "laydown" and commenced to slip into their equipment. None had undressed; they had slept as they stood, fit for action.*

*All was tense excitement, yet not a sound was made. The Boys had undergone a thorough and severe training and none but the hyper-fit had survived, and as two bed chums stood facing one another ready for parade, "At last," blurted out one, which was heard by all in the hut, and the humorous grins of satisfaction eloquently indicated how aptly the speaker had voiced the temper and spirit of the Boys in that "At last!"'*

Oliver Hopkins, at that time a private, writing to his mother, commented on the early start to the day. So too did then Lieutenant Alec Mack, in a letter to his mother. Mack, formerly an undergraduate at Jesus College, now a junior officer ready to take his place in the front lines, began a series of letters to his mother from his arrival in France. He hoped, one day, that they would be published as *'Drivellings of a young Officer at the Front'*. He died barely six months after going abroad, but the letters were privately published by his family after his death and constitute an excellent account of the early days in France.

Mack does not seem to have been the most organised of people. The time before departure was spent desperately trying to pack his 35lbs of luggage that was the officer's allowance. His first attempt maxed out the scales at over 55lbs, and he ultimately ended up with 45lbs, hoping no one would check; apparently he was justified in this hope for his luggage arrived all right in France. He tried to sleep that night in an armchair with the rest of the officers, but instead spent the night staring into the fire and *'seeing the pictures of men and horses you always see in fires'*.

The following morning's schedule for Mack was:

> *'At 3-30 we got up, 4-0 a hasty breakfast,*
> *4-45 I began to go to the lines to fall in,*
> *4-46 I came back for my glasses,*
> *4-48 I return for my identity disc,*
> *4-50 I return again for my day's rations,*
> *5-0 I fall in a quarter of an hour late.'*

The local newspaper was pleased to report that the Cambridgeshire Kitcheners did not depart unseen, despite the early hour:

> *'As the end of the column disappeared under a murky haze of rain down the road, a keen observer would have noticed at the side of the road, in front of the hospital, two nurses standing in their white uniforms. One had in her uplifted hand a handkerchief waving a last farewell to the column, but which in the uncertain light of the morning seemed more than a benediction. So the Sons of Cambridge have not gone forth without a woman's farewell; these two Ladies of the Lamp had acted proxy for the Women of Cambridge.'*

Mack saw several women out of their cottages who came to wave them off in spite of the early hour – he was impressed that despite having seen many thousands of soldiers pass by, they still rose to wave off the 34th Division.

The journey to France did not go as smoothly as might have been hoped. Half of the battalion was delayed when their train broke down. B and D companies remained an extra night in England, staying at Folkestone, as they were too late to catch the boat. Oliver Hopkins wrote that they *'put us all in the big hotels what is in front of the sea but there is no one lives in them now'*. This was a continuing great adventure for a young man who might otherwise have gone no further away from his village than Cambridge. Their subsequent crossing of the Channel was fairly smooth. Oliver Hopkins said they *'got on the boat and had a nice rode to it took us a 1 hour and a half on the water it was a nice boat to'*.

For the half of the battalion that had reached Folkestone undisturbed by broken engines (A and C companies), an entirely different 'treat' was in order. The crossing was rough, with one man in the division becoming so seasick and disorientated that he missed the arrival in France and ended up back in England, returning to France again the following day with the rest of the battalion. Mack was on this crossing and tried to avoid seasickness by eating a big lunch. He wrote that *'I paid three shillings for my lunch, and discovered afterwards that I had not bought it, only hired it for a short while.'*

After a night in tents near Boulogne, they moved to the Armentières front, sleeping in farm buildings near the lines. W.J. Senescall recalled:

*'We slept in farm buildings mostly and managed to keep fairly warm. I remember owing to being crowded two of us went into a cowplace to sleep. There was a cow and calf inside. We laid down with them. We could not sleep as the calf would not be still. Anyway we got a few winks in when in came the farmer and his wife with milk for the calf. My pal said "They have come to feed that bloody calf." In an instant the old girl said "Yes, "bloody calf", "bloody calf".'*

Sidney Beeton had a similar experience, being billeted in a pig place. He wrote to his mother that the war seemed far off even though they were now in France, but they could hear the guns which sounded like an *'everlasting thunderstorm'*.

Finding billets could be tricky for officers too, or even for the whole company.

*'When we were finally in bed and almost asleep comes loud knocking. Brown puts his head out of the window. "For the love of Heaven, come and show us our billets." B and D Companies have just arrived a day later than us and their guide is deficient in common sense. We are quite old soldiers now and past such excitement; we could billet ourselves in China if necessary. However, Brown goes to help.'*

Before the 11th Suffolks had even seen the trenches, their brigade suffered its first casualty. Brigadier General Fitton was wounded on the night of 19 January and died the following morning in the Casualty Clearing Station. He was accompanied by then Brigadier General C.L. Nicholson, who described the incident in his diary.

> 'General Fitton commanding a Brigade in 34th Division turned up to be attached for instruction. Went up to trenches with him and Tower after dinner. Passing behind the Forward cottage, Fitton got hit by a Sniper through both thighs. Got hold of stretcher bearers, and then went to get hold of KSLI doctor at La Brigue. Tower brought him down with the KSLI stretcher bearers. A bad job, as he was a very big man. Got back to HQ about midnight.'

Though Brigadier General Nicholson would pass for a time from the lives of the men in the battalion – and he likely put the incident out of mind too – they would meet again later when Nicholson was promoted and placed in charge of 34th Division after the Somme.

Alec Mack remarked of the loss of Fitton: 'We are all extremely sorry to lose him; he was such a priceless old man although he made us work. It was extremely bad luck for him.'

Not all senior officers were ignorant of trench conditions, and many, like Fitton, would lose their lives. In many ways this made things more difficult for their subordinates and units – the loss of a man like Fitton, who had stamped his character on the brigade he commanded, was sorely felt. It also meant that while newly in France, Colonel Somerset had to take temporary command of the brigade, leaving Major Farquhar, who had transferred into the 11th Suffolks as second-in-command on 15 January, in charge of the battalion. Doubtless everyone was relieved when R.C. Gore arrived to take command of 101 Brigade and Somerset could return to his men.

On 2 February 1916 the 11th Suffolks had their first spell in the trenches. They were attached for instruction to 69 Brigade. Up till this point they had done additional training in France, but now it was time for more practical training, in the lines that they would later man alone.

W.J. Senescall wrote of these trenches:

'We moved up to a smashed up village, La Boiselle, and on along the road to the trenches. The trenches here were not dug owing to low lying land but built up sandbags. That's why we had such cold feet. It was all mud. Several had frozen feet. Mine went numb and I remember when the warm weather came how the soles of my feet were throbbing as the feeling came back. Then we heard our first shots. Jerry kept up a steady fire on this road. However, none close to me were hit and at last we were in the front line. We were in a salient which was made during the battle of Loos. We were very close together here and could shout at each other on quiet days. We gradually got used to the crack of bullets during the night and doing four days in and four days in reserve. There were several dead men lying in "no-man's land". They had been lying there since September – about five months. They did a feint attack during the Battle of Loos. As the lines were so close together they did not get cleared up. There was one, a Scotsman, whose kilt kept flapping in the wind. We could see the front of course quite plainly with periscopes. A pal of mine said "I am going to creep out tonight and have a look at him." Sure enough he did and came back with a tin of machonachie stew from Jock's haversack. This stew was a really good brand and we did not get much in place of the eternal bully beef. He opened the tin and we had a small piece each. We said, at the time, it would be something to talk about. I did not dream that I should be writing about it about sixty years later.'

This account illustrates well some of the problems with accounts written sixty years after the fact – or even some that were written much nearer the time. The battalion first went into the lines near Erquinghem, not La Boisselle. La Boisselle was where they moved to in May and where they attacked on the first day of the Somme battle. However, Erquingham was close to where the Battle of Loos took place, unlike La Boisselle. Place names and exact dates are the most common casualties of time; stories such as that about digging through Jock's haversack, although impossible to prove, are more likely to remain close to events.

Private C.M. Newman wrote to his mother of the same first period in the trenches, and the letter was published in the local newspaper. People in Cambridge were eager for news of the battalion and, despite censorship, a good deal of detail can still be gathered from the press. This is particularly true when the war diary and other sources can be used to supply details that were censored out, namely where the battalion actually was in France.

Newman wrote:

*'We were put into the reserve trenches with the —, and on our way there we went through a village which was once in the hands of the enemy, and which, during an advance, our artillery blew to bits. We also had to go over some open ground, and were fired on by snipers, but no one was hit. We also passed many a grave of soldiers.*

*That night and next day was very quiet, and at 6 o'clock we were moved up into the firing line. All the work is done at night, such as building up the trenches, going between the lines to put up barbed wire, etc. We were kept very busy all night, and I fired about 200 rounds during the night. Next day we were busy filling up sandbags, as we thought that the enemy were going to bombard us. They started at 2.30, but our artillery soon shut them up with one or two shells which blew up some of their trenches. For an hour before sunset and an hour before sunrise we have to stand to.*

*The artillery are having a fight between themselves. As far as I know, we have only had one man hurt; he was wounded in the arm, so we have been lucky. These Germans are very funny people, but they are good shots. The trench I am in is only 200 yards from their trench, and in some places the trenches are only 60 yards apart. We can hear them talking, and often they shout across to us. When the Saxons are in they always call out, "good evening, English: we are here again."*

*We have just had an order that we are going to be relieved this evening by the —. As I am writing this the artillery are popping the shells over to the Germans but they are not making any reply.'*

Before the first spell in the trenches, Alec Mack had been transferred to the trench mortar battery. He would still be on the rolls of the 11th Suffolks and was still in the same division, though he might not be in the trenches at the same time as the rest. He also continued to have a good relationship with officers across the division. On 7 February, he wrote to his mother that:

*'The battalion has just returned to-day from the trenches for a week or so
before we return to them to take over part of the line. Where we are going
is, I believe, a fairly nice peaceful spot. I shall try and stir them up if I
have half a chance. What happens in trenches is: that if the Germans get
nasty and shell us, or send a few bombs from trench mortars, we try to make
ourselves nastier still and send over twice as many. Then the Germans get
nastier still, till both sides have got thoroughly bad tempered at having their
parapets spoiled and trenches messed about. Then it gradually wears out.'*

Although sometimes 'Tommy' might shout to 'Fritz', and the fraternisation
on Christmas Day 1914 is well known, this sort of tit for tat retaliation does
not seem to have been uncommon. Some battalions had a reputation for
being more 'active' than others; Alec Mack's attitude to firing the trench
mortars suggest that the 11th Suffolks might have been one of them. Mack
continued:

*'I have just seen Brown. He says he was going up to the trenches in rather
a nervous state of mind when the Officer Commanding the trenches into
which we were going for instruction met him, told him his serjeant-major,
would look after our men and took him to have a wash and then to have
dinner in mess. They had soup, meat, sweet and savoury, all to the strains
of a gramophone. Not bad for the much-abused trenches. The battalion was
in about a week and lost nobody.'*

Conditions in and out the lines were better for officers than for the men –
only to be expected. But, by the same token, casualty rates among junior
officers were incredibly high. The Brown mentioned in this letter as being
nervous would lose his life in action towards the end of 1916, while Alec
Mack was killed on 1 July.

Captain Tuck also spoke later of this early time in the trenches:

*'After training and equipping near the base … we marched by easy stages
to a quiet section of the front near Armentieres. There we went into the
trenches for instruction with another Kitchener battalion, and four days
later we took over that part of the line. Trench life in that sector just then*

*was a sort of domesticated warfare. During the three months we were there I should say that 30 per cent of the men never saw a German at all.'*

Colonel Somerset wrote to Charles Adeane on 12 February, to let him know how the battalion was getting on, and the letter was published in the press. In common with the rest of the country, Cambridgeshire men and women were desperate for news from the front.

*'We have been up in the trenches attached to other regiments for instruction, and have now returned to billets, some 30 miles from the firing line. I regret to say that we had six men wounded, and one man accidentally wounded by a bomb. No officers were hit.*

*The men are very fit and well, and conducted themselves splendidly in the trenches under all sorts of fire, both gun and rifle. I feel proud of them, and I am sure you will be too.*

*Yesterday Lord Kitchener inspected our Brigade, and expressed himself well pleased. I happened to be commanding the Brigade, as our new G.O.C. is on leave, and Lord Kitchener remarked to me that the 11th Suffolk (Cambridgeshire) Battalion were a fine body of men.'*

Undoubtedly the inspection was a proud moment for Somerset and the men he commanded.

On 21 February they returned to the trenches, this time on their own. Battalion snipers are mentioned repeatedly in the war diary at this time – if their count was accurate they hit seven Germans in the four days they spent in the trenches. Later in March they were commended for their good attitude in the lines and for the activities of their snipers. Sidney Beeton was one of the men who went on a sniping course, writing home on 1 May: *'I have been on a special course for a reserve sniper and it is a nice little job, we do not have to work too hard at it and it is about the safest job anyone can get in trench warfare.'*

This seems to have been Mack's first occasion in the trenches, though he had visited them before, and he sent a lengthy letter home, part of which gave details of the Germans' attempting to work on their front lines. He explained:

'*I nosed round and noticed some of the wretched Germans were having the cheek to work by day time, throwing earth out of their trenches. You could see on the snow on the parapet, so I sent them four rounds with my compliments and they then saw their mistake and stopped. I then watched their return of compliments with a battery of field guns; they were quite cruel to a small bush a hundred yards behind our line. I thought it rather a funny object to vent their spleen on. Yesterday I inspected the whole of the brigade trenches to see where I could make myself unpleasant to Fritz, and to-day we started making a beautiful emplacement in the salient.*'

The retaliation that trench mortar batteries brought on troops unfortunate enough to be near them sometimes made them unpopular with other troops. However, they would be glad of the additional fire power when they were in a more active part of the front. A few weeks later, Mack reported:

'*This afternoon a major in command asked me to get on to a dug-out in the German lines, the roof of which was showing over the parapet and from where a sniper had killed one of his men. I did so. We fired four shots, all landed in the trench, the fourth blowing up the dug-out. That sniper snipes no more. The infantry were awfully bucked and several men have spoken to me as I wander along the trenches about our good shooting. It was a long-range and there was a difficult wind. I was very pleased. The Germans retaliated with mortars, but fell short of our front line.*'

Though several amongst the battalion had been wounded in the trenches (one of them accidentally), the first man killed in action within the battalion did not die while in the front line. Instead, Private Harry Wilkins was killed while on a working and carrying party on 28 February. He was shot through the head while filling sandbags. Born in 1893 in Arrington, to Ellen and Rule Wilkins, he died on his twenty-third birthday. He worked on the Wimpole Estate before enlisting in Cambridge. His death shows how duties at 'rest' or out of the line could be just as strenuous and dangerous as ordinary front line service. Working and carrying parties often involved laying wiring in the front line (a shame that the rocket-propelled grappling hooks had not succeeded for they would have saved much work) or taking up ammunition or stores as trains and pack animals could only get so far forward.

Their first officer casualty was about a week later, when they had returned to the lines. Lieutenant Ian Drummond Claughton was killed on 2 March, at morning stand-to. Every morning and evening – the times when an attack was most likely – the front line trenches would be fully manned and everyone would peer together into no man's land; at other times this task would be given to designated sentries. Lieutenant Claughton's death was reported in the *Cambridge Independent Press* on 17 March. He was born in Bury, Suffolk, the son of a school inspector, and attended King's College Cambridge, graduating with a BA in 1912. He then joined the 11th Suffolks in September 1914, having been a school teacher at Dean Close School in Cheltenham.

At some point during this early period in the trenches the battalion faced a gas attack, or perhaps a rumoured one. Mack wrote home:

*'As we were passing him to go to the C.T. (communication trench) I noticed something funny about his face, so I asked him what was the matter with it. He answered that he was wearing a gas helmet. I asked him if it was for amusement, or because he thought his face would frighten the passers-by. He answered that there was a gas attack on. Then an infernal din broke out, artillery, rifles, machine guns, &c., Very lights. I can tell you we got our helmets on pretty slick. Of course, Kitty (that's Kitton) had forgotten his (he's getting the other battery in the brigade, a Scot – a topping chap), but as I had two I lent him one of mine, keeping the prettiest, a blue and white striped one, for myself. Then we proceeded up the C.T. Well, you have never worn a gas helmet. It smells like ten hospitals and nearly suffocates you. I could not breathe out of mine at first and the windows got misty, but it got all right soon. You can imagine what it was like, nearly suffocated, hardly able to see or hear, and slithering about in army rubber boots on the ice in the bottom of the C.T., catching my cloak in everything, never knowing who was coming towards us, whether it was a fat, greasy Fritz or what it was, not having the faintest idea what was happening in the front and the firing line we were making for, unarmed except for the moral effect our gas helmets would create by their hideousness.'*

Up until 31 March 1916, it was comparatively easy for the local papers to print news of all local war casualties, but after that date the War Office forbade publication of men's units, allowing only regiments to be published. It was thought that this information was too helpful to the enemy, and so families were requested to send in details of their war dead for publication. It is often possible to tell whether they were in the 11th Suffolks or another battalion of the Suffolk Regiment from other details in the accounts, but where it isn't, all fatalities are listed by the Commonwealth War Graves Commission. There were also some newspapers which ignored the War Office ruling – throughout 1916 the *Herts and Cambs Reporter* gives battalions for most of the casualties it lists, although it doesn't give all the casualties of the 11th Suffolks.

Part of April was spent with the division behind the lines in a training area. According to the divisional history, *'a thorough brush up and polish was commenced at once, and there was some grumbling among the war-tried warriors at having to go back to "Right turn, left turn, take the begger's name down" sort of work.'* Not surprising for a battalion that had seen at some action, had its first casualties, and been commended for its coolness in the lines. Of course, the men remained comparatively green, and higher command had far less confidence in their new found experience than the men themselves.

Early in May they returned to the trenches, this time going to an area near Albert. It was in this area that they would take part in the biggest attack of the war to date, the 'Big Push' that everyone knew was coming. Here there was some concern from the French woman that owned the land they were to be billeted on. Mack wrote home that *'Madame was in tears at having so many soldiers all over the place, but we soon pacified her, and did all she wanted, and now she cannot do enough for us, especially as I send Fuller, my servant, who is a gardener, to work in her garden every day.'*

A few days later, when they were in the front lines again, Alec Mack wrote home to describe the changed situation:

*'I am writing this in my dug-out. It seems very comfortable at present. We have one large dug-out in which Carroll slept with two machine gunners. I was going to sleep there too, and as I have a new officer, Ingle, with me he was going to sleep there. But by the greatest stroke of good fortune I spotted*

13574 Private Ernest Phillips of Longstanton. Died of wounds 15 March 1916. (Cambridge Weekly News *7 April 1916*)

9124 Private Ernest Mole of Burwell. Awarded a red card for gallantry at the front in early 1916. Later promoted to serjeant. (Cambridge Weekly News *14 April 1916*)

21893 Private George Kidman of Girton. Wounded in May 1916. (Cambridge Weekly News *2 June 1916*)

17522 Private Alfred Reynolds of River Lane, Cambridge. Died of wounds 24 May 1916, five minutes after being admitted to the hospital. (Cambridge Weekly News *2 June 1916*)

16301 Private George Brown. Died of wounds 2 April 1916. (Cambridge Weekly News *9 June 1916*)

15792 Private William Saxby of Madingley. Killed in action 24 May 1916. (Cambridge Weekly News *16 June 1916*)

16601 Lance Corporal Anthony Isaacson of Trumpington. Killed in action 23 May 1916. (Cambridge Weekly News *23 June 1916*)

15657 Private Bertie Oliver Woodcock of Catherine Street, Cambridge. Killed in action 22 May 1916. (Cambridge Weekly News *23 June 1916*)

*this one just near. It is the best dug-out I have ever had. The other dug-out is swarming with mice and rats, who scratch earth into you all the time, and come and expire on you at night. One fell down and died on the table while we were having tea. But in this I have only seen one mouse so far, and it has got about ten feet of solid earth over it. I sleep on a comfortable folding bed, in my clothes, of course. It is well back six or seven hundred yards from the firing line. The firing line is more unhealthy than other trenches we have been in. They will keep sending the oil cans I told you of over into the front line. If you manage to get away from them round a traverse they come rolling round the corner after you; I don't love them at all.'*

17358 Private Walter Lambert of Fen Drayton. Died of wounds 29 February 1916. (Cambridge Weekly News *24 March 1916*)

## Chapter 6

# Preparing for the 'Big Push'

On 21 February 1916 Allied plans for a joint offensive across all fronts were put on hold. The Germans had pre-empted them by attacking at Verdun. This French fortress was strategically and emotionally important to the French; they had to hold it. General Falkenhayn, the German commander, had selected this point deliberately. His intention was to bleed the French army white and thus force France to make a separate peace.

This changed the plan on the Western Front from a mostly French joint attack, with a British preliminary operation to begin wearing down the enemy, into a mostly British attack with French assistance. Right from the start, it was conceived as an operation to help relieve pressure on Verdun, though Haig's later justifications for the battle and the form it took probably made out that this was more important in the initial planning stages than it was. In essence, the Battle of the Somme stemmed from the commitment at the end of 1915 that all the Allies would attack on all fronts at roughly the same time and with as great a commitment to the fight as possible.

With the British now taking the lion's share of the battle, and having taken over parts of the French line in to assist their Allies as far as possible, the planning for the battle was carried out by the British with limited French input. Haig gave the task to his Fourth Army, commanded by General Sir Henry Rawlinson. While General Rawlinson had, by this time, a great deal of experience, he also disagreed with Haig on various points about how the operation should proceed. Rawlinson was, arguably, already ahead of his peers in his conception of tactical conduct on the battlefield. He did not hope for a breakthrough, as Haig did, and had no illusions about using cavalry to exploit a sudden shattering of the German lines. Instead, he planned a 'step by step' approach to the battle, a technique later known as 'bite and hold'. In essence, the German system would be very heavily bombarded, the British infantry would capture a small and manageable portion of it, and then the guns would move forward and the next portion would be heavily bombarded and then captured. This technique gave greater assurance of success, though a much smaller success would be achieved.

As far as Rawlinson was concerned, the greatest difficulty would be in holding the trenches once they were captured. Stationary Service pamphlet 112, 'Consolidation of Trenches after Assault and Capture' stated: '*The capture of a system of hostile trenches is an easy matter compared with the difficulty of retaining it. A thorough knowledge of the principles, a careful study and correct use of the natural features of the ground, and a detailed preparation and organisation of the work, are necessary; but success will only result if there is also an absolute determination on the part of all ranks to get the work done promptly at all costs.*' This was why troops carried so much equipment with them, from entrenching tools through to barbed wire, so that they were ready for the inevitable German counter-attack. Unfortunately, this presupposed that they were able to get into the German trenches.

According to 'a casualty', whose *Notes on Minor Enterprises* was published in extract by the War Office, particularly the portion relating to an attack on entrenched positions, there were four stages to an attack. While his pamphlet was based upon the principles to be employed in a local attack, many of the problems facing the 11th Suffolks would be the same. The four stages were:

1. Deliberate advance up to within assaulting range.
2. Obtaining a lodgement in enemy's network.
3. Maintaining the lodgement in enemy's network.
4. Extending the lodgement in enemy's network.

The biggest problem on 1 July 1916, would be the second step. 'A casualty' wrote that:

'*The enemy's strong points, keeps and above all his machine guns and their emplacements, must be located beforehand by every means at the disposal of the staff.... This work is of the utmost importance and fully justifies the employment of a special Staff Officer whose sole duty is to locate these strong points. When it is considered that few machine guns, well wired in, can arrest the attack of a whole division, it is impossible to exaggerate the importance of this point.*'

Sadly, the importance of this did not seem to have been taken in; or, where it was, the ability to do anything about it was lacking. The capability of the artillery to adequately deal with not just machine guns but hostile artillery was severely limited by poor weather in the lead up to the assault. Although this is most commented on in terms of delaying the attack and leading to a seven, rather than five, day bombardment, it also significantly limited the ability of the Royal Flying Corps to observe the fall of artillery fire and thus correct it – and to discover where hostile machine and field guns were located.

Haig, rather than hoping for small gains followed by German counter-attacks that would allow the British to inflict heavy casualties on the enemy, instead wanted to see a major breakthrough. After the Battle of Loos in 1915, Rawlinson had determined that more guns than that per portion of trench would be essential. Unfortunately, the deeper objective meant that the number of guns per section of trench was much lower than it needed to be – and lower than Loos, which had been assessed as inadequate already. Some work had been done on making the artillery more effective with the publication of a study on how best to cut wire based on both experimentation and practical experience. After the shell scandal of 1915, leading to the creation of a coalition government with Lloyd George as Minister for Munitions, much work had been done on supplying the Army better. However, the new factories churning out shells were doing so without the benefit of many skilled workers, who had often enlisted, and with poor quality control procedures in place. Estimates put the number of dud shells as being up to a third of all those fired in the preliminary bombardment.

The task of taking the front line, intermediate line and a zone of defence east of Contalmaison, plus the outskirts of Pozières was allocated to the 34th Division. This put them around the middle of the British lines, not far from Thiepval, where many of the battalion's casualties are commemorated. According to the plans for the battle, found in the 34th Division war diary, the battalions were to advance with a 300-yard front per battalion in four waves. The first two waves were to form up for the attack in no man's land, while the next waves would follow on from them. The 11th Suffolks were the second battalion on their front, following immediately behind the 16th Royal Scots. After the first battalion took the first line of the German defences, the second battalion was to go through them and take the intermediate line; 103 (Tyneside Irish) Brigade was to then go through both sets of troops and take the final objective. If one or other of the groups got held up, men were to be pushed forward to assist.

As the plans filtered down the levels of the British Army, additional details were added, often with input from the levels above. Battalion orders insisted that there was to be no use of the word 'retire' and that no one was to search for souvenirs or to help wounded comrades back to their own lines. Men doing so would be subject to court martial. The emphasis on not saying retire or retreat was a strong one; it was claimed that the Germans had caused much confusion by shouting 'retire' and hoping the British troops would obey. If a tactical withdrawal was considered necessary, it was only to be conducted with written authorisation, again under penalty of court martial. This could lead to a firing squad, though it must be stressed that not all courts martial did lead to death sentences – they were used for serious offences, but not necessarily ones that carried the death penalty – and many death sentences were commuted.

Men were to carry a huge variety of stores. The battalion orders listed that every infantryman was to carry:

• Rifle and Equipment less pack (Haversack on back).
• 2 extra bandoleers of S.A.A.
• 2 Mills Bombs.
• 1 Iron Ration.
• 1 Days Ration.
• W.P. Cape.
• 4 Sandbags in belt.
• 1 Gas Helmet and 1 pair Goggles in satchel.
• 1 Gas Helmet will be worn on the chest pinned to the shirt.
• Box respirators will be carried by all those in possession of them.
• A yellow triangle pinned base upwards on outside of haversack.
• 1 pick or shovel (proportion to be equal).
• An adequate supply of Rifle oil (oil can as well as bottle).
• 1st Field Dressing.

This was a huge amount to carry across uneven and muddy ground, churned up by the seven-day bombardment. But, because Rawlinson was convinced that the hardest part of the task should be holding on to the ground once they had captured it, the list makes a degree of sense. It is also worth noting that in many parts of the battlefield it became incredibly difficult to move supplies up after battle had begun, despite the allocation of carrying parties from reserve troops.

The first wave of the 11th Suffolks was to leave a secondary British line (Kingsgate line) at two minutes after zero. There would be a mine exploding at two minutes past zero too, and *All ranks should be warned that the concussion will be considerable.'* If all went to plan, the 11th Suffolks would be ready to consolidate the trenches that they had captured, with strongpoints already mapped out in advance for them. This enormous mine explosion was the one that made the Lochnagar crater, which is now a memorial in France.

The huge quantity of paperwork that make up these plans has to be seen to be believed. There are pages and pages of details, about what men would wear, how communications would be established, where headquarters would move to and so on. All headquarters clerical staff, including Bernard Hammond, would have been incredibly busy typing out and correcting orders, ensuring they reached the right place; much of this work at battalion and brigade level would have been carried out within range of the guns.

There was little contingency planning for disaster, but many expected that the artillery would be effective enough to get the infantry through at least the first parts of the defences. The reason for all the details was simple: Rawlinson and others in the British High Command believed the New Armies were incapable of acting without it. In *Fourth Army Tactical Note*, Rawlinson explained:

*'Owing to the large expansion of our Army, and the heavy casualties in experienced officers, the officers and troops generally do not now possess that military knowledge arising from a long and high state of training which enables them to act instinctively and promptly on sound lines in unexpected situations. They have become accustomed to deliberate action based on precise and detailed orders.'*

He went on to stress the need for careful and consistent practice, including what men should do when their officers and non-commissioned officers were unavailable. He asked that men practise what to do if they had to deal with *'a portion of a line being held up, impassable obstacles encountered, or local counter-attacks by themselves or the enemy'*. This was excellent advice, in theory. Unfortunately, very little time was available to battalions to practise these kinds of situations and so men were forced to rely on just the plan, rather than having been given the time, training and knowledge to improvise around it. Rawlinson was adamant that men must obey the orders they were given, something that he too may have struggled with, given his disagreement with Haig about the methods to be used on 1 July. He told his subordinates that *'it must be remembered that all criticism by subordinates of their superiors, and of orders received from superior authority, will in the end recoil on the heads of the critics and undermine their authority with those below them.'* He seems to have followed his own advice.

The biggest problem of all with *Tactical Notes* was that the advice on attacking was not followed by Rawlinson and the generals when it came down to planning the Somme. The author of *Tactical Notes* wrote: *'Under present conditions the limit of the artillery will sometimes include the second system of trenches, but not the third line. This second line should usually also be within the limit of endurance of the troops.'* Rawlinson, under pressure from Haig, then expanded the 1 July objectives to include areas beyond not only the intermediate line, but areas well beyond it.

The 11th Suffolks first began intensive training for the assault on 5 June. The battalion war diary records that *'Attacks were carried out daily against flagged trenches to represent the enemy's lines between Albert and Contalmaison.'* Although this was not as realistic as it could have been – they were probably 'attacking' across fields of corn or tall grass, not across crater-scarred mud – it did go some way towards preparing the troops for what they would have to do. Alec Mack wrote of this training to his mother:

*'As I told you in my last letter we are now resting, and we are doing it very vigorously indeed…. When you are having a thoroughly good rest you rise at 6 am, parade at 6.45 every day, and charge across country, practising the assault for the day that has always been coming (is always in a fortnight)*

*and never comes off – the great Spring Offensive. That's what we have been doing the last few days, walking five or six miles out, then walking two miles or so across country, and then marching home. Every day we receive orders in the afternoon that the brigade will go somewhere, to the trenches or to some other village, but they are always cancelled in the evening.'*

This was to be his last letter home. He was on leave from 15 to 22 June, and did not write again between his return to the front and his death less than a fortnight later.

A number of new men joined the battalion at this time, to replace early war casualties. Amongst them was Private James Albert Bays, whose service record survived both the First World War and the bombing of the National Archives in the Second World War. He had joined the 13th Suffolks on 6 November 1915. This was the reserve battalion raised in Cambridge, in part from the extra two companies of the 11th Suffolks that had been raised. He was significantly under age, having been born on 14 March 1899. A well-built teenager at 5 foot 7½ inches, and with a 34-inch chest measurement, he would have been bigger than some of those who were the right age to serve. It is quite possible, though, that doubts about his age meant that he was put into the reserve, rather than service, battalion at the beginning. After the Battle of the Somme, in mid August, he was taken away from the battalion – it is not clear whether this was his own choice or whether it was that of his parents – and placed into an under-age reserve battalion in England. The day after his nineteenth birthday, when he was officially old enough to serve, he returned to the front, initially as part of the Northamptonshire Regiment, and then the 12th Suffolks. A few weeks later he was reported missing, but had become a prisoner of war, returning to England after the war and, most likely, continuing his pre-war career as a butcher's assistant, perhaps running his own business one day.

By the night of 15/16 June, the training was over. The whole battalion was sent to Bécourt Wood, where they spent several days digging assembly trenches for the coming advance. This was strenuous work, and not without its dangers. Lieutenant R.V. Burrowes and Captain Angus Kidman Bird were both wounded during this time, men that the battalion could ill afford to replace this close to an assault. There were also three other ranks killed and nine injured in the weeks immediately prior to the attack.

The Chateau de Bécourt, headquarters of the 11th Suffolks during the first day of the Somme. (*Author's collection*)

One of these men was Private Leonard Hagger, the oldest son of Mr and Mrs Walter Hagger, of Thriplow. He died in hospital in France from wounds received while in the trenches. He had enlisted with his brother, George, in early October – the two had almost consecutive regimental numbers (Leonard's was 15610, George's 15608). The lieutenant in charge of their company wrote home to his parents with the news, the letter being printed in the *Cambridge Independent Press* the day before the assault, saying:

*'Leonard has been in my platoon ever since I took charge of it in 1914, and I have always had the highest appreciation of his good qualities. He has always been very quiet and unassertive, but I have learned to know him as one of the very steadiest, most intelligent, and hardest working men in my platoon. Especially since we have been in France I have formed the very highest opinion of him, and I shall miss him more than I can say.'*

Another was Gadsby Dring, who was killed by a shell on 21 June. The Reverend Canon Adderly wrote home to give the news, saying: '*I deeply*

*regret to have to tell you that your son was killed last night in action, and I buried him this afternoon in the military cemetery. Please accept my sincere sympathy with you and your family in your sad loss, and my God comfort and sustain you.'*
His captain and second lieutenant also wrote, the latter telling his parents:

*'He was killed by a shell which burst in the trench. I can only offer you the consolation that he died for his country. His cheerfulness in trying times will be missed by all of us, his comrades. We buried him behind the wood not far from where he has been doing his duty as a true British soldier.'*

Gadsby's father had been a soldier in the Afghan War, and three of his brothers also fought in the war. Gadsby had been a Scout, and so on the Sunday afternoon after the news was received a special Scout memorial service was held at Chatteris Parish Church with the Scouts parading with black bands as a token of respect. The hymns were 'Abide with Me', 'Fight the Good Fight' and 'For all the Saints', and a short talk was given by the Scoutmaster (the Rev. H. McNeice) on 'Running a Straight Race'. To conclude the service, the Dead March from Saul was played and the Last Post was sounded by Corporal F. Freeman.

Captain Tuck recalled of this period that *'we were relieved by some Anzacs from Gallipoli, and marched back to a training area to prepare for the Somme offensive. We arrived in the Somme area in May, where it was obvious that extensive preparations were in progress, and every man realised that we were in for something big. That was one of the worst trench sectors in France, and harried by trench mortars, mines, and gas, we were not sorry when the offensive began.'*

On 24 July 1916, the bombardment began. Following a carefully constructed artillery programme, shells rained down on the German defences. The hope was to kill all the Germans and for the infantry to then be able to walk across and occupy the enemy trenches, before pushing forward with cavalry to create a great hole in the German lines and perhaps win the war. However, although the bombardment looked impressive, it was weakened by poor weather, poor quality shells, exhausted guns and gunners and by a low emphasis on anti-artillery fire. This would have grave consequences when the troops came to attack; not only was the weight of shell on the German trenches inadequate (especially with the depth to which the Germans had dug), but the German artillery was able to lay down a massive bombardment on no man's land.

On 26 June the 11th Suffolks received their orders for the attack. Everyone had known it was coming – hard not to with the rehearsal of attacks on mocked up German lines and the digging of new assault trenches. However, it seems surprisingly late in the day for such complex orders to be issued, even if aspects must have been known about beforehand. The assault was to take place on 28 June and so, on the night of the 27/28, the battalion moved up in battle order to their assaulting trenches. The order was then given that the attack had been postponed forty-eight hours, due not to inadequate bombardment, but the weather. Although in the earliest plans there was talk of not attacking until all the wire was definitely cut and all defences definitely damaged, with such a large assault this proved impractical. So, although in places along the Somme front the German wire was reported as not cut, or poorly cut, the attack was going ahead as soon as the weather cleared.

The 34th Division was to make an advance of about 3,500 yards, on a front of about 2,000. This advance included around six lines of trenches, plus two fortified villages. In describing the attack, the 34th Division's history commented: *'Truly might the representative of Army Headquarters, who came to address the officers tell us that if we carried out the whole of the programme we should do uncommonly well, and that we ought not to be disappointed if we only achieved partial success.'*

It was 26 June, too, when Arthur Elbourne was awarded his Card of Honour, for *'Gallant work in Albert in relation to an ammunition wagon'*.

The 11th Suffolks waited for the assault in trenches somewhat overcrowded, despite HQ and one company moving into the RE dug-out to ease this. The weather was poor and the men were doubtless nervous about what the assault would bring.

Ominously, on the night of 29/30, the Summary of Operations reported that *'3 parties of the 34th Division tried to get into the hostile trenches but were stopped by M.G. fire.'* In neighbouring 8th Division, *'patrol reports wire cut very well nearly everywhere. It found the enemy trench fairly strongly held and the enemy very alert.'*

Some of the officers were cheery about the prospect of a great attack; Mack had written home earlier in the year that:

*'It is so difficult to hurt anyone actually in trenches; I think a mortar is the only thing that can do so. With dozens of shells sent over in the last ten days or so (40 yesterday morning) there has not been a single man in the brigade wounded by shell fire, and rifles and machine guns are the same. The casualties occur only in a push when one goes over the parapet, and that is not war, only a big field day. I was talking to a serjeant-major who had been through Neuve Chapelle, and said that it was just like a field day in Salisbury Plain, men marching in fours in all sorts of formations. His battalion halted after a little, ate its lunch, and then went on, got a bit too far forward, returned and dug themselves in, and trenches again. It is a hole and corner affair.'*

Corporal Leonard Samworth of Balsham. He was badly wounded on 16 June 1916. After recovering he served in the Royal Army Medical Corps and survived the war to become a farmer. (*With thanks to Mrs Anne Kiddy and Janice Ellam*)

Portrait of Corporal Leonard Samworth. (*With thanks to Mrs Anne Kiddy and Janice Ellam*)

Leonard Samworth's Medical Transfer Certificate. (*With thanks to Mrs Anne Kiddy and Janice Ellam*)

Corporal Leonard Samworth on horseback. (*With thanks to Mrs Anne Kiddy and Janice Ellam*)

Leonard Samworth's Medical Certificate on transfer to the Reserve. (*With thanks to Mrs Anne Kiddy and Janice Ellam*)

Letter notifying Leonard Samworth's mother that he had been wounded. (*With thanks to Mrs Anne Kiddy and Janice Ellam*)

However, not everyone was so optimistic, and it must be remembered that Alec Mack was writing home to his mother, naturally he wouldn't want to worry her with too much information on what might go wrong.

Even where the wire was well cut, it seemed that the Germans knew what was coming and were ready for it – hardly surprising, given the length of the bombardment and the very visible preparations for assault. What should perhaps have given cause for concern was that these Germans were evidently not all killed by the bombardment and were able to mount effective resistance. However, it was by now too late to stop the attack that was in motion. Haig and Rawlinson had to deliver an assault to satisfy the French of their commitment to the war and Haig still had high hopes of a cavalry breakthrough.

*Chapter 7*

# The First Day of the Somme

From 5am on 1 July the 11th Suffolks began to move to their jumping off points. They were slightly delayed in getting into position as 102 Brigade extended too far and took up some of their allotted space. However, the confusion was sorted out and by 7am all were in position and ready. The concentrated artillery barrage began at 6.25am, with an intense fire falling on the German trenches. In the 34th Division area, the artillery plan called for the heavy guns to move in a series of lifts, while the lighter ones would rake back slowly over no man's land, with troops staying as close behind the barrage as possible. Later known as a 'creeping barrage', this tactic could produce good effects, enabling the troops to get as close as possible to German lines without losing the protection of the artillery barrage.

Overnight, light trench mortar guns were moved forward into no man's land and into other forward trenches. The brigade papers record that *'it is difficult to collect evidence of the number of rounds fired by these guns as Lieutenant Kitten and the personnel with him subsequently became casualties, but it is understood that the fire was effective.'* The same was true of Alec Mack's party. At 7.22am, eight minutes before zero, these guns began to fire. Six minutes later, the mine opposite the left of 101 Brigade was exploded, and then at 7.30 the assault began. There was nothing left for headquarters staff to do but wait and watch and try to make sense of the confused reports that began to filter back to them.

Simultaneously across the nearly 18-mile long front, men rose up from their forming up trenches or, in some cases, from shell holes in no man's land, and began to advance on the German lines.

*'No braver or more determined men ever faced an enemy than those sons of the British Empire who "went over the top" on 1 July 1916. Never before*

The Advance up Sausage Valley. The troops are unidentified, but the date and location strongly suggests that this shows the 11th Suffolks. (*Author's collection*)

*had the ranks of a British Army on the field of battle contained the finest of all classes of the nation in physique, brains and education. And they were volunteers not conscripts. If ever a decisive victory was to be won it was to be expected now.'*

So wrote Brigadier General Sir James Edmonds when he composed the section on this battle in the British official history.

Captain Tuck recalled: *'On Sunday morning, 1 July, we gathered in the assembly trench soon after daybreak. Everything was against us. Our trenches had been badly knocked about, for the Boche had seen our preparations during the past two weeks, and must have had a good idea of what was going to happen.'*

The 11th Suffolks wouldn't have reached no man's land immediately. Instead, they had to move forwards, behind the 10th Battalion of the Lincolnshire Regiment (the Grimsby Chums), and then attack. Senescall believes that the assault started at 8am, but it is difficult to be sure whether it took half an hour after the first lines beginning to move for the 11th Suffolks to reach the front lines or not. Oliver Hopkins, writing to his parents from a hospital in France on 3 July, said that they had gone over at 7am.

From the start, things began to go wrong. The lack of emphasis on counter-battery fire during the preliminary bombardment meant that the German gunners were ready and waiting for the moment of the assault. As soon as it was launched, they began to lay down heavy fire on the British front lines. At divisional headquarters, Ingouville-Williams could see that the barrage was heavy and accurate, falling mainly on the front line trench, which the 11th Suffolks would have to advance through to reach no man's land.

Due to the mine explosion, the 10th Lincolns and 11th Suffolks were starting out further from the German trenches than other 101 Brigade troops. The further they had to cover in the open, the more difficult the assault would be. From the moment they left the assembly trenches, both battalions were met with heavy machine-gun and rifle fire. *'In spite of the fact that wave after wave were mown down by machine gun fire, all pushed on without hesitation though very few reached German lines.'*

Early reports from observers were that the 10th Lincolns and 11th Suffolks were able to reach their objectives; however, it soon became clear that this was wildly optimistic, or at best based on only a handful of troops getting forward. Similar problems with reports were experienced all across the Somme battlefield. The 11th Battalion East Lancashire Regiment, better known as the Accrington Pals, attacking at Serre, were reported to have made it to the village. This report seems to have been based on a small number of troops who somehow got through heavy fire all the way to their final objective, only to be cut off and all become casualties. The confusion

14432 Corporal George Percy Driver of Elsworth. Killed in action 1 July 1916. (Cambridge Weekly News *4 August 1916*)

15813 Lance Corporal George Allgood of Barton. Died of wounds 3 July 1916. (Cambridge Weekly News *11 August 1916*)

15471 Private Albert Bradnam of West Wickham. Died of wounds 30 July 1916 after suffering 'extreme agony'. Patient at the 2nd Western Hospital, Manchester. Buried in West Wickham, St Mary's Churchyard. (Cambridge Weekly News *11 August 1918*)

15901 Private William Joseph Wilderspin of Histon. Killed in action 1 July 1916. (Cambridge Weekly News *11 August 1916*)

of the battlefield was intense – communication systems were primitive, and relied on aerial observation, signals and runners. Radios were too heavy to carry into battle. Nearly a hundred years on, it remains difficult to piece together what happened and where troops got to.

Field telephones were brought forward and wires laid, but these were easily cut by shell fire, especially given how intense the bombardment was. W.J. Senescall, though not originally meant to be doing so, ended up pushing a drum of wire forward for the field telephone:

> *'I pushed the drum along as well as I could as I had to negotiate by corpses, shouting wounded men and large lumps of earth. Puffing and panting I kept this up for a long time as I was crawling along on my stomach and progress was slow. At last I thought I must have a look round – I had got some thirty yards from Gerry's trench. I could see the Gerry hats moving about their trench top. That settled it – no use taking the wire to them.'*

He lay down in no man's land to shelter as best he could, while all around those who moved forward, or attempted to do so, were mown down by machine guns. Shells continued to fall, though the open parts of no man's land became quiet and still, no one daring to move. W.J. Senescall lay there all day until he was able to get back to the British trenches.

Matters were made more difficult for the whole division by the fact that some troops which had pushed on to reach further objectives had left behind groups of German soldiers. These soldiers were then able to emerge from their dugouts and cut off advancing troops – rather than the result hoped for in the plan, which was that the German troops, cut off from the rear, would be forced to surrender.

Most of the casualties to the battalion probably took place in the first hour of the attack. Within an hour of the assault being launched, the Divisional History records that the units of 101 Brigade *'ceased to exist as effective units'*. Serjeant Dellar, a cook in the battalion and thus not directly involved in the attack, wrote home to his wife that *'our boys went over splendidly, just as if it was a manoeuvre or a grand field day. We knew we had a dangerous job on, as we "copped" all their spare fire, but none touched us. Well, we had the kitchens back up the line, but we could not get up to them as they had got farther on than was*

15357 Private George William Pink of Boxworth. Killed in action 1 July 1916. (Cambridge Weekly News *18 August 1916*)

13661 Private Ernest Cox of Willingham. Killed in action 1 July 1916. (Cambridge Weekly News *1 September 1916*)

13573 Serjeant Smith Stevens Poulter MM of Willingham. Killed in action 1 July 1916. (Cambridge Weekly News *1 September 1916*)

13649 Private Robert Wilson of Weston Colville. Killed in action 1 July 1916. (Cambridge Weekly News *8 September 1916*)

*expected. We got up the next day, however, and I had some grub ready for them, and they had a feed – not half!'*

Carrying around 66lbs of equipment each – more if they were in a specialist section and were expected to carry additional materials – there was no way that the men could move quickly through the falling shells and hail of machine-gun fire. The weight of their equipment also made it difficult to make use of cover. Though the intensity of fire was such that heavy casualties would have been sustained regardless of how quickly the men moved, the ability to travel faster across no man's land would have reduced casualties and might have enabled more of the fire-swept ground to be covered before the Germans could get out of their dugouts and start shooting.

Serjeant Wright wrote:

*'I was with the company the night before the attack took place and had a chat with Joe. I quite expected I should see him again all right, as we did not think for a minute that they would meet with very much resistance. But, as we now know, they were faced by very heavy machine-gun fire. They advanced bravely as if only on parade, and met their deaths like the heroes they were. Our losses were very heavy, but a high proportion of the wounded were only slightly hurt, and we hope will soon recover.'*

Joe Mason was just one of the 188 men of the battalion who were killed on that day.

Montague Cutter's brother wrote to his sister with what news he could get, *'All I can find out is that he went out of the trenches all right; of course every man was for himself after that. It was those machine-guns that thinned us out, for it rained bullets. He was killed going across no man's land. Poor old boy, he was in good spirits that morning, and he saw no fear of anything.'*

Private Fromant, by contrast, was probably killed by a shell:

*'I am sorry to say I can tell you very little of your son, Private J.H. Fromant, of our Battalion, as none of his section are left with me. On 1 July we took part in a big attack on the German trenches, and from letters received from wounded men it seems almost certain that your son and others of his section were killed instantly by a shell shortly after leaving*

16412 Lance Corporal Herbert Edwin Webb Cornwell of Horningsea. Killed in action 1 July 1916. (Cambridge Weekly News *8 September 1916*)

13777 Serjeant Reginald George Bareham of Newton. Killed in action 1 July 1916. (Cambridge Weekly News *15 September 1916*)

13785 Lance Corporal William Horace Humphreys of Cambridge. Killed in action 1 July 1916. (Cambridge Weekly News *15 September 1916*)

16357 Private Stanley Gawthorpe of Stow Cum Quy. Killed in action 1 July 1916. (Cambridge Weekly News *15 September 1916*)

*our own trenches and while advancing quietly and steadily against the Germans.'*

Reports in the local papers seem to show casualties split about evenly between those from machine-gun fire and those from shells, making it clear that although the battle is best remembered for machine guns mowing down lines of infantry, the German artillery played just as great a role in causing the heavy casualties.

Corporal R. Harley had a narrow escape, and wrote home about how a letter from Major M.G. Townley (a Conservative candidate for North Cambs) helped to save his life.

*'I had always carried the letter in my left-hand top tunic pocket along with several pocket books. On 1 July the 11th Suffolks were on the right of Albert when at 7.30am we left our trench to tell Mr Germany that it was time he got moving. A great many of our brigade not being bullet-proof fell before they reached the German first line, for the Germans were mowing the grass with machine gun fire. I managed to cross the enemy's first line, when I halted and looked round for my comrades. The nearest of them were about fifty yards to my right and left, so I thought I would wait for the reserves to come up. As I was standing there I felt something hit my left-hand top pocket, which reminded me that I had better move. I did so, and a few minutes later a bullet passed through my left wrist. I decided to return to the dressing station, which I did, and later when I examined my tunic I found that a bullet had passed through your letter and two thick pocket books, continued its journey between my tunic and chest, and passed out again through two more books and a pocket mirror which were in my top right-hand pocket. Where it went to next I am not at all interested in, but I thought I would return the letter to you so that you could have a memento of the big advance…. It was just splendid to see the lads jump out of the trench that morning – altogether just like a field day in England.'*

Second Lieutenant C.O.F. Jenkins and Private W.H.E. Pearson also got as far as the first line. Second Lieutenant Jenkins wrote to Pearson's mother:

13795 Private John Henry Fromant of Landbeach. Killed in action 1 July 1916. (Cambridge Weekly News *15 September 1916*)

15760 Private Alfred Arnold Day of Comberton. Killed in action 1 July 1916. (Cambridge Weekly News *22 September 1916*)

13586 Private Reginald Charles Impey of Foxton. Killed in action 1 July 1916. (Cambridge Weekly News *22 September 1916*)

13814 Private Albert Conquest of Over. A Royal Navy veteran who enlisted in 1914 with the young men of his village when he was 36. Killed in action 1 July 1916. (Cambridge Weekly News *29 September 1916*)

*'Dear Mrs Pearson, You will have heard long ago of the sad news of the death of your son Private Ernest Pearson. I would have written before, but I was wounded, and have only recently received my kit and have managed to get your address. Your son was my servant ever since the time the battalion was at Cambridge, and I felt his loss very keenly. We were together during the attack on 1 July until the end. We reached the first line German trench, just before entering which I was wounded. He helped me to put on a bandage, and also did what he could for one or two other wounded in the trench. A little while later, incautiously exposing himself above the trench, he was struck by a sniper's bullet, and was killed instantaneously. You will, I am sure, be glad to know this – that he suffered no pain at all.*

*I'm afraid I am unable to tell you where he was buried, but it is probably in a little British cemetery in a wood a little behind our original lines. I sympathise very deeply with you in your loss, as I knew and liked him very well. He always served me excellently, and it was in doing his duty and in doing it well that he fell. He followed me bravely in the attack, and never faltered though under heavy machine gun fire. England is very proud of all those of her sons who from a high sense of duty came forward and offered themselves in the hour of her need.'*

At 8.30, *'the carrying companies of the 10th Lincolns and 11th Suffolks were fired on by machine guns from La Boiselle and failed to get across. The loads carried by these companies were too heavy and it is evidently impossible to push forward stores with any chance of success while the route they have to follow is under hostile fire.'* This meant that the troops which had got through were without supplies other than those they had carried themselves and those that could be scavenged from the wounded.

Although it had seemed impossible, from the fire laid down on no man's land, a number of troops had got into the German lines, and were holding out between Wood Alley and Round Wood. Amongst these men was Captain O.H. Brown of the 11th Suffolks and Lieutenant Robson of the 15th Royal Scots. They commanded a composite party of survivors of 101 Brigade troops, and a second party of men were also nearby, also with a lodgement in the German lines, but both parties were oblivious to the presence of the other. By 9am the following morning, the situation was known to be that one group of 101 Brigade, plus 50 men of another brigade under Major Temple were in contact with the 21st Division to their left, and had the Germans further along from there. The detachment numbered around 250 men – about 100 from the 15th Royal Scots, 80 of the 16/Royal Scots, and 20 from the 11th Suffolks, under Captain O.H. Brown. Captain Brown was awarded the Distinguished Service Order for his part in this, the citation reading: *'with only one orderly, proceeding to the enemy's third line, where, collecting details of all units, he drove off two hostile counter-attacks and repelled a strong bombing attack.'*

A fellow officer, Maxwell-Lawford, wrote after his death that *'everyone who was left said they would have retired but for him'*; this was the same Captain Brown who was, understandably, nervous before his first spell in the trenches. Captain Brown had been wounded in the advance, with a bullet in his arm, but determinedly remained at duty until they were relieved. His earlier nervousness was replaced with determination and ability, and even ignoring the tendency to eulogise about the dead, it's clear that he did his duty and more.

Lance Corporal Victor Pamment was probably with him and he received the Distinguished Conduct Medal. The *Ely Standard* gave as many details as it had to hand about the award which was for distinguished service with a machine gun on the first day of the British offensive:

*'He showed the greatest bravery and an utter disregard of the perils which surrounded him. It appears that the battalion had orders to take a certain place at all risks, and the men as they went over the parapets, met with a deadly fire from the enemy. Some idea of the nature of the fighting will be gleaned from the fact that Lance-Corporal Pamment was the only one of the machine gunners left of his Company who advanced to the second line of the German trenches, the majority having been cut off by the Germans. Unaided, the Lance-Corporal kept up a rapid fire until reinforcements reached him, and through his great bravery and fearlessness the position was held…. Among those who fell wounded was Serjeant Barber, who also lives on the Back-hill. He has now recovered from his injuries, and has been home for a few days. He spoke in glowing terms of Pamment's bravery. Bullets, he said, were flying all around him, and it was really marvellous how he escaped unhurt. Several gave him up as lost.'*

Captain Tuck was aware that some had got through in spite of casualties:

*'Zero hour came (7.30) and the Battalion went over the top. Casualties began in the very first minute, whole lines of men being swept down by machine-gun fire from La Boiselle, where the Boche emplacements had not been knocked out by our bombardment in consequence of their very clever system of dugouts and pulleys. However, in spite of tremendous casualties, a small handful of men reached the first line of the Boche system and held on, in spite of repeated counter-attacks, for three days, when we were relieved.'*

He was doubtless referring to the small party commanded by Captain Brown. Tuck continued:

*'By the sheer magnificence of the men, things were accomplished that day that were almost impossible, and I believe the Germans have themselves paid tribute to the splendid way in which small bodies of men held positions long after they were isolated. In villages that we did not capture until three weeks later little groups of bodies were found – sometimes one man by himself – who had penetrated far into the German defences when the rest of their Battalion were casualties.'*

There was also another detachment of about 150 men, mostly 16th Royal Scots, slightly further along, under the charge of Captain Armit. Colonel McCrae was given orders to take charge of all the troops in those two detachments and to try to clear out Scot's Redoubt and be ready for the 19th Division to launch an assault on La Boisselle, given that it was clear the small numbers remaining of the 34th Division would not be able to take it alone. By 4.50 that evening, McCrae was able to report that they had bombed out Scots Redoubt, but couldn't make any further progress as the Germans were too strong. That night 400 men were sent up as reinforcements to the detachment, which was not able to clear out any additional German trenches, but was successful in holding on to the gains they had made. They would hold on for a further day, before being relieved on the night of 3/4 July.

Throughout 2 July, it continued to prove difficult to get supplies up. There were two covered communication trenches, but this was very slow owing to

13813 Lance Corporal George William Whittaker of Babraham. Killed in action 1 July 1916. (Cambridge Weekly News *29 September 1916*)

16325 Private Frederick John Prime of Harlton. Killed in action 1 July 1916. (Cambridge Weekly News *29 September 1916*)

Serjeant Reginald George Bareham. Killed in action 1 July 1916. (Cambridge Weekly News *12 May 1916*)

15583 Private Harry George Norton of Burwell. Killed in action 1 July 1916. (Cambridge Weekly News *11 August 1916*)

congestion and it was impossible to travel outside them as German machine guns were still active from La Boisselle. The battalion headquarters spent 2 and 3 July gathering up the wounded as best they could. Stretcher-bearers were hard pressed to meet the needs of the mass of wounded men in no man's land; many of them lay for hours or even days before being picked up. Among the stretcher-bearers was Drummer Benjamin Robert Thompson who was awarded the Military Medal. He was wounded around 4.30 in the afternoon of 2 July, having spent the day moving around no man's land and tending to the wounded. He was just leaving the trenches to carry in more men when a shell burst close at hand, severely wounding him. He was sent to England where he had one leg amputated. However, he was not able to survive his wounds and succumbed on 4 August. After his death he was brought back to Cambridge and was buried at Mill Road Cemetery.

Private Sidney Rolls was also wounded, in the chest and arm, while helping to bring in a wounded comrade. An officer in his company wrote to his mother:

*'He was one of a few men whom I had with me in a captured German trench, which we were holding, and I am very glad to tell you of his gallant conduct while we were there. He is only a small lad, but he was always one of the first to volunteer for any bit of work that I wanted done. I remember asking for volunteers to carry in a wounded serjeant whom we found lying near the trench, and he was the first one to offer himself. He was very tired, for he had been through our attack on the previous day, and had been without sleep for two or three days and nights, but he never stopped working all the time we were there, and I admired his pluck very much. The poor serjeant whom he was helping had been without food for two days and nights, and he was so grateful to those who were helping him and very sorry when your husband got hit on the way down. He is one of the men of my platoon whom I miss very much, and I do hope he will soon recover and have a good holiday at home.'*

From the context, it seems likely that the officer who wrote (his name is not included in the *Cambridge Independent Press*'s reprint of the letter) was Captain Brown, and that Sidney Rolls was with him in the captured portion of trench.

## For King and Country.

Pte. R. WILSON, Trumpington
(Suffolk Regiment),
Killed in Action in France, July 1st. 1916.

Killed in action, our hearts are sore.
For King and Country, we miss him more,
His cheerful smile, his loving face,
No one on earth can fill his place.

Grieve not dear parents, but be content,
For I to you was only lent,
For love I lived, for my country I died,
You asked my life but 'twas denied.

Private Robert (Bob) Wilson, killed in action 1 July 1916. Postcard produced with his picture and a commemorative poem. (Cambridgeshire Collection, Cambridge Central Library. T.G.K16 23429)

13662 Private Harry Adams of Over. Killed in action 1 July 1916. (Cambridge Weekly News *30 March 1917*)

16440 Private William Bertie Fox of Chesterton. Killed in action 1 July 1916. (Cambridge Weekly News *4 May 1917*)

## Chapter 8

# Those Who Fell

The ranks of the 11th Suffolks were decimated on the First Day of the Somme: 188 men were killed and the total rises to over 215 when those who died of wounds received on that day are included. The war diary gives the casualty figures for the three days in the line as: 4 officers and 148 other ranks killed, 12 officers and 387 other ranks wounded and 2 officers and 75 other ranks missing. Only the officers' names are given in the war diary, so it is difficult to know who was reported missing and who was reported killed at first. Not all of those missing were killed, though few if any were taken prisoner. The missing who turned up were probably wounded and stuck in no man's land, or got separated from the battalion in the confusion of battle.

It is impossible to give all of the stories, but some are included below.

Fred and Eliza Worland, of Cottenham, were parents of a fighting family. Of their sons listed in the 1911 Census, all served during the war. Arthur Thomas, born 1889, was wounded on 1 July as part of the 11th Suffolks. Herbert, born 1891, died on the same day, as did the second youngest son Harry, born in 1899. Of their other brothers, Edwin Frank, born in 1893, died in action December 1915 with the 2nd Suffolks, Frederick Charles born 1897 was in another battalion of the Suffolk Regiment and was wounded twice, and Kimberley George, born 1900, joined the Navy in 1916.

The news of Herbert and Harry's deaths was not received until early August, over a month after they had died. They were initially reported missing, leaving the family in a state of anxiety as they waited and hoped for news. All three of the brothers in the 11th Suffolks served in the same platoon; it is quite possible that they were hit by the same shell or by the same machine gunner. However, the uncertainty as to their fate makes it likely that they were separated from Arthur before they were killed, otherwise he would have been able to give his family definite news much earlier.

# For King and Country.

**Pte. H. WORLAND, Cottenham,**

**(11th Suffolks).**

Killed in Action in France, July. 1st, 1916.

He who dies quick with his face to the foe,
    In the heart of his friends must needs die slow.
And over his grave shall be heard the call,
    "The battle is won by the men that fall."

When peace reigns over the countryside
    Our thoughts shall be with the men that died.
Ah, brave hearts, could you hear us tell.
    How peace was won by the men that fell.

Postcard commemorating 15633 Private Harry Worland of Cottenham, killed in action 1 July 1916. (*Author's collection*)

The local MP, Mr Montagu, wrote to the family:

*'Dear Mr Worland, I hope that you will not feel that I am intruding upon you in a time of sorrow if I venture to send you this brief note of sympathy in the grievous loss which has befallen you by the death in action of two sons on the same day. I know of no family which has made a greater sacrifice than yours in the country's cause, and I can only trust that you may find consolation in the thought that your three sons laid down their lives willingly for their country.'*

Private Sidney Beeton sent home his last communication on 25 June 1916, a field card indicating that he had been admitted to hospital, possibly with a minor wound sustained in the bombardment of Bécourt Wood. He was back in the lines by 1 July, however, and the initial location of his grave indicates that he managed to get forward around 200 yards, though he had gone about 500 yards in total. His mother was not to hear any details as to what had happened for some time and continued sending letters to him. On 30 July, when the battalion returned to the line near Bazentin-le-Petit, they relieved the 10th Battalion The Worcestershire Regiment – the battalion in which Sidney's brother Arthur served. Arthur wrote home with what details he could get, which was only that Sidney was missing. The letter informing the family of his death was dated 2 August 1916. His body had been found; in 1921 it was moved from a small, unnamed grave site to Ovillers Cemetery, where he now lies next to an unknown member of the Suffolk Regiment.

After his death, his mother kept all his letters, as well as his death penny, medals and photographs. The death penny was placed into a shield, possibly made by a member of the family, while his medals and a photograph were placed into a specially made frame. In 1921 his mother wrote this haunting poem in remembrance of him:

In loving memory of my Dear Son Pte Sidney Ed Beeton
who was killed July 1st 1916

Five years have passed our hearts still sore
As time rolls on we miss him more
Some may think that we forget him
When at times they see us smile
But only those who have lost can tell
The pain of parting without a farewell

Goodbye Dear Son thy toil is over
Your willing hands will work no more
You did your best for all of us
Till God called you home to rest-billets

Peaceful be the rest Dear Son
Tis sweet to breathe your name
In life I loved you dearly
In death I'll do the same

Loved one gone but not forgotten
And as dawns another year
In our lonely hours of thinking
Thoughts of him are always dear

Although five years have passed away
Since our great sorrow fell
Still in our hearts we mourn the loss
Of him we loved so well

In the bloom of life death claimed him
In the pride of his manhood days
He like our Saviour died of wounds
That others he might save.

SIR,

It is my painful duty to inform you that a report has this day been received from the War Office notifying the death of

(No.) *1566.*  (Rank) *Private*

(Name) *Sidney Beeton*  (Regiment) *11* SUFFOLK REGT

which occurred at *place not.*

*stated.*  on the *1st*

of *July 1916*, and I am to express to you the sympathy and regret of the Army Council at your loss. The cause of death was *Killed in action*

If any articles of private property left by the deceased are found, they will be forwarded to this Office, but some time will probably elapse before their receipt, and when received they cannot be disposed of until authority is received from the War Office.

Official letter notifying Sidney Beeton's death. (*With thanks to Tony Beeton*)

Death Penny of Sidney Beeton, displayed in a shield. (*With thanks to Tony Beeton*)

Medals and photo of Sidney Beeton in home-made case. (*With thanks to Tony Beeton*)

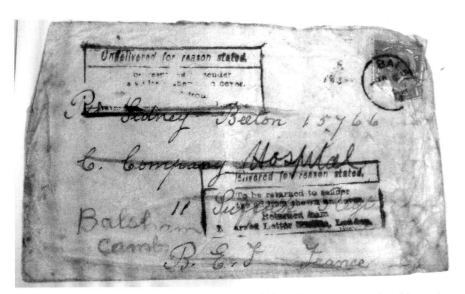

Envelope which contained the last letter sent to Sidney Beeton, returned to his mother. (*With thanks to Tony Beeton*)

Private Jonas Dodson was 39 when he died. He lived in Swavesey and left a widow and ten children, seven of whom were under fourteen when he was killed. The news was sent home by Lance Corporal A.A. Linford, also of Swavesey, who found both him and Lance Corporal James William Prior together on the battlefield. James Prior was already dead, but Jonas Dodson was saying the Lord's Prayer when he was found, before he passed away. Before the war he had worked as a bricklayer. One has to wonder why he decided to go to war, leaving his young family, when he was close to the maximum age for enlistment. Had he not chosen to volunteer, he might well not have been called up to fight.

Another who left a young family was Private James Cole. Initially reported missing, by mid-August the War Office notified his wife that he had been killed in action. He had enlisted later than many of the other men, perhaps because of his family and a sense that the young men without family commitments should go first. However, in June 1915 he joined the 11th

16333 Private James William Prior of Swavesey. Killed in action 1 July 1916. (Cambridge Weekly News *21 July 1916*)

16374 Private Jonas Dodson of Swavesey. Killed in action 1 July 1916. (Cambridge Weekly News *21 July 1916*)

Suffolks, and was sent to France on 30 May 1916, probably having served with the Reserve Battalion, the 13th Suffolks, until that point. Before the war he had been employed at Messrs Elgood's Brewery in Wisbech. The brewery is still in operation today, having been owned and operated by the Elgood family since 1878. He married Susannah Maria in 1900 and the couple had three children in 1911 – Florence Louisa (1901), Bertha Lillian (1903) and George Robert (1905).

Corporal Joseph Mason of C Company was another father. After leaving school he worked in the offices of Messrs Button and Aylmer, solicitors, at Newmarket, where he was a clerk. He then went on to be a clerk at the Rutland Livery Stables and was one of the first to offer himself for enlistment at the outbreak of the war. He was rejected on his first attempt, though the reason is not clear. He would have been 32 at the time, so while older than many other recruits, he was still within the maximum age limit. He tried again to enlist and was accepted into the army in October 1914, joining the 11th Suffolks. Perhaps surprisingly, he does not appear to have been pulled in to work in battalion or brigade headquarters, but he may have undertaken clerical duties at a company level.

Serjeant F. White, in a letter to Miss Mason (Corporal Mason's sister), dated 24 July, said:

*'Further to my promise concerning your brother, Corporal Joe Mason, I very much regret to inform you that nothing as been seen of him and he is now posted as killed. It pains me very much to have to tell you; but no doubt you will be able to break the news to his wife... I beg to offer you and his father and all other relatives my sincere and deep sympathy in your great loss. Your brother had been closely associated with me ever since joining. I liked him very much and appreciated his good qualities. All the members of the Company join with me in deepest regret and sympathy.'*

He wrote again to say:

*'Your brother had been with me so long that we had become quite friends. I was with the Company the night before the attack took place and had a chat with Joe, and quite expected I should see him again all right, as we did*

*not expect for a minute that they would meet with very much resistance. As we now know they were faced by a very heavy machine gun fire, but they advanced bravely, as if only on parade, and met their deaths like the heroes they were. Our losses were very heavy, but a high proportion of the wounded were only slightly hurt, and we hope will soon recover.'*

When he died he left his wife alone with five children and she was ill at the time. Two of the children were born after 1911 as they are not listed in the census, and one was born in 1911, so she had three children under five to look after. To make matters harder the pension for an Army corporal was unlikely to favourably compare with the pay of an experienced clerk in a racing stable.

By contrast, just starting out in married life was Private William Henry Palmer, who died a year after marrying Mabel Lilley. He was born in 1889 to Martha Ann and Frederick Palmer in Ramsey, Huntingdonshire, though by 1911 the family had moved to Peterborough. Instead of starting out on a new life with her soldier

15662 Corporal Joe Mason of Newmarket. Killed in action 1 July 1916. Left a widow and five children. (Cambridge Weekly News *15 September 1916*)

husband, Mabel Lilley was widowed within the year. His death does not seem to have been reported in the local newspapers, possibly because he was not a native of Cambridgeshire.

Captain Isaac Alexander Mack, some of whose detailed letters home about the battalion have been included earlier, died on this day too. He was with the Trench Mortar Brigade, which was to move forward and go into action to cover the advance and assist with consolidation, after sending off a heavy fire in the moments before the advance. He, and everyone else with his gun, was killed, perhaps by a shell.

Market Street, Peterborough. At least five men enlisted in the battalion from this town, probably more. These included 16383 Private William Henry Palmer who was killed in action 1 July 1916. (*Author's collection*)

Isaac Mack was born in 1892 in Liverpool and attended The Leys School, Cambridge from the age of 17. He was a prefect, won First Colours in football, and was awarded an Exhibition to Jesus College Cambridge, where he read history. He hoped, on graduation, to join the Indian Civil Service. However, when war broke out he obtained a commission in the Suffolk Regiment instead.

Isaac Mack's parents published his letters home after the war. At the end they included letters sent to them by officers who served with him. One wrote:

*'The last time I saw him was on Friday afternoon, 30 June, in the cellars of the Chateau. He was gaily talking to his Officers and giving them one or two final instructions. "Have some tea of dog biscuits and bully beef", he said to me just as I had finished a wash. I said "Good-bye" to him, and then crept along the dark passage to the Chateau. He was one of the real enthusiasts for war amongst us as a regiment. Most people had joined*

*because it was their duty – he joined because he was a soldier by nature as well. If there was to be a scrap he was sure to be in it. He wanted to go out before the battalion on July 1st, but the C.O., of course, would not hear of it. At Armentières I was told that when the Corner Fort was bombarded he was hit on his helmet by a huge piece of shell, but just carried on. I feel certain he died in the forefront of the battle, for his pluck was proverbial. "Whoever else gets the wind up – Mack won't", I heard an Officer of the regiment say one day during a bad spell in the trenches. I do not believe he was afraid of death, and I am sure he fell as far forward as the German leaden hail would let anyone get alive.'*

Brothers Arthur and Henry Hancock had joined the battalion together, on the same day and at the same time, as shown by their consecutive service numbers. Arthur was the oldest, having been born in 1887, while Henry was born in 1890. Arthur married Lucy W. Plumb in 1913 and left her and two young children to mourn his death. His death was not reported until early August. At the same time, it was reported that Henry had been taken prisoner and was in Germany, holding out hope to his grieving family. This changed to missing and then, at the end of October, Mrs Hancock was told that her son Henry was also dead and had died on the same day as his brother.

Company Serjeant Major Thomas Jolly had been born in 1873, and when war broke out he was working for a solicitor as a messenger. However, prior to this he had served in the Army and so he rejoined the Colours. As an old soldier, his experience would have been invaluable in building the battalion almost from scratch. His regimental number (3/1092) suggests that he was transferred across from another of the Suffolk battalions, in order to bring his experience to the new formation. He left a wife and two children in Norwich.

Another old soldier was Serjeant Simon Jacklin, who had previously served in the 1st Suffolks. He rejoined the Colours in December 1914, leaving behind a wife and four children. He was born in 1880 and worked as a farm labourer after he first left the Army. His wife was initially informed that he was wounded. However, a few weeks later she received a letter from his officer, stating:

*'I am deeply grieved to have to tell you certain news of your husband's death. I have not heard officially that it is so. No words of mine, I know, can make any difference to you, but I hope that in time it will be a comfort to you to think that your husband died nobly for his country, and that his loss is felt by the company he was in and by the officers who are left. We all thought very highly of him, and can sympathise with you, though we cannot comfort you in your loss.'*

Private Percy Victor Harper lied about his age to enlist, as he was only 17 in 1914. He was reported missing; then on 20 July his parents received a letter from Private Butterworth, of the Gloucester Regiment. Butterworth who wrote:

*'He was found by my corporal and myself on the field and we have no doubt he died almost immediately and suffered no lingering pain. He has died like a man, doing his duty, and you can rest assured we gave him a decent burial, as we hope we may ourselves get if it is our lot to die out here. I am keeping a couple of photos which were in his pocket, and which you may have any time you care to write. I shall be only too pleased to give you any further particulars if you should care to know, and in the meantime we send you our deepest sympathy.'*

Despite the letter from Private Butterworth, it was not until February 1917 that they received official notification from the War Office of his death; prior to that he was reported as missing. Before the war, like many in the battalion, he worked as a farm labourer and lived in the village of Comberton.

He was not the only one; in fact he wasn't the youngest. At least thirteen of the Cambs Kitcheners soldiers who died on 1 July were born in 1898, and so were just 18 when they died.

Private Ernest Edwin Pridham was amongst them. He and his brother, Lance Corporal C. Pridham, sons of Mrs John King of Willingham, were both reported as missing. Lance Corporal C. Pridham was in the Northamptonshire Regiment and was missing from 9 May 1915. His brother, Ernest Pridham, was subsequently reported missing from 1 July. Mrs King made great efforts to trace them, and published an appeal in the

*Cambridge Independent Press* for news. *'After journeying to London and making wide inquiries, and writing to all likely places and individuals who might know anything of her boys and help to trace them, she has failed to secure definite information and is compelled to presume that both are killed. Should this meet the eye of anyone who could give any information to Mrs King, it would be gratefully received.'*

Frederick Papworth had had the difficult and dangerous job of being a company runner. Like many others, he was initially reported missing and it was not until some time after the battle that the captain for whom he had been a runner heard officially that he had been killed. The captain wrote *'Your son I always knew as an excellent fellow. He was a company runner, a position which is only given to the very best of men. I sympathise with you very deeply in your loss, and hope that your sorrow will be comforted by pride in the way your son met his death.'* He had enlisted in November 1914, when he was 20 years old. Before the war he had worked as a farm labourer and lived in Soham.

The parents of another 18 year old, Private Edward Harknett, had particular difficulty in getting news about their son. He died the day before his nineteenth birthday, but his parents received conflicting information about whether he had survived or not. He was initially reported to have been wounded and in hospital, though no details about the wound were forthcoming. The following week, the *Cambridge Independent Press* reported that he was missing, and that nothing had been heard of him up till 20 July amongst his friends. Someone had mentioned him as wounded, but that now appeared to be incorrect. The week after that, the official information of his death was received.

Lieutenant Robert Quilter Gilson, born in 1894, attended King Edward's School, Birmingham, the same school as J.R.R. Tolkien, with whom he was good friends. His father R. Cary Gilson was the headmaster of the school. After a distinguished career at King Edward's, he went on to study at Trinity College, Cambridge, matriculating in 1912. He studied Classics and was a good scholar; at the end of Part I, he was awarded first class honours. He hoped in the future to become an architect, and both in France and in England spent a good deal of time sketching out trench constructions. In 1914 he cut short his studies and was commissioned in the 11th Suffolks.

He was promoted from second lieutenant to lieutenant in March 1916, while serving overseas. Before the war he had been a member of both his school OTC and then the CUOTC, where he would have been in the same year as Gerald Tuck, and the two men probably knew each other well before they served together in the 11th Suffolks.

Another two sets of brothers also died on the same day, both with surnames of Day, however these brothers do not appear to be related.

Private Alfred Day and Corporal Walter Day were the sons of David and Agnes Day of Comberton. Walter Day was attached to the Trench Mortar Battery, and was reported to have been killed by a piece of shrapnel which pierced his heart and killed him instantly. Lance Corporal Hopkin was in the battery with him and wrote to his mother, saying: *'All in the Battery loved him so well, and we deeply deplore his loss. He was thought very highly of by his officers. Only a few months ago he was awarded a card of honour, for coolness and steadiness in working a trench mortar while under shell fire.'*

He was a shepherd and an amateur footballer, and for several years before the war was the honorary secretary of the Comberton Football Club.

At the same time, the newspaper reported that *'Private Alfred Day, a brother of Corporal Day, and in the same company, is also unofficially reported missing from 1 July, and his parents would be glad of any information respecting him.'* A month later, his picture was published in the newspaper with a request for information from his parents.

Born in 1897, Alfred was another lad who lied about his age to enlist, leaving his work as a farm labourer to join the army. His regimental number is significantly different from that of his brother, suggesting that they did not enlist together, but instead that Alfred joined up some weeks later, perhaps inspired by his brother's example. It was not until late August 1917 that the *Cambridge Independent Press* could report:

*'Mrs D. Day, of Comberton, has received official information from the Army Council that her son, Lance-Corporal Alfred Day, of the Suffolk Regiment, who was previously reported missing since 1 July 1916, is now presumed dead. In a letter received from the British Red Cross Society Mrs Day is informed that after questioning every reliable witness who could be found, the Society have reluctantly had to give up all hope of hearing*

*anything of Lance-Corporal Day's fate, though they have unceasingly watched the prisoners' lists from Germany for the names of all the missing. It will be remembered that an elder brother, Corporal Walter Day, of the same regiment, was killed on 1 July. A younger son is also now serving.'*

Although she lost two sons on the same day, Mrs Day did not find this out for certain until over a year after the event, leaving her and the wider family suspended in a state of hope and fear for Alfred's fate.

The other Day brothers in the battalion were Serjeant Jack Day and Private Walter Day. Both died on 1 July 1916. They were the sons of George and Agnes Day, who lived in Comberton. Walter was the elder, having been born in 1881, while Jack was born in 1894. Jack was the first to enlist, followed about a year later by his brother. Not long after the attack, George and Agnes received a letter from Private G. Warren, of Cottenham:

13791 Corporal Walter George Day of Comberton. Killed in action 1 July 1916. (Cambridge Weekly News *15 September 1916*)

17266 Private Warren Ivan Cook of Reach. Killed in action 1 July 1916. (Cambridge Weekly News *22 September 1916*)

*'I am sorry to tell you the sad news of your sons, who were both in my platoon, and whom we were very sorry to lose. Serjeant Jack was very good to us. He did his duty, but we do not like losing him. Walter we cannot hear anything of, but I do not think he is dead. If we hear anything about Walter we will write and let you know. Do not worry about Jack. He did his best. In fact, our battalion held out well, and was praised by high people, as you might perhaps see in the papers.'*

The family had another two sons in the army – Clifford Day in another battalion of the Suffolk Regiment, still training in England in 1916, and Leonard Day who was training with the Canadians, having emigrated to Canada before the war.

Unlike some of the other serjeants, it is clear that Jack Day was promoted on merit after joining the battalion, having little or no military experience until that point. Before the war, he was a butcher. Walter had been a railway porter.

Official news was received that both sons had died towards the end of August 1916.

In Bottisham, Private Alan Dockerill and Private Harry Goody, brothers-in-law, both died as a direct result of 1 July. Alan Dockerill died from the wounds he received on that day on 8 July, while Harry was killed in action. Dockerill left behind a wife and two young children, who learned within the space of a month of the deaths of her brother and of her husband.

Serjeant Robert Marking White died on 6 July at a base hospital in France, of wounds sustained in the attack. The news was unexpected; he had sent a postcard to his father saying that he was getting on well. He originally served in the Territorials while working in Messrs. H. Johnson and Nephew, a shop on St Andrew's Street, but joined the 11th Suffolks when war broke out. He was captain of Chesterton United Football Club before the war and captained the battalion's football and cricket teams. In May 1915, he was one of the men who boxed in the tournament organised in Cambridge, fighting Corporal Morris, the champion of the Welsh Division. Serjeant White (then Corporal White) did well in the first round, less so in the second and by the third round he was obviously tired and lost the bout. He had been fortunate enough to get leave in June 1916, but it is unlikely anyone expected not to see him again.

William Alsop, who enlisted with three other men from his village (including his brother Sidney) in response to the vicar's pleas, was another man who died in the advance. Sidney had been wounded in the same action in the head and shoulders. Sidney was discharged due to his wounds on 30 May 1917, when it was clear that he would not be fit to fight again. He probably returned to the family building trade – his father was a builder in 1911, and he and his older brother William were his assistants. After the war, he married Marguerite M. Hovell in 1922; he died in Ely in 1983.

The oldest soldier in the battalion who died on 1 July was Company Serjeant Major William George Brooks, who had been born in 1869. He was orphaned before his twelfth birthday, living in Dry Drayton with Mary Ann Binge and Cornell, two elderly widows, two of their children and his younger sister. He joined the Army and served for several years. He married Agnes in 1906 and they had four children between 1907 and 1911. Second Lieutenant Andrew Wright, the only officer of D Company who was not killed or wounded, wrote to his wife with the news of his death, saying:

> *'It is with feelings of real sorrow that I write to tell you that your husband was killed in action on the first morning of the British advance (1 July). The roll of our regiment was heavy, but few losses will be felt more deeply than that of Serjeant Major Brooks. Loved and respected by the men, he was a permanent pillar of strength to D Company, and there can be no doubt that his efforts, as well as his personal example, did wonders towards the making of that fine body of men which went forward to the attack on the fateful day.... It is not then as representative that I speak these few poor words, but as a friend whose sympathy, though insufficient, is nevertheless sincere. I can only trust that strength will be given to you and his children to bear this blow, and that you will build a wall of just pride able to prevent the bitterness of memory.'*

Drummer Benjamin Robert Thompson did not die straight away, although his death was a direct result of 1 July. Born in 1896, he was the son of Police Constable Robert Thompson and Ann Elizabeth Thompson, née Smith. His father died in 1902 and his mother remarried, to another policeman, Francis Holmes. Despite his policing family, Benjamin worked as a painter and decorator and was among the first to enlist in the 11th Suffolks. He went through the attack on 1 July without being wounded. As a drummer in the battalion band, he would have been detailed as a stretcher-bearer right from the start. On the following day he and Corporal Billing spent four hours in no man's land dressing the wounded who could not be moved, and rescued a wounded man of another regiment from the enemy's barbed wire. He and Corporal Billings were both awarded the Military Medal and both were wounded by the same shell.

Benjamin was brought back to England and taken to hospital in Whalley, Lancashire. He died on 4 August from the wounds he had received, aged 20. He was buried in Mill Road Cemetery with military honours, with three volleys fired over the grave. The Last Post was sounded, and amongst the buglers was Corporal Billing, who had been in the battalion's band with Benjamin. He was in Cambridge on convalescent leave on 4 August, returning to the front on 11 August. His grave can still be seen in Mill Road Cemetery and is part of a trail of other soldiers who died during the First World War and are buried or commemorated in the cemetery. As part of the commemorative events for the First World War, a monologue was written based on his life and can be downloaded from the Mill Road Cemetery website.

*Chapter 9*

# Reporting the Somme

Families at home in Cambridgeshire, and across the UK, were desperate for news of loved ones. The reporting in the local newspapers was often more graphic than in national papers, fuelled in part by the publishing of letters from local men. It took a long time for news of casualties to filter back to England and for news of what happened on the Somme to become clear. The War Office seems to have had a tendency (understandable) to report the best results they could.

According to the *Cambridge Daily News*, published on 3 July, *'The first news of the attack was published in the Cambridge Daily News on Saturday, when it was officially reported that British troops had broken into the German*

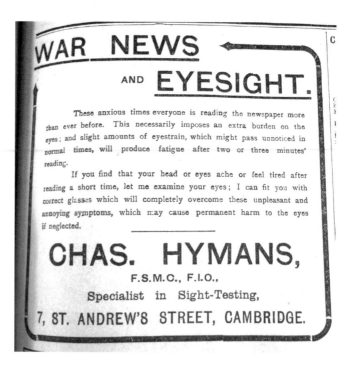

WAR NEWS ← AND EYESIGHT.

These anxious times everyone is reading the newspaper more than ever before. This necessarily imposes an extra burden on the eyes; and slight amounts of eyestrain, which might pass unnoticed in normal times, will produce fatigue after two or three minutes' reading.

If you find that your head or eyes ache or feel tired after reading a short time, let me examine your eyes; I can fit you with correct glasses which will completely overcome these unpleasant and annoying symptoms, which may cause permanent harm to the eyes if neglected.

CHAS. HYMANS,

F.S.M.C., F.I.O.,

Specialist in Sight-Testing,

7, ST. ANDREW'S STREET, CAMBRIDGE.

Advertisement from the *Cambridge Weekly News* 17 March 1916.

*forward systems of defences on a front of 18 miles and that a French attack on the immediate right of the British was preceding equally well.'* [Unfortunately the copy of the *Cambridge Daily News* on 1 July recorded on microfilm was damaged, and the left half of the column about the attack was missing.]

*'The satisfaction with which this news was received has been deepened during the week.... [damaged line] which record considerable progress. The Allies have captured many villages and positions heretofore held by the enemy. The Germans have lost heavily, and down to yesterday afternoon the British Army had captured 3,500 and the French 6,000 prisoners, a total of 9,500.... After a great bombardment from the Allied artillery, the offensive was launched on Saturday morning and the first German positions along the whole of the front attacked were carried. The British left wing, north of the little River Ancre, stormed the village of Serre, 1½ miles north-east of Hebuterne. South of the Ancre our centre pushed in so as to cut off Fricourt, a railway junction two miles east of Albert, La Boiselle, 1½ miles north-west of Fricourt was stormed. Mametz and Montauban, two strongly fortified villages three miles east of our old line, were captured, with a German labyrinth of trenches near them. Our gains at this point were held though north of the Ancre German counter-attacks during Saturday recovered some portions of the ground lost by the enemy. The village of Fricourt, which held out when it was cut off by our troops, was carried yesterday, and progress was made to the east of it.'*

La Boisselle was definitely not taken; neither was Serre. In both cases, however, there were reports of British troops in or near the villages, so although the reports were overly optimistic, they were not outright lying. These official reports were distributed quickly, going to the big national newspapers, and to the local papers from there, on the very day of the battle. The first reports of the Somme were ready for the evening papers on 1 July.

According to the *Herts and Cambs Reporter*, this news was *'a great and welcome change from the tedious trench warfare to which we had been accustomed for some months past.'*

*'To the man in the street it came as a great relief, and to all branches of the Armies in the field, at home, and at the Front, it came as an inspiring tonic for which all had been eagerly waiting.... To have received, from day to day, for over an extended period, only brief accounts of trench bombing and exploding of mines, without any indication of change of front, may have been a little trying to the patience of some of our people at home, who in the absence of fuller information from the front, may have thought the long-looked-for offensive movement a long time coming, but if that was so there was never any doubt that such an effort was to be made in due course. In fact, during the past month there had come to anxious friends at home significant hints from the fighting line that "big things" were imminent, and when last week there came echoes of the continuous thunder of British artillery on the enemy's lines it was generally felt that the psychological moment for the great push was near at hand.'*

It must be remembered that people were almost entirely reliant on the written word for their daily news. There were no radio stations and so the press and talking about it with friends, were the only ways that people in Cambridgeshire would get news of the war. What's written in the papers therefore gives a good idea of the state of knowledge at home. Although these reports are overly optimistic about how well the battle was going, they did to an extent reflect what the Higher Command initially believed to have happened, as they too were hampered by poor communications.

However, detailed reports were not forthcoming from official sources. In part, this was down to restrictions on military information that could be of use to the Germans. It has been suggested that the War Office deliberately staggered the release of names of killed and wounded in order to hide the true scale of the cost. This seems unlikely, especially given that it merely meant that the issue was kept in the paper for weeks and months after the attack, with a significant number of casualties not being reported until the end of August or even September. More likely is that the sheer number of casualties swamped the official reporting processes – families often received news of loved ones from soldiers in the same battalion from the same area, or from wounded men, before they got official notification. Many of the soldiers were not definitely known to be dead, especially where a shell had killed everyone in the vicinity who might have been able to say for sure, and there was a tendency amongst survivors to hold out any hope they could to families.

Of course, sometimes there were other signs that a loved one might be wounded or killed. On 21 July an article in the *Cambridge Independent Press* stated:

*'Much anxiety is being felt by relatives and friends concerning the fate of Private Walter Barton, 17512, of the Suffolks. Up to 25 June he wrote regularly every week to his parents, Mr and Mrs Fred Barton, of the Caxton Common Farm, but since the latter date no tidings have been heard of him. He was in the Trench Mortar Battery attached to the Suffolks, and was engaged in the recent fighting, and although enquiries have been made of his chums in the regiment, so far no one appears to know anything of his whereabouts. Neither has any news been heard as to Corporal Charles*

15353 Lance Corporal Charles Keep of Bourn. Killed in action 1 July 1916. (Cambridge Weekly News *18 August 1916*)

17512 Private Walter Fred Barton of Bourn. Suffered from spinal meningitis while in training, but recovered and went to the front to join his comrades. Killed in action 1 July 1916.

*Keep, of the same regiment, whose case was reported in last week's paper. It is to be hoped that evidence of some sort will soon come to hand to relieve the great anxiety naturally felt by their relatives.'*

Both Private Barton and Corporal Keep were killed on July 1. Charles Keep was reported to have been killed in the local newspaper on 11 August, 18-year-old Walter Barton on 4 August. They are commemorated on the Thiepval Memorial as their bodies were never identified.

From the early stages of the battle, people were already being warned not to get their hopes up too high for rapid results. The editor of the *Cambridge Weekly News* told readers:

*'Patience is the quality which the progress of the Franco–British offensive on the Western front will perhaps demand more than any other from those who stay at home. We must not expect any such sweeping or spectacular advance as that of our Russian Allies in Bukovinn. The conditions in the West are different, and the strategical steps in any advance are closer together. But when this warning is remembered, we have every reason to be satisfied and even jubilant at the first-fruits of the longed for offensive... the first step, which might have cost so dear, has been achieved with, we believe, comparatively small losses on our side, and with conspicuous damage to the enemy's strength and moral... It is worth noting in this connection that the simultaneous offensive on the three fronts lends an extraordinary importance to the actual figures of the German losses. And even if the offensive of the allies fails to reach its ultimate aim, the failure will have cost the enemy so dear in manpower as to have all the colour of a success.'*

Haig's later rationalisation of the Somme, as being a necessary stage in a battle of attrition, was already being publicly aired on 7 July – in the case of the *Cambridge Weekly News* this was the first time the attack could be mentioned at all.

From 14 July, reports about casualties began to be published in the local weekly papers. These reports gave the best indication of what had happened, especially when coupled with the printing of letters from officers in the battalion who were notifying casualty's families, or from the wounded soldiers themselves. The editor of the *Cambridge Weekly News* summarised the news so far available with the following:

> *'"All the men were heroes"', writes an officer who took part in the battle in which the men of Cambridgeshire suffered so heavily and carried themselves so gloriously. The list of casualties which appears on another page, tells more eloquently than any verbal description could convey what a terrible fire our men had to face, but they never wavered for an instant. Singing and cheering they charged over the fire swept zone, and though many fell, those who remained charged on into the German trenches and not only captured them but held them. The time has not come yet, we regret to say, when the full tale of their deeds may be told, but we are able to state, on the best authority, that the regiment lived up to the best traditions of the County in which they were born and bred, the County that provided Cromwell with so many of his Ironsides and Wellington with many a stalwart fighter in the Napoleonic Wars.'*

It was now becoming clear that the attack had not been as free from casualties as the optimistic reports the previous week had suggested.

Some of the smaller papers ignored the War Office regulations about not printing battalion numbers. The *Ely Standard* reported:

> *'Never since the war began has it been our regrettable duty to record on one occasion so many casualties among local men as are published in this issue. Week by week throughout the lengthy period during which the war has been waged news of casualties has come to hand; sometimes few and of a minor character, sometimes numerous and accounting for a sad toll of life or serious injury to those who have fallen to the assaults of the enemy. On the memorable occasion when the Cambridgeshires were in action at St Eloi the county suffered many losses, and once again Cambridgeshire men appear to have been in the thick of the fighting, though this time in a different unit, the 11th Suffolks.*
>
> *This Battalion of the Suffolk Regiment is one of those formed during the war, and consists of Cambridgeshire men. Judging by the casualties the Battalion appears to have been called upon to take part in the "big push",*

*and it is stated that the men acquitted themselves magnificently, showing great coolness under fire and spirited dash when called upon to advance. It was only to be expected that in such heavy fighting as has taken place the casualties would be numerous, but it is very satisfactory to note that the number of killed is small in proportion to the number of wounded. The official lists so far issued report two officers in the Suffolk Regiment killed and twelve wounded. As to the rank and file the full list has not reached us, and in addition to those we publish there are probably others that have not come to our knowledge. In due course fuller details will probably become available, and we may learn something of the character of the fighting in which the Battalion engaged, and how the men acquitted themselves in helping to drive back the foe.'*

The initial hope that the killed were so significantly fewer in number than the killed seems to have been down to how families were notified of casualties. Casualties amongst officers were the first to reach home. And, in truth, there were many more men wounded than killed, although the proportions were not quite so skewed as those at home first thought. The wounded would often report to families themselves, as in the case of Oliver Hopkins, who wrote home on 3 July:

*'Dear Mother Father Brother and Sisters; i now fine time to rite you a few lines hopeing it will find you qute well as it leaves – [crossed out] and i am sorry to tell you that i have been wounded no dought you have herd about it before now well i got wounded on the first of July if you look in the papers you will see what happened on that day and besides full of [crossed out] Died and Wounded for there is some poor chaps gone to rest there is not many of our Battalion left to till the tale Cpl Day is Killed and i don't now nothing about the Wilburton Lads at all i got 4 bullet wounds, in the left arm and 3 down my right side i am pleased i am alive i can tell you but downt worry about me for i am goneing on as well as you can expect we went over the [crossed out] top at 7 oclock on the 1st of July and we was in the 34 Division so look in the papers and see what it says about us and the Battalion but i think we have got the Germans on the run now it is a lot worse than the Battle of Loos was well i can not give you my address but i*

*am in a Hospital in France and we mite get moved any time from here so dont rite to me i will rite to you the best i can so i must close now tell all my Palls i am still alive i remain your ever loving Son Oliver'*

Oliver Hopkins' letters, excluding this one (though he nearly wrote it anyway!) almost invariably start with the line *'hoping it will find you well as it leaves me'*. Most of Sidney Beeton's letters also contain the same line. Interestingly Alec Mack, in a letter to his mother, mentioned that the letters he censored nearly all started in exactly the same way. It seems that in a schoolroom somewhere in Cambridgeshire all the men were taught that this was the proper way to open a letter.

Although this particular letter wasn't printed in a local newspaper, many were. This would give families an additional point of contact with their loved ones at the front – not only did they receive direct letters, but they could view the letters sent to others from men in the same battalion, and gain a better picture of what their sons and husbands were going through.

Letters weren't all that was published. Private James Sallis, of Chatteris was engaged to marry Florence Barnes. The couple were hoping to marry as soon as they could, dependent on when James could get leave. However, it was not to be. James Sallis lost both his legs and died on 6 July of his wounds. As he died, he composed a poem which he sent home, and which was then published in the *Ely Standard*.

## THE DYING BUGLER BOY

Hark! What means that Heavenly music
Sounding sweetly on my ear?
Can it be that I am dying?
Heaven seems so very near.
Come dear mother, come yet nearer,
Kiss your dying soldier boy;
Jesus calls, and I must answer,
For I'm not afraid to die.

Chorus

The heavenly music pealing,
And the gates are open wide;
I will wait for you, dear mother,
Over on the other side.

You have often prayed, dear mother,
For your loved and darling child;
And your heart was near the breaking,
By his conduct rough and wild;
But at last the loving Saviour
Met your wayward, wandering boy;
now he calls and I must answer,
For I'm not afraid to die.

Since I've joined the Army, mother,
In the battle I've been true,
And though tried by sore temptations
My dear Lord has helped me through;
Now I come to Jordan's river,
With the angels standing by;
Take me, Jesus, I'm Your soldier,
And I'm not afraid to die.'

With the high number of casualties, it is unsurprising that the local newspapers attempted to reassure those who mourned that their loved ones had not died in vain and to offer what solace they could. The *Ely Standard* wrote:

*'Many additional casualties – the price which must be paid for great victories – among Cambs. men at the Front have come to hand during the past week. Mingled, however, with the expression of deep sympathy with the relatives of those who have fallen, and the earnest hope for the recovery of the wounded, is a feeling of great pride in our gallant county lads and their*

*valiant conduct in the Great Push. Fearlessly, and "in a storm of shell, rifle bullets and machine gun bullets" – to use the words of one of them – the lads of Cambridgeshire leaped out of their trenches when the word was given in the early hours of the morning of 1 July. Many fell, but "most of the boys got there," and gloriously did they acquit themselves. Town and county have cause to be proud of the part played by their sons on this memorable July morn. And before then, too, and since.'*

The families were encouraged to be proud of their sacrifice, and the sacrifice of families who lost loved ones was linked with that of those who died in the trenches. The Territorial Force Association held a special meeting to offer their condolences to families and express their pride in the men who had fallen. Part of their minutes were published in the press:

*'Especially at such a moment do we think of those at home who grieve for those they have lost. The long list of casualties shows that they were in the forefront of the attack, the place of the greatest danger, but of the greatest honour, and that they acquitted themselves like heroes – heroes every one of them. The county is indeed proud of these men, for whether sitting in the trenches under a storm of shell or advancing on the enemy positions, they are always the same, cool and brave, and although nothing can compensate any one of us for those who fall, yet the glorious manner of their death must bring some consolation. I do not suppose there is any part of the county which has not felt the weight of some loss, but it is bravely borne by those who are connected with the heroes out there.'*

The same message of sympathy to the bereaved whilst encouraging them to take pride in their loved ones, was expressed by the editor of the *Cambridge Weekly News*:

*'To the relatives of the men who have fallen, the heartfelt sympathy of everyone of us is extended. Their loss is indeed great, but they have the consolation and pride of knowing that their dear ones died as men, fighting a cruel and implacable foe, in the great cause of civilisation and humanity. We hope those villages that have not yet begun to keep a roll of honour,*

*will make a start without delay, so that a permanent record of our heroes may be set up, not only as a memorial, but as an example and a stimulus to generations yet unborn.'*

Meanwhile, Dr Josiah Oldfield, writing in the *Huntingdonshire Post*, offered somewhat less sympathetic advice to mourners:

*'Most sorrow is selfish, and therefore the greatest consolation against such sorrow is unselfishness.... It is because there is a blank or a raw place left in my own life, that my heart aches so badly.... To-day there is a call for work – and ever more work; and for those whose souls are torn with great gaping wounds, there is no drug more potent to bring ease, no balm more soothing, no treatment more healing than the active day-long night-long caring for the broken and wounded comrades of those who have gone.'*

He wrote of how some suffered painful deaths, but: *'then I see a fair young knight, full of the joy of sacrifice for honour and home sturdily footing it with comrade men, and singing gaily into the very face of death, flushed with the thrilling gladness which comes of brave work bravely done and fear outmastered, and in a moment – painless, sudden, beautiful – the triumphant soul is set free by a bullet or a shell, and the Great God of Battles has crowned the sacrifice with the hallowing touch of golden fire.... Let us, then, mourn our dead sons and brothers, but let us mourn them sweetly and proudly, and with well-ordered garments and faces anointed with the oil of a great peace, let us take up our work and march on.'*

Not quite as sympathetic, perhaps, but it did offer the same message of glorious and worthy death, and the need for families to keep going regardless, that was offered elsewhere.

For families in Cambridge, many of whom would never go overseas, the work of the Commonwealth War Graves Commission, and its precursor, the Graves Registration Commission, was often too remote. Though pictures might be sent home of the graves of family members, and though the families might be able to add some text to the grave of their soldier son or husband (if his body had survived his death, was identified, and his grave marker was not lost in subsequent battles), for many this was not enough. Thus, local cemeteries often have the names of soldiers added to family memorials, regardless of whether they were buried there or not. Mill Road Cemetery has eighteen Commonwealth War Graves Commission headstones from the First World War, where the soldiers are actually buried having died in England (all who died overseas were buried overseas, as close as possible to where they fell). However, there are over a hundred and twenty other graves which have casualties commemorated on them, and these could provide a focus for family grief. It is not clear whether there would have been a ceremony of some sort when the graves were inscribed with the soldier's names – there is no mention of it in local newspapers – but there were memorial services held for soldiers who died in France. These might be for individuals, in small parishes, or collectively.

Sometimes the burial of one soldier was used to stand in for others who had died. The *Ely Standard* records the funeral of Private Harold Thomas Royston, who died on 1 August, aged 18. He had been seriously wounded on 1 July, suffering two broken legs, a fracture in his back, and a bullet wound to the body. He was brought to hospital in England, but succumbed to his wounds and was brought back to Ely for burial. This was the only way in which families would have their loved ones buried close at hand, if they were wounded and died in England. In those cases, it seems to have been the policy to let them be buried at home, hence the Commonwealth War Graves Commission headstones that can be found in cemeteries across the UK.

'He was a member of the Countess of Huntingdon Sunday School, and there now hangs in his parents' house in Silver-street a framed copy of the Ten Commandments which was presented to him by Mr Bearcock, his teacher. It was, therefore, fitting that the Rev A.G. Bradford, the Pastor of the Countess of Huntingdon's Church himself attired in the uniform of the Ely Volunteer Training Corps – officiated at the funeral. The fact that such an event was taking place – the first interment of a war hero in Ely – was not generally known in the city, or a very much larger attendance would have been present. As it was, the funeral was numerously attended, and due honour was paid to the memory of the young soldier, members of the Volunteer Training Corps, the wounded soldiers, and several khaki-clad Ely men home on leave, following him to the grave.*

*The cortège started from the house of deceased's parents in Silver-street at half-past one, and the blinds were drawn, not only at many houses in the locality, but also en route to the cemetery where the funeral had become known.... The Rev A.G. Bradford, in a short address, paid a tribute to the young soldier who had laid down his life for King and country. The rev gentleman said their sympathy, of course, went out to the deceased's home, and for those to whom he was most near and dear. They also sought to do him honour that day, he having been one of millions who came forward a year or two ago and joined the Army with a clear idea of the issues at stake. They believed the life of the nation was worth purchasing at the sacrifice of their own life, and their friend of whom they were now thinking, with many others, were moved by the impulse of a motive greater than themselves, and were prepared to do all they could for their God, their King and their country. The offer of their friend, now departed, had been accepted. Let them thank God or him, and for all like him, who ware sacrificing so much for them at the present time. Let them learn to value their freedom, which had been preserved for them at such a great price, and, if the demand was made upon them, to make sacrifices for the great cause which they believed to be the cause of God.'*

# Chapter 10

# After the First Day

O ver the night of 3/4 July, the 11th Suffolks were relieved from the trenches they had managed to occupy and cling on to. They moved gradually back from the front lines, where the work of rebuilding the battalion began. With over 600 casualties, this would take some time, though some of the wounded probably remained at duty. Captain Osbert Brown certainly did, and so would some of the lightly wounded other ranks.

W.J. Senescall recalled that: '*We few who were left after 1 July 1916 had the job of going through all the other fellows packs and sorting personal stuff from military stuff. The stuff they carried – photos galore, small souvenirs. All the personal stuff was sent to their homes.*' In other units, men remembered sharing out the food parcels amongst those who were left, as they could not be sent home.

Despite the high casualties, messages of congratulations were in order, first from Brigadier General Gore, who wrote to Colonel Somerset, asking him to express to his battalion his '*admiration for their gallant conduct in the attack on 1 July, theirs was the hardest task of any, having the farthest to advance before crossing our own front line in face of a deadly fire, their courage was magnificent as in spite of wave after wave being mown down they fearlessly pressed forward towards their objective and got well into the German line but unfortunately their numbers were too few in the end to gain it. No troops could have done better and I am sure that their advance in this battle will go down to posterity as one of the most gallant actions of the War.*'

They also received a message from the Divisional Commander, congratulating his troops '*on the fine reputation they have earned for themselves. With them he mourns deeply for our absent comrades.*' The officer commanding III Corps addressed the brigade and said he was pleased with their performance, while Rawlinson sent a wire with a message to be passed on: '*Please convey to the 34th Division my hearty congratulations on their successes. Whilst regretting their heavy casualties I desire to express my gratitude for and admiration of the determination and gallantry with which they carried out their difficult task.'* Although it hardly made up for the casualties, the message was that they could be proud of their performance and the fact that those who had died lost their lives gallantly, the same message that was being proclaimed to grieving families.

Casualties amongst senior officers meant that the command of the battalion and brigade was shifted around. Major Farquhar, the previous second in command, was moved to command the 20th Northumberland Fusiliers. Captain Gerald Tuck was appointed second in command of the 11th Suffolks in his place and Second Lieutenant W.H. Parker was appointed adjutant. Reinforcements to the rest of the battalion were also brought in – between 6 and 30 July, thirteen officers and 520 new men were brought in from various sources. Some may have come from the 13th Suffolks. Some of the men who initially enlisted in the 11th Suffolks had been moved to this battalion for further training, it is possible that these now went overseas to rejoin their original battalion. Senescall believed many of them to be Derby recruits and some may have been conscripts too. On the whole these men were probably older, perhaps with families, and so would have been less willing to join up in the early stages of the war.

On 22 July, Major General Ingouville-Williams, the commander of 34th Division, was killed in action. He was replaced a few days after his death by Major General C.L. Nicholson, who had originally served in the East Lancashire Regiment, before being promoted to the Staff.

The officers that remained were crucial in rebuilding the battalion. Captain Tuck wrote to Captain Brown's parents after his death that Brown *'helped us to build up a battalion from nothing to the splendid thing that it was before our battles on the Somme, and is rapidly becoming again.'* Lieutenant Anthony Maxwell-Lawford, who served in the same company as Captain Brown, came to the same conclusion about him: *'the Company was run wholly on hero-worship, since it consisted of men of many different regiments put together and worked into a really splendid Company as it is to-day.'*

Captain Tuck reflected:

*'The original Battalion had grown up together and was like a huge family, in which the system of discipline was tempered by very strong feelings of affection and local sentiment. That was characteristic of Kitchener's Army. When reinforcements came out to replace our losses, it was a question whether this bond of union could be maintained. To me it is very wonderful that it has survived as well as it has done. Fortunately there has always remained a sufficient bedrock of the old Battalion to keep up something of the same spirit, though it would be unwise not to admit that it has been necessary to attach less importance to that and more to discipline. Our present Commanding Officer was able, by knowledge of discipline and military life in pre-war days, to see just how the Battalion should be treated. By the force and magnetism of his personality he has made the Battalion as good as it ever was.'*

Conscription was brought into force in January 1916. Britain was forced to accept that the voluntary principle was not bringing in sufficient men to keep the armies up to strength, and this was before the heavy casualties of the Battle of the Somme. On the first day alone there were over 57,000 casualties, and though subsequent days took nothing like such a heavy toll on lives as the first, casualties remained high until the official end of the battle on 18 November.

Recruitment had gradually slowed and was no longer able to keep pace with casualties. However, that was not the only motivation for introducing it. With the need for increased war production, it was vital to direct all the manpower resources of the nation. In the initial rush to the Colours, particularly in the north of England, skilled men who were needed in the factories had enlisted, leaving the factories dangerously short of people who knew what they were doing. In Cambridgeshire, a much more agricultural area, this problem was less acute. However, it was important to increase food production as much as possible, even before unrestricted submarine warfare took the necessity to new heights. It was for this reason that Tribunals were set up, bodies of local men who determined whether a particular man could be spared from his work. Many agricultural workers were able to claim exemption on the basis of their work, though not all were granted exemption if it was believed the farm could continue without them, by such expedients as using prisoners of war, conscientious objectors, young boys or old men, women, or the specially constituted agricultural companies. Some men would also be given leave during the harvest period if they had particular agricultural skills.

On 31 July, the 11th Suffolks took up a position in the lines once again, at Bazentin-le-Petit. This portion of the Somme had been taken by a successful dawn attack on 14 July, but the early success was not exploited. Here they found the artillery active, on both sides, and the battalion war diary notes that there were *'constant complaints of our own artillery firing short'*, which can't have improved the position. Many of the trenches used for shelter by the British would have been captured from the Germans and so all the defences would be facing the wrong way. Work had probably been done to alter the trenches by putting a fire-step on the correct side and to establish strongpoints to resist counter-attack, and the German trenches were often of superior quality to the British ones. In large measure this was because the Germans were occupying enemy territory – they did not need to advance further to have a good bargaining point. By contrast, the Allies needed to drive the Germans out of their own territory and so trenches were more likely to be seen as temporary.

Around this time, an incident occurred which demonstrated the fatalism which could infect ordinary soldiers. One of the officers observed *'one of our men, stripped to the waist, calmly washing himself in a shellhole at the bottom of which was a dead German, at Bazentin cross-roads, the most heavily shelled point I have ever known. He was apparently quite unconscious of the danger he was in: at any rate he was oblivious to it.... It is difficult to know how far such behaviour is due to lack of imagination, and how much to that philosophical outlook on life characteristic of sons of the soil.'*

W.J. Senescall wrote:

*'About the third day the Colonel received orders that we were to capture a bit of trench opposite. As soon as it was dark our guns let fly and blew the Jerry trench to nothing. The Adjutant leading, forward went our new recruits and flopped into the trench such as it was. These chaps – two days in the trenches and then sent on an attack like this. As soon as Jerry realised we had taken over he did the same thing and started to blow our chaps out. By a miracle*

*the wire they took with them was not cut. The Adjutant rang through and put it to the Colonel. I could hear the Adjutant shouting against the shell fire asking could they evacuate as the position was hopeless. The answer was "Come back". They did, just a handful, and we were so many hundreds less once again. Another silly bit of strategy if you can call it that.'*

Captain Tuck wrote of the same attack:

*'We moved up on 30 July to Bazentin-le-Petit. This was the first experience the New Army had had of what might be called the wastage of war. Here, instead of the mathematical exactness of trench warfare, we had the remains of ruined villages, land on which there was not a vestige of grass or cultivation, trees torn up by the roots, human bodies, debris of all kinds, and terrible smells that could not be avoided. One had to get accustomed to eating and sleeping in places that in ordinary circumstances one could not have faced. It was a very great test of the moral [sic] of the soldier.*

*We had two terms (or tours, as they are called) in the battle trenches, and at the end of the first tour took part in an attack, which, though confined to the Brigade, was a great test for the men who had just come out. About 150 yards in front of us was a Boche trench of great importance, and we were ordered to take it. The stolid East Anglian temperature [sic] proved of great value in this operation. Only two companies of ours were actually engaged. They got to their objective in the face of machine-gun fire, and remained there for two hours until a staff officer decided that as no troops had got up to them on either side, they must retire. Not until then did they budge, tough during the whole of the time they were in the Boche trench they were being bombed from both flanks and heavily shelled from the front.'*

Both of these accounts fit closely with the war diary's account of the attack. Orders were received for the attack at 5pm on 3 August, with a conference of company commanders being held at 8pm. Shelling overnight and during the early morning led to the death of Second Lieutenant V.K. Mason and four other ranks, with one other dying of wounds. Even those not selected for an attack were not out of danger. One of the 'other ranks' who died was Private Victor Sayer, who had enlisted on 7 September 1914, meaning he must have been one of the first men in the battalion. Lance Corporal W. Caden wrote home to his parents to describe the circumstances. Victor was *'sound asleep in a dugout'*, when he was killed instantly by a shell.

The plan was for parts of 101 Brigade (two companies of the 11th Suffolks, and two of the 16th Royal Scots) to attack and consolidate the enemy's Intermediate line, with zero hour at 1.10am on 4 August. One of the criticisms often made of the attack on 1 July was that it was done in broad daylight, giving the enemy gunners an easy target. However, attacking at night did not necessarily make things any better. The attack would be supported with an intense bombardment beginning a minute before zero, lifting thirty seconds before the attack was to be launched and moving back, except on pre-selected strongpoints, which would be bombarded for an extra fifteen seconds. The Trench Mortar Battery, re-equipped and with new officers and men, would also go into action from thirty seconds before to thirty seconds after the attack, after which they would focus on the communication trenches and barrage behind the German trench which was to be taken.

The intention was for the companies to enter the German trenches under cover of the barrage. There was good reason for the shortness of the barrage: experience had shown that in this sector at least the enemy artillery was quick to retaliate. It was hoped that by keeping the barrage very short, surprise might be obtained. 101 Brigade received a report from the officer commanding 57 Brigade that also informed them of where the enemy's barrage had fallen in response to the attack. Additional accommodation for the attacking troops was therefore dug beyond where the barrage had fallen. Though the popular impression of British generals is one of incompetence and ignorance of their men's lives, it is clear that some, at least, tried to learn from previous mistakes. Other lessons that had been learned from experience included the order to fire in front of the enemy's trenches to clear snipers and just behind them to target machine guns.

Initially, the attack was to be launched in conjunction with attacks on either flank. However, on 3 August, 34th Division Headquarters informed 101 Brigade that this would no longer be the case. In consequence, they were not to push on quite as vigorously if all went well. When the time came for the assault to be launched, B Company of the 11th Suffolks, under Captain

Brown, moved off as expected. However, A Company of the 11th Suffolks, and the two companies of the 16th Royal Scots did not leave the trenches. There had been some confusion when they were moving to their assembly positions, and so they were not ready at zero hour and failed to carry out the attack.

General Nicholson believed that the failure of the attack was down to *'very bad company leading.... One company got in with greatest ease on the top of the artillery barrage, the other 3 did not. The 11th Suffolks' left company got in, the next on its right did not start and for some reason the 2 companies of the 15th Royal Scots, thinking they had to move by their left, did not start. These two companies did start later when it was nearly light and got very roughly handled.'* There was a later, handwritten addition to this account that the right company commander of the 11th Suffolks *'completely lost his head'*, being transferred shortly afterwards to a training school.

B Company was able to achieve its objective, and began bombing to the right, where they should have been supported by the other companies meant to attack. In the attack with Captain Brown was Corporal Desborough. According to a friend who wrote to his mother, he was acting as corporal in charge of the battalion bombers during the attack. When the writer reached battalion headquarters, having seen him and the others leave, *'the report came through that the party had been hit by a shell and that all were killed. Later two came back suffering severely from shell shock – they know nothing of what happened. Next morning the rumour went round that Corporal Desborough had been seen going to the dressing station, but I am afraid this is false as I can find no definite person who saw him, and he went to none of our Brigade dressing stations. I am afraid it is almost certain that your son was killed instantly by the shell.'*

Lance Corporal L.J. Brown was also in the attack and, after being wounded, he wrote home to describe it to his sister:

*'We had been holding a trench for five days when we had the order passed along about 11 o'clock that we were to be ready in battle order by 12.45 to go over the top and take the Huns' front trench about 150 yards in front of us. We had got into position, I in charge of my company's guns (machine), and for ten minutes we opened fire; the noise was deafening. Then, just as*

*we started to go over the top of the trench, the Bosches started strafing us, and they gave us hell too.*

*It was the worst engagement I have been in after being here for seven months. I think they dropped a shell every yard in our front trench, and we expected to go sky high every minute. Then just after the first line were over and we were waiting for an order I got mine; at first I thought it had taken my arm clean off, as it went in my forearm, smashing the bone, and came out under my wrist, so you may guess I have a nasty hit. It was one of his heavy black ones that burst right on the top of the trench. Well, I handed my gun to a comrade and crept round to another lad, and he put my field dressing on, but, of course, he could not stop the flow of blood. Then came the worst job, which was to get to the dressing station, as they were shelling us heavily, but I managed it somehow. Thank God it was in the early hours of morning, being about one o'clock, so it was not light, otherwise we should have been sniped. I managed to get through at last to the station, and was sent to —, where I was made a stretcher case, then was put on the boat for good Old England, where I am now.'*

Private Albert Edward Miller was with Captain Brown and made it as far as the German trenches. According to Lieutenant Maxwell-Lawford, '*it was while actually standing on the German parapet that the platoon commander, Second Lieutenant Tallon, and your son were killed. They were the only two to be hit, and in your son's case a rifle or machine-gun bullet passed through the centre of his forehead, killing him immediately, so quickly in fact that he could have suffered no pain whatever.'*

He continued: '*It may comfort you to know that he regularly attended all church parades out here, and that the great victory which we are bound to obtain can only be gained by the sacrifice of such gallant lads as your son had proved himself to be. I can only end by offering you my deepest sympathy, and wishing the best of success to his brothers in the Army, to his sisters and other relations.'*

Private Miller had joined the battalion in June – it is unclear if he fought on 1 July, but he would have been a replacement for a casualty in the early days of the battalion's time in France.

Private Gordon C. Freestone also took part in the attack, and instead of (or, more likely, as well as) writing to his family, he wrote to his local newspaper, the *Newmarket Journal* to describe the attack:

*'Dear sir,--I am writing from the Red Cross hospital, Gloucester, where I have been sent from the front wounded. I was wounded on Saturday, 5 August. It was a big night. We were meant to be getting back some more of the German trenches, and glad to say we did. We came up with good hearts, crept up under heavy shell fire to our trench after getting orders to go over into the German trenches. We were not satisfied with one, so with the help of the Royal Scots we were all willing to get to the next, and did. I had put ten rounds in my rifle, and got within two yards of the German trench when a tall German tried to bayonet me and my mate; but no time was lost, and before he could say Jack Robinson he was lying dead.*

*We had to crawl over dead Germans, and took three nice little trench and machine guns. After getting wounded in my left knee I found that I could not walk, so my mate got me back into a dug-out, where I lay till Sunday morning, when I tried to have a little sleep, but could not, for shells and bombs were bursting over my head. I made the best of it, my cig was blown to pieces. I made myself as comfortable as I could by putting on a German overcoat. At 8 o'clock Sunday morning I was carried out by two of the Scots stretcher bearers and arrived at Albert, where my wounds were dressed, and was then taken to Rouen Hospital, when I went under an operation. Am now in England and getting on as well as can be expected, but cannot bend the knee. I hope to be home soon for a few days. The Germans had the cheek to say "have mercy comrade"'.*

Orders were given for the 16th Royal Scots to reorganise and carry out the attack as originally ordered. There was so much confusion in the front lines that it was not until 4.45am that they were able to attack. A report was sent back that the troops were able to advance only about 30 yards before being met by very heavy machine-gun fire, which was *'quite impossible to pass through'*. By now it was daylight and German machine-gun fire beat off the attack, causing heavy casualties.

Captain Brown's men had suffered heavily amongst the trained bombers, most of them becoming casualties. At 5.15am, the order was given by the brigade to withdraw. Captain Brown did so and was able to bring most of the wounded men with him. He was later awarded the DSO for his actions. The citation read: *'for conspicuous gallantry in action. He commanded the only company which succeeded in reaching its objective, and beat off many bombing counter-attacks, until he was finally ordered to withdraw. He sent a fine example of coolness and courage, and carried out the withdrawal with great skill.'*

Two German machine guns were captured, but the lines had not advanced – and to make matters worse, the British heavy artillery put down a strong barrage on the British front line trenches.

The cost of the attack was high for the lack of results: one officer and three other ranks killed and one more who died of wounds. Two officers and seventy-one other ranks were wounded and nineteen men were found to be missing.

The following evening Lieutenant Tempest took fifty volunteer bombers up to the German lines to assist the 15th Royal Scots. The attack was unsuccessful and two other ranks were killed, another died of wounds, nineteen were wounded and one was reported missing. Ernie Spendelow was one of those killed in the attack. His platoon commander wrote to his mother to give her the news of his death, and what details he was allowed to share, reporting that *'your son, with some other of our fellows, went up to the front line as a bombing party to help another battalion, and I am afraid Ernie was killed while doing his duty as every soldier should. I am sure no one can be sorrier than I, for although I have not been very long with*

15702 Private Walter William Huckle of Willingham. Killed in action 17 July 1916. (Cambridge Weekly News *1 September 1916*)

16327 Lance Corporal Basil Augustus Reeves of Cottenham. Awarded the Military Medal for his actions on 1 July 1916. (Cambridge Weekly News *18 August 1916*)

15818 Private Albert Wilderspin of Histon. Killed in action 3 August 1916. (Cambridge Weekly News *31 August 1917*)

*this battalion I had made great friends with him, and discovered him to be a very lovable fellow, always willing to do his best and to help other people, and for that reason I feel his loss terribly.'*

His friend Private G. Clanty also wrote to Ernie's parents, on behalf of his friends to tell them:

*'what a good soldier and a jolly mate he was. When out of the trenches he was very jolly, and kept us from thinking of trench life. He was a good bomber, and on 1 July he was brigade bomber. It is ill-luck for our battalion to lose such men, as I don't believe we shall get fellows up to his standard again. In action he was fearless and Fritz had to look up if he got near him. I should like to let you know he died a soldier. He was sent out with a party of bombers in a trench to shift some Boches out, and after throwing*

*his hardest, a rifle grenade landed in front of him. It will ease your minds to know that he suffered no pain.'*

On the evening of 6 August, the battalion was relieved. The Germans opened fire and it was at this time that W.J. Senescall was wounded, his wrist being broken by a piece of shrapnel. He was taken to the medical officer's dugout, had his wrist put in a sling, and then went back to the lines for the night. Later, his arm was badly swollen and he was sent back to the first aid station, then to Le Havre in a hospital train, and finally he returned to England. After his wrist had healed, he moved to another battalion of the Suffolk Regiment, and saw out the rest of the war in Salonika.

*Chapter 11*

# The Somme Continued

After the attempted night attack, the 11th Suffolks had a fairly quiet rest of the year, though various incidents took place and the battalion was not without further casualties. They were relieved on 6 August, but then returned to support lines from 10 August. Although this was not quite as difficult as being in the front lines, it did not mean they were out of danger.

On 12 August, the *'enemy shelled intermittently, doing some damage. Three other ranks killed. Second Lieutenant W. Curtiss, Second Lieutenant R.T. Poles, thirteen other ranks wounded.'* Amongst the three other ranks killed was Private William Cupit Rash, of Babraham, who had enlisted in September 1914, and had married in June 1915. Killed at the same time, and likely by the same shell, was Private Arthur J. Hart, who worked with his father as a fish and fruit merchant, visiting the various villages around Longstowe and being well known in them.

Arthur's Company Commander wrote:

*'I am so sorry to have to tell you that your son, 23762 Private A.J. Hart, was killed at dusk on the evening of 12 August. He was killed instantly by a shell which burst over our trenches. We said a prayer over him and buried him just behind the trenches, putting up a small cross. I am afraid it was all we could do. He had only been with us for a short time, but I knew him slightly as very keen and willing to do his best, and a great favourite with his platoon. We all sympathise so much with you in your great loss, but he died bravely for his King and country.'*

It seems likely that he was one of the draft of men sent over to replace those killed on 1 July.

Private Looker also sent a letter home to Arthur's family, writing that he was killed around 8.30 pm, as they were on sentry duty together.

> *'I was on, and he was the next to come on, and he had just got two letters come and he was in the trench and I was on the fire trench. Two shells came, one behind the other. He dodged the first one, but the next one came so quick he got a piece on the head and died instantly and never spoke. We were the best of mates, and he was a good mate and a chum that never seemed frightened of the Huns, as he has seen some rough business since he has been out with me, but he was always cheerful.... I feel lonely without him now.'*

The following day, another private was wounded – George Lee from March who was one of the battalion signallers, having enlisted in November 1914. He was sent to hospital in Manchester, and wrote home:

> *'Dear Mother and Dad,--I am just writing to let you know how the thing happened. We were up in the front line when Fritz started shelling, and I happened to get in the way of one of them. That is the reason that I am here. I caught it in several places – in my left leg and foot and right arm and back, but am getting on as well as can be expected. Don't worry, for I am not.'*

In a later letter he added: *'Don't worry, for it is all for the good of the country.'* Despite the hardship of the Somme, soldiers still believed in the cause for which they were fighting – or at least told their families that they did, perhaps in the hope of encouraging their parents not to worry too much.

On 15 August the battalion was relieved and, together with the rest of their division, moved to the area around Erquinghem. Much of this journey was completed by route march, putting to good use their early training in Cambridge. Going into the line on 21 August, they found the trenches in poor condition. Much work would need to be done before winter set in. Living outdoors during the winter would lead to casualties from sickness, often much more difficult to identify than those caused by enemy action as they tend not to be reported in the battalion war diary. Higher level war diaries sometimes mention the number of sick across the whole brigade or division, but it is difficult to separate this out to battalions. Much emphasis was placed in training and in books dealing with how to be a good officer on looking after the health of the men, perhaps a reaction to previous wars where the British Army had suffered more casualties through sickness than through enemy action. The First World War was the first war where this was not the case.

The area that they moved into was fairly quiet, but there were three enemy searchlights which hampered patrols at night. Senior commanders in particular were keen to see constant patrolling and a constant 'offensive spirit' amongst those in the line, in order to prevent troops growing stale and accustomed to hiding behind parapets. It was also believed that active patrolling would keep up morale. The grass had to be cut in front of the trenches, having grown long thus, presumably, obscuring vision. The battalion snipers were active again, claiming one hit on 25 August. Three days later, on encountering a German patrol, bombs were thrown but nobody in the 11th Suffolks was killed or wounded. This quieter sector was a welcome change for the battalion and the comparative quiet continued into September.

On 5 and 6 September the battalion war diary recorded that *'Enemy very inactive in every way, only using .77 mm shells, and doing practically no damage. He appears to use his truckle tram very freely by night.'* and *'JOCK'S JOY shelled with 40 5.9 shells. Very little damage. His artillery were active generally, also his trench mortars did some shooting. We are doing a great deal of work to make the line more comfortable for the winter. One other rank died of wounds.'* The 11th Suffolks likely returned the favour – both sides sometimes co-operated to make parts of the line almost peaceful, though this was officially frowned upon.

A book of advice for platoon commanders, framed as a series of questions, asked at the beginning and end:

*'I AM HERE FOR TWO PURPOSES – TO DO AS MUCH DAMAGE AS POSSIBLE TO THE ENEMY, AND TO HOLD MY PART OF THE LINE IN ALL CIRCUMSTANCES. AM I AS OFFENSIVE AS I MIGHT BE WITH ORGANISED SNIPING, RIFLE GRENADES AND PATROLS? AM I DOING MY BEST*

*TO MAKE "NO MAN'S LAND" OUR LAND? AM I DOING ALL I CAN TO MAKE THIS LINE AS STRONG AS POSSIBLE? HAVE I DONE ALL I CAN FOR THE COMFORT AND SAFETY OF MY MEN?'*

The answer to the first parts of those questions might very well have been 'no, not really', although the continuance of the Somme offensive elsewhere in the line means that it is also quite possible that the artillery lacked the shells to be particularly active. But, to the latter, there were certainly significant efforts going on to improve the trenches. Even at brigade level, which had the reports of several battalions to view and summarise, there are a number of days in September (when battalions of the brigade were in the front lines) reported as *'All quiet. Nothing to report.'*

On 7 September, the Germans opposite put up a board over their trenches, reading *'3 Generals, 21,000 Romanians captured, 1000 cannons taken. Don't mind for the rest.'* Patrols were sent out to try and capture it, but were unsuccessful. This was a reference to the fact that although Romania had joined the side of the Allies, they had not proven a particularly useful additional ally, and were all but defeated in a few weeks.

The remainder of the month was spent alternating between the quiet front lines and being at 'rest', though time in rest was largely spent on working parties. A number of patrols were sent out, but they rarely met the enemy and it seems that no man's land was largely dominated by the British. The battalion was not without casualties, and the fact that they were much fewer in number than in previous months would have been no consolation to the families. Private Charles Patten, for instance, was killed on 21 September. He had enlisted early in the war, leaving a wife and four children at home. They now mourned his loss, having received the news of his death from an officer who wrote:

*'Dear Mrs Patten, I am awfully sorry to have to inform you that your husband, Private C. E. Patten, 16814, was killed in action on Thursday, 21 September. He was killed instantaneously by a 'whiz-bang'. He was buried in the British cemetery on Friday by the Church of England minister. A cross is being made for his grave. Please accept the deepest sympathy from myself and the officers and men of his company. He was liked by all.'*

24224 Serjeant Alfred Grant Rule Few of Willingham, awarded the Distinguished Conduct Medal for his actions on 26 September 1916. (Cambridge Weekly News *3 August 1917*)

Of the five men who died in September, four of them were married and at least three had children.

From 4 October Major Tuck began training a volunteer raiding party, made up of himself, Second Lieutenants F.M. Higen, K. Scott-Walker, Grand, and thirty other ranks. They were going to attempt a silent raid, without any artillery assistance. Meanwhile the rest of the battalion continued with working parties to improve the trenches ready for winter, which was beginning to set in. The raid was probably motivated by an order passed down from 34 Brigade: '*With the object of assisting our operations elsewhere by inflicting as much damage as possible on the enemy's personnel and defences increased activity is to be undertaken on the Second Army front.*' This activity was to take the form of artillery shoots combined with dummy raids and actual raids. Prior to the raid, the trench mortars would fire on the German trenches, with '*apparently accidental shots dropped on the wire especially near the point of entry.*' Gaps were to be kept open by machine-gun fire, and regular patrols into no man's land would check for German sentries and work out where additional 'accidental' rounds needed to fall.

The preparations that went into this raid almost seem to rival the preparations for the Battle of the Somme (certainly at the battalion level where it was planned), which might be why this one would be a success, while 1 July was of much more questionable effectiveness. Arrangements were also made for Lewis guns to be ready and waiting in position in no man's land to deal with any enemy machine guns that fired on the raiding party.

The Silent Raid was first attempted on 11 October. At 1.15am, when it was fairly dark, they went out into no man's land, but at 2am reported that *'the belt wire found the previous night close up against the parapet was still uncut, and that the Medium Trench Mortars which had fired during the afternoon had been short, as the ground in front was all shell holes.'* There was also a sentry where the wire had been uncut, firing occasionally into the wire. Major Tuck ordered them to return and look for an opening elsewhere in the enemy's wire.

Second Lieutenant Myers found ten Germans on his expedition up the line, to see if there was another way through, so he tried to get the main party up to attack these men. While he was making these arrangements, someone else from his party came after him to say that there were now twenty Germans in the wire. Major Tuck, believing it might be a wiring party, ordered them to try and cut them off. Returning to do so, Second Lieutenant Myers and the rest of the party could no longer find any party of Germans at all, but did see sentries waiting where the wire had been uncut. They were unable to cut the remaining wire. As it was now 4.15 they returned to the British front lines.

The following night was darker, so they tried again. There were other raids taking place and so the idea of a 'silent' raid with no artillery support was scrapped. Instead, they crept into no man's land at 7pm, and then at 7.30 a barrage began, lasting for three minutes and providing cover for the raiding party. The barrage was *'wonderfully accurate and effective'*, and succeeded in considerably damaging the wire that had been uncut the previous night. At 7.35pm the barrage switched to a box barrage – firing on all the areas around the raiding party to prevent reinforcements being brought up. Having cut the remaining wire by hand, they *'entered the German trench and one party proceeded to the left and another to the right, a third party waiting at the point of entry.'*

*'The party proceeding to the right, under Second Lieutenant Scott-Walker, found a dug-out and bombed it..... . One German tried to bolt but was shot, two wounded Germans were dragged out, one of them was brought back alive and sent to 102 Field Ambulance, the other caused so much trouble in the trench that he was shot, the three other occupants of the dugouts were killed.*

*'The party under Second Lieutenant Grand found the trench very much damaged, and could find no enemy dugouts. They brought back two rifles and a steel helmet. At 7.38 pm, on the whistle being blown, the whole party returned with their prisoner, having suffered no casualties.'*

The prisoner, a 42-year-old man *'was rather badly wounded in the leg, and was carried back in a specially constructed light stretcher and two poles, this proved very effective as the poles nearly met over the man and prevented struggling and made carrying quite easy.'*

As they returned to the British lines, a German machine gun opened up on the party. However, it was immediately attacked by two Lewis guns and a Vickers machine gun that had been taken out into no man's land and were ready and waiting for action. Enemy retaliation once they were back in the British lines *'was unexpectedly intense, both with artillery and Trench Mortars, chiefly on the front line and behind the Support Line.'*

In his report on the raid, Major Tuck wrote that *'undoubtedly the success of the raid was very largely due to the excellent patrolling which had been done by the raiders, all the officers had been over the ground five times, and all the other ranks four times, and the information obtained on the night 11/12 was most valuable.'*

Major Tuck also later wrote of the raid:

*'We spent a comparatively quiet winter, except for a successful raid we carried out. This resulted in exactly what was required – the destruction of a number of dug-outs and the capture of a prisoner. During this raid a notable incident occurred. In spite of good preliminary bombardment, the Boche wire was not all cut, and the officer who was leading the raid had to cut it himself before the raid could carry on, which he did in extraordinarily cool fashion.'*

After the excitement of the raid, the remainder of the month – and, indeed, the remainder of the year – was much quieter. The sector of the line where they were located remained quiet, and though on occasion the British artillery fired heavy barrages, the Germans seemed disinclined to return them that vigorously. Casualties remained light, though they included

Harry Hines, who lived on Cambridge Place, in Cambridge, who died on 12 October, after being hit on the head by a piece of shrapnel. Another of the original members of the battalion was lost.

There was also the more noted death of Captain Brown, though Harry Hines's family no doubt suffered just as much from his loss as the wealthier Browns. He was killed on 1 November while inspecting his company in the front line. He did not fall leading a raid, and in fact his death seems almost implausible given his actions on both 1 July and 4 August. Lieutenant Maxwell-Lawford wrote home to his mother as follows, the letter being passed on to Osbert Brown's family:

*'We were laughing and talking in the front line men's dug-out about 6 pm one evening and he went out to see the sentries. The post arrived and I had just got your long letter from Rottingdean open in front of me when a servant came in and told us he [Osbert Brown] was hit. Grey and I went to where he was lying, shot straight through the brain. Since we left the Somme every night there have been sentries standing in every bay looking over the top and not one has been hit. Brown stands up for one minute beside one and is killed. Just before he went out he was talking about his future. He already had a job in the Treasury which he had never taken up. He was only twenty-four, and had a brilliant career at Cambridge, Pembroke, BA and BSc at the end of his second year. Beginning in the Civil Service with a DSO would have meant immediate promotion.... He was buried last night (All Souls' Day) just behind the firing line. It had to be a simple ceremony as it was under observation of a Bosch balloon.... It doesn't take long to make friends when one first comes out here, and as I told you, I realised I had found a great friend in Brown during my first week on the Somme; how great I never understood, and I cannot yet realize that he is dead.'*

Cyril Sheen also wrote home about Captain Brown's death: *'How he got through all I don't know, but it seems too cruel that he should now be killed by a stray shot. Everyone will be frightfully upset. He was very efficient and popular, everyone regarding him as a personal friend.'*

Captain Brown's men missed him too; Corporal Kitson wrote to the family, while the mother of Private Hutt also wrote to Mrs Brown, sending

her sympathy and telling of how she was grateful to Captain Brown for his
kindness to her son:

*'I can't tell you how much the boys loved your son, and it does make so much
difference when the officers are kind to the men serving under them.... Will
you accept all my heartfelt sympathy. I understand all you are suffering.
God's ways are perfect and past finding, but, although sending you this
sorrow, He will comfort you. When I think of him so young, so bright, being
cut off in this war, my heart aches for you. His giving his bright young life
for his Country. May God in His great mercy strengthen you and give you
courage to face this your great sorrow. I understand your great loss. I have
lost my eldest in the war.'*

*Chapter 12*

# A New Year Begins

New Year's Day 1917 and the first few days of the year, were occupied with working parties. At home, the newspapers reflected on the year passed and looked ahead to the year to come.

A special service was held in Great St Mary's to mark the Day of National Prayer and Resolve and to open the week of prayer arranged in Cambridge by the branch of the Evangelical Alliance.

> *'The Bishop of Ely preached a stirring sermon, in which he uttered a warning against war-weariness and premature peace. A united prayer meeting took place in the Guildhall in the evening, when addresses were given by the bishop and ministers of the town. Prayer meetings at the Henry Martyn Hall begin to-night, and will continue during the week.'*

The bishop told the congregation that they should thank God, not for the fighting, but for the fact that they had been brought through great dangers and had seen great successes. The whole nation had been brought together, and *'our men, those living and those who had laid down their lives, had encountered unmentionable dangers with a noble courage, self-sacrifice and tender consideration for others which no human words could possibly describe.'* He also emphasised that the war was a righteous one, fought not because of national ambition, *'but because of a deep and awful sense of duty, and this sense must still remain strong as at the beginning…. We must not shrink from self-sacrifice, however hard and long-drawn-out the war proved.'* Lastly he called on his congregation to return to God, to seek forgiveness for wrongs and to pray sincerely for not only their soldier sons and husbands, but also for the enemy that they too might turn to God.

The same week, the local newspapers printed Douglas Haig's despatch about the Battle of the Somme. He claimed a victory, but continued:

*'The enemy's power has not yet been broken, nor is it yet possible to form an estimate of the time the war may last before the objects for which the Allies are fighting have been attained. But the Somme battle has placed beyond doubt the ability of the Allies to gain those objects.*

*The German Army is the mainstay of the Central Powers, and a full half of that Army, despite all the advantages of the defensive, supported by the strongest fortifications, suffered defeat on the Somme this year. Neither victors nor the vanquished will forget this; and, though bad weather has given the enemy a respite, there will undoubtedly be many thousands in his ranks who will begin the new campaign with little confidence in their ability to resist our assaults or to overcome our defence.*

*Our new Armies entered the battle with the determination to win and with confidence in their power to do so. They have proved to themselves, to the enemy, and to the world that this confidence was justified, and in the fierce struggle they have been through they have learned many valuable lessons which will help them in the future....*

*It is... justifiable to conclude that the Somme offensive not only relieved Verdun, but held large forces which would otherwise have been employed against our Allies in the East.'*

Despite the casualties suffered by both the French and the British, at Verdun and the Somme respectively, there was no thought amongst the politicians and the generals of not attacking once again, as soon as the weather was favourable. German offers of peace, based on negotiation, though not particularly favourable to the Allies, were rejected out of hand. Those who supported them, it was claimed by the *Cambridge Independent Press*, had become anti-British:

*'So anxious are these people to pull down the credit of their own country that they are careless if they pull down the whole edifice of civilisation with it. So Mr Ponsonby tells us that the idea of punishing wrong-doing is a low motive for continuing the law. Mr Bonar Law annihilated his position by immediately asking him upon what social order rests if not upon the vindication of justice and the punishment of wrong. It is a sure indication that any cause has become panic-stricken when its advocates will, intellectually, run amok in this fashion. The mere extravagances of*

*controversy may be excused. When Mr Trevelyan speaks of the war as being continued for the purpose of putting Russia into Constantinople, he is merely indulging in a little special pleading which deceives nobody. He does not provide anarchy and all anti-social forces with arguments for their evil work. The distortion of facts carries with it its own remedy in the long run, and rarely does much harm where expression is free. But to debase the currency of moral ideas is an altogether grievous offence. It is a desperate thing to set out to discredit a Government and end by discrediting civilised humanity. Surely such an end is also the* reductio ad absurdium *of the proposition with which contemporary pacifism begins.'*

The civilian population, as well as the soldiers, were undoubtedly growing tired of the war, but newspapers made an effort to keep up morale. A jaunty little song was published:

### DO YOUR BIT

The objects of these verses are
To emphasise that we're at war,
Entreating all to do their best,
Lloyd George and Co will do the rest.

'Lend your money,' that's the cry;
Make the German Kaiser sigh;
Empty your purse to the very last penny
(That is if you really have got any).

You are all, I know, prepared to own
The many advantages of this Loan.
So do your bit for Tommy and Jack,
And help to bring your loved ones back.

The German Loan has long been spent,
They find it hard to raise a cent;
Theirs was a bunch of curious mystery,
Let ours make a page of British history.

So don't forget this little plea,
Think it over at dinner and tea,
And every time you pass your plate,
Remember the boys and the Hymn of Hate.

The 'Loan' referred to was the War Savings Loan, which the British public was encouraged to invest in, in order to help pay for the war.

The British Official History begins the volume on 1917 with an overview of what had gone before, and stated: *'The Allies had every right to look for a much larger measure of success in the year 1917. They had experimented with various methods and had gained vast experience, though at a vast price.'* The British Army now had significantly more artillery at its disposal. At the opening of the Battle of the Somme, the British had 761 heavy guns and howitzers. With the improvements in production of both guns and ammunition, they now had 1,157 available for operations in France.

In France, the 11th Suffolks began to train for the coming offensive. The plans had to be significantly altered after the Germans withdrew from large parts of the Somme, conceding ground they had previously fought hard to retain, and took up station at the Hindenburg Line. Through January, time spent training was alternated with time in the lines, but the area remained quiet and stints even in the front line did not lead to any casualties.

Captain Tuck wrote of the time:

*'At the end of January, 1917, we went out of the line and started practising for the Spring offensive. We were placed north of Arras at the southern end of Vimy Ridge, and for a month prior to going over the top we were occupied night and day in carrying up, through trenches knee-deep in mud and under heavy shellfire, ammunition to trench mortar emplacements necessary to the bombardment.'*

In February, training was stepped up significantly in preparation for the coming attack. The first half of the month was spent doing bayonet fighting, physical training, musketry, company and platoon drill, and battalion attack drill. After moving to the area around Houvelin, the battalion continued training through the rest of February and in March, although they also spent a good deal of time providing working parties. Houvelin was near Arras, where the battalion would go into action in April, taking part in two significant attacks during the month. February and March, while the weather was still often poor, were spent preparing for those attacks. This took the form not only of training, but of carrying stores, especially artillery ammunition, to the places where it would be needed, and to form dumps further forward ready for an advance.

To assist with training, the General Staff issued several pamphlets to explain what was needed in an offensive, and how battalions should train to achieve success.

*SS 143*, issued in February 1917, was aimed at platoon commanders, and emphasised that the platoon was the key unit in the assault, being the smallest unit containing all infantry arms. A platoon was made up of four sections and a headquarters, each section having a different specialty. These were bombers, who fought with grenades and were usually placed in the first lines of an assault, in order to throw bombs at possible machine-gun nests; rifle-bombers, who were often also in the front lines of an assault, and used rifle-grenades; riflemen, who were not meant to be just anyone else, but instead would specialise in accurate rifle fire and sniping, and would do additional practice in bayonet fighting; and Lewis gunners, who manned the platoon's Lewis gun – a light machine gun designed to be at least moderately portable.

Although acknowledging that it was impossible to cover every situation, it was *'hoped that a careful study of the instructions herein contained may assist subordinate commanders to act correctly in any situation.'* In training their men, platoon commanders (and above) were to focus on the following areas:

(a) The Offensive Spirit. All ranks must be taught that their aim and object is to come to close quarters with the enemy as quickly as possible so as to be able to use the bayonet. This must become a second nature.

(b) Initiative. The matter of control by even Company leaders on the battlefield is now so difficult that the smaller formations, i.e., platoon and section commanders must be trained to take the necessary action on their own initiative, without waiting for orders.

(c) Confidence in Weapons, necessitating a high standard of skill at arms.

(d) Co-operation of Weapons, is essential on the battlefield and is the corollary of (c).

(e) Discipline is most necessary at all times, and particularly on the battlefield.

(f) Morale must be heightened by every possible means; confidence in leaders and weapons goes a long way towards it.

(g) Esprit de Corps. True soldierly spirit must be built up in Sections and Platoons. Each section should consider itself the best section in the platoon, and the platoon the best in the battalion.

In order to attend to these requirements, platoon commanders were to work progressively, from saluting etc (which, one would hope, most of the men in the 11th Suffolks had long since figured out), up through to complex tactical exercises. There was a particular focus on musketry and physical fitness, which could be encouraged through *'recreational training, such as football'*. Football was a particularly popular pastime amongst troops on the Western Front, and it doesn't seem to matter where they came from or what their previous background was. Though football was considered a particularly working class pastime, the agricultural labourers amongst the 11th Suffolks seem to have enjoyed it just as much.

This new approach to training was not particularly different from the emphasis and manner of carrying out the initial training, although as the war progressed there was an increasing reliance on platoon commanders, and increasing calls for them to use their initiative. Moreover, the men being trained now had weapons and were able to practise actually shooting, rather than aiming dummy rifles or using miniature rifle ranges.

During March the area around Arras, in which the battalion was training and providing working parties, became increasingly active. Towards the end of the month several men were killed and wounded while out on working parties. Four were killed on 24 March by a shell which hit the British front line. Private Ernest Revell (43517) was one of the conscripts who had joined the battalion. Born in 1889, he lived in Woodbridge, Suffolk, and probably went to the front after 1 July 1916. Also killed by the same shell was Private Alec Bailey, who had been one of the first Boy Scouts at Lakenheath, where he was born in 1895. Private Ashman wrote to his parents that *'I am sorry to inform you that your son Alec was killed instantly on 24 March. We had not been in the trenches only a few hours when it happened. I was not far away at the time, and I went as soon as I heard what had happened, but he and two of his comrades had passed away.'*

Another friend, Lance Corporal Levitt, also wrote to the family:

*'It is with my deepest sympathy and regret that I write to inform you of the death of your son Alec, who was my own chum. He was killed by a shell in the first line, and I can honestly assure you his death was instantaneous, and he could not have suffered any pain, because there was assistance at hand at once and he had passed away. He was taken from the line and buried in a British cemetery. He was very much liked by all the platoon, and they all desire that I should offer you their deepest sympathy.'*

Orders were issued, and filtered down through the levels of the Army, for an attack on the German Hindenburg Line. The British Third Army, of which 34th Division was now a part, was ordered to *'break through the enemy's defences on the front CROISILLES (7 miles S.E. of ARRAS) – COMMANDANT'S HOUSE (one mile South East of THEULS). The Canadian Corps is to deliver a simultaneous attack with a view to capturing the VIMY RIDGE northwards from COMMANDANT'S HOUSE.'*

XVII Corps was to attack between the River Scarpe and the Arras–Lille Road, aiming to capture the German third line system. Despite the failure to break through on the Somme, this was still the aim of British strategy, though at lower levels there was a recognition that more limited attacks, well planned and executed, which aimed at gradually forcing the Germans back, might be more successful. This was, in fact, what the first part of the Arras offensive (and in particular the attack on Messines Ridge) would be.

There were some changes in British tactics. A 'creeping barrage' would be used and supporting fire from machine guns. Although this technique had been trialled in the past, it was now to be applied uniformly and improvements through experience had been made to the pace of the barrage. There were also four tanks available to the 34th Division, to help capture a section of the German second line trench system. Tanks were a comparatively new weapon, first going into action during the Somme battles on 15 September

1916. They were not a war-winning weapon in themselves, despite hopes that they might be, and despite post-war theorising that they had been ill-used and ignored. Early tanks were prone to mechanical failure and were still available only in limited numbers.

The eventual assault was to take place on 9 April. Up until that day, *'two brigades of the 34th Division were in the Forward Area, one holding the line and the other in rear in huts at Ecouvres, while the third brigade was in training the Back Area in and around the vicinity of Chelers. Each Brigade in turn had about 10-12 days training in this Back Area.'* The two brigades in the forward area spent the time digging new communication and assembly trenches and carrying up stores and ammunition. They also had to spend time fixing trenches, which were in poor condition thanks to the rain, snow and the thaw after heavy frosts. The men were also called upon to carry trench mortar ammunition to forward dumps.

The preliminary bombardment was begun on 4 April. The day before, a minor raid, consisting of Second Lieutenant F. Puller and twelve other ranks, had taken place. Unable to take any prisoners or make any identifications, they at least suffered no casualties in their unsuccessful attempt. They had aimed to take a prisoner and obtain any other information that they could get. They formed up in a sap leading into no man's land at 4am, and then moved forwards under a barrage, getting within 40 yards of the German front line before the barrage lifted. Entering the German trenches, they found a rifle left on a firestep which they brought back, but although they saw one or more figures moving away from the front line did not find anyone to take prisoner, despite moving around over about 50 yards of trench. The resulting intelligence was that the German front line was only lightly held, but that the barrage had not been strong enough to force the Germans to stay put.

Careful note would be taken over the next few days as to the state of the wire in front of the German lines. At Third Army Headquarters, this was believed to have had good results and the enemy retaliation to have been weak. However, at 34th Division Headquarters, the picture was one instead of gradual improvement. Thus, on 5 April, the 34th Division war diary noted that the *'bombardment* [was] *still continuing, not very encouraging reports about the wire received.'* however, two days later the wire was *'reported completely cleared in front of enemy front line'*.

That same night the 16th Royal Scots were sent out on a raid, to check on the wire and the state of the enemy's defences, and they were able to take one prisoner. It is not entirely clear what would have been done if this was not the case in terms of delaying the advance. On the Somme, though emphasis had been laid in the plan on waiting until all wire was cut, no provision was really made for this in the plans. However, in the plans for the Battle of Arras, there was some provision made for this, though the attack would not be delayed. In response to the concern about uncut wire, special instructions were issued on what to do if the wire was found to be uncut when the attack was launched.

*'Although the advance must be made <u>in the very boldest possible manner</u>, troops cannot be expected to capture enemy trenches covered by uncut wire and occupied by the enemy.*

*When uncut wire is encountered and no opening can be seen, the following procedure will take place:—*

*(a) Leading troops to at once take up a fire position and push wire cutters forward to cut the wire. As soon as a passage is made, troops will at once press forward.*

*(b) If wire cannot be cut owing to enemy's fire, patrols must at once be pushed out to the flanks to ascertain where openings exist, and rear troops must at once take advantage of these to pass through and turn the enemy's flank.*

*(c) If no openings exist, word must at once be passed back and openings made with the aid of Stokes Guns.'*

Notes were also available on how to deal with hostile machine guns. The pamphlet began by explaining what was probably already well known to every officer, non-commissioned officer or private who had seen action during an attack: *'At the present stage of operations one of the enemy's chief methods of defence consists in holding strong points immediately in rear of his defensive systems. These strong points usually contain one or more machine guns and are arranged chequer-wise so as to be mutually supporting. They are frequently concealed in hollows so as to be difficult to detect from the air and for artillery to deal with.'*

However, it went on to give advice on how to deal with them, which included the fact that, '*to continue a general advance under these conditions in attack formation, as has sometimes been attempted, is therefore usually inadvisable.*'

> '*Small tactical advance guards should be pushed well forward, charged, among other duties, with locating and, if possible, dealing with hostile machine guns.*' *It might then be necessary, if the machine guns discovered are well entrenched, to delay for an artillery preparation, perhaps including a creeping barrage. Once located,* '*information* [about hostile machine guns] *should be passed as quickly as possible to any artillery that may be within reach and able to assist. This information should also be passed to Machine Gun Commanders, who must act with boldness, making every effort to engage the hostile machine guns, and provide covering fire for the advance of infantry and 3" Stokes Mortars. This can be effected, even if the exact position of the hostile machine gun has not been accurately located. The employment of cross-fire, from two or more sub-sections of machine-guns, to sweep the locality by means of either direct or indirect fire has proved very successful.*'

It was also hoped that the new platoon formations should be able to deal with isolated machine guns, particular use being made of the Lewis gunners, who should open fire from cover to keep the German machine gunners' heads down. Riflemen and rifle grenade men, as well as in some situations, bombers, should then be able to flank the machine gun and attack it. The pamphlet concluded: '*The suitability of the recently introduced organization of Platoons for dealing with the situation indicated has been demonstrated, and successful results in recent fighting from the tactics mentioned above have frequently been reported.*'

The British Army was beginning to learn its lessons and provision was being made for ineffective bombardment, rather than assuming that the artillery would be able to completely destroy all the German defences. Also, in contrast to 1 July, a good deal of emphasis was placed on counter-battery work. The Royal Flying Corps reported that they had flown a number of patrols in support of this objective, and '*many direct hits and damaged*

12183 Private Fred Rose of Exning,
Suffolk. Killed in action 2 April 1917.
(Cambridge Weekly News *27 April 1917*)

*emplacements are reported and 11 explosions were seen.'*

General Nicholson was less impressed with this plan. In a letter written after the attack to an unnamed male relative, he said that he thought beforehand that they were given too much to do, and would still think so *'if the Hun had fought as he used to'.* He added later that *'the plan wasn't mine and I didn't like it and don't now even though it came off.'* However, he could show none of these doubts to his men. Instead, his special order was guardedly optimistic, admitting that the task before them was a difficult one, but not, he claimed, so hard a task as they had faced on 1 July. The 11th Suffolks moved up to the front lines, taking position in their assembly trenches on 8 April. The special order from Major General Nicholson was read out immediately before the move:

*'In a few days' time the Division will be called upon to take part in an attack on the German Positions in front of us. The preparations for this attack have gone on continuously since the Division arrived in this Area, and in spite of many difficulties and trying weather conditions, they are now complete. This result is due to the never failing zeal, energy and cheerfulness, which all Ranks have put into their work, and I wish to put on record my very high appreciation of the efforts of all.*

*The attack we have to carry out, details of which have been communicated to all ranks, is part of an operation in which large British and French Forces will take part. The task before us is a difficult one but in many respects, especially with regard to the weight of our Artillery Support, it is easier than that allotted to the Division in the early days of July last year when it won for itself a reputation for gallantry and determination second to none in the British army. I have full confidence that the same gallantry and determination and devotion to duty will be shown again, that the Division will enhance its already high reputation, and that, under God's providence, a victory will be won which will go far to shorten the war.'*

*Chapter 13*

# The Battle of Arras Begins

Prior to the attack, the barrage to be fired at zero hour was rehearsed, in order to confuse the Germans about when the assault would actually take place. The hope was to pause the bombardment as though an attack was coming and then to catch the German defenders as they rushed to man the parapet. After a couple of tries at this, it was hoped the Germans would be slower to react to pauses in the bombardment.

As on 1 July, the two leading battalions were to take the first portion of the objectives, and then the remaining two battalions were to advance through them and take the German third system. Unlike on 1 July, efforts were made to advance into no man's land prior to the assault – the operation orders insisted that '*during the process of assembly the whole of No Man's Land must be in our possession and the forming up of battalions for the actual assault is to be protected by covering parties.*' Instead of starting from behind the British front lines, the troops were starting much further forward and had a shorter distance to travel. Special 'assaulting trenches' had been dug and, although this had meant extra work for the infantry, it was almost certainly worthwhile.

By 2.30am on 9 April all the companies of the 11th Suffolks were able to report that they were in position, and '*all men had had hot tea and rum*'. The final part of the barrage commenced at 5.30am and the 11th Suffolks, along with the rest of their brigade and division, left their forward trenches to attack. They left their trenches at zero, forming up under the barrage.

After action reports state that the company commanders were all '*enthusiastic about* [this barrage], *only two guns firing at all short; but all company commanders state that the salvoes of shrapnel to denote the lift of the barrage could not be recognised. The pace of the barrage was considered correct. The men were at first alarmed by our machine gun barrage, thinking it was German machine guns opening on them, but afterwards it gave them confidence. Owing to the darkness there was some loss of direction and it is suggested that the tapes be run forward from the jumping off trenches to give the line of advance; also owing to the darkness waves were almost immediately merged into one another.'*

Lance Corporal Arthur Gauge, of Old Chesterton, wrote to his wife from hospital of the advance:

*'Of course you know by the papers that we had some sport on Easter Monday, and, as usual, we were in it, and I ran into a bit of shrapnel in my right shoulder. It is very painful, but I think it will go on all right. It is not very big. We copped "Fritz" fairly on the hop. At half-past five the artillery opened, and we went over the top. Got to his first line and found only dead bodies; went to his second line, and found the same there; and then on to his third line.'*

By 6.10am reports were being sent back that the 11th Suffolks had reached the German second line, suffering only slight casualties; an hour later it was reported that 101 Brigade had captured their objectives in the German first system (referring to the set of trenches, not individual ones) and was consolidating there. The third line was more difficult to capture; Arthur Gauge wrote that *'we saw some get out of the trench and run like rabbits. There were we "potting" them over. We got into his third line and bombed his dug-outs and got a lot of prisoners. We stopped there for an hour, and that was where I got hit, but I was too excited to notice it much.'* This would have been a pause to consolidate and reorganise. At 7.16, the *'artillery reported that the enemy appeared to be massing for a counter-attack from the BOIS DE LA MAISON BLANCHE: nothing further was heard of this counter attack.'*

At the Black Line – the limit of the third German trench – the record of operations reports:

*'There was considerable confusion for several reasons: (a) it was not recognised; (b) the supporting Battalion had closed up on the Assaulting Battalions; (c) a large party of South Africans charged in from South of the BAILLEUL road after the position was occupied by this Brigade and got intermingled. It was found impossible to reorganise into waves on the BLACK LINE in time so the advance commenced as the troops stood.*

*The wire in the valley was not much damaged – only small lanes, which the troops got through in small parties. There was a certain amount of rifle and machine gun fire from the BOIS DE LA MAISON BLANCHE and the Railway Cutting, but this was soon neutralised by rifle and Lewis Gun fire. Our Artillery Barrage during this advance was considered to be much weaker than that up to the BLACK LINE, and the protective barrage was too close, preventing troops getting up the hill where they could get a view toward the PONT DU JOUR, and preventing the line being dug in advance of the Railway Cutting until it moved off.'*

As far as Arthur Gauge was concerned, there was still little opposition as they moved on to the German fourth line:

*'We captured a tremendous lot of stores in a sunken road. It was a road in a valley with a railroad running down it. Well, we got down there and couldn't see a soul. All at once I saw one put his head out of a hole in the bank. I pointed my rifle at him and said, "Come out". He came out with his hands up. Then another came, and another, until we got 85 and an officer, all out of one dug-out. I should think we got 150 out of it altogether, and sent them back. They were glad. Some of them had got pockets full of cigars. We went on a little further and dug ourselves in.'*

At 9.08am, the men at the railway were able to set off flares to notify the contact aeroplanes where they were. These contact patrols had been attempted during the Somme, but the lack of progress, and the fact that at times isolated parties had made it much further forward than the majority before setting off flares, meant that they had not been particularly successful. However, part of the brigade's training before Arras had included making contact with aircraft and they were able to do so on the day in accordance with the plan.

In 101 Brigade's area, all objectives were captured in accordance with the original timetable, with feeble enemy resistance. The left of 34th Division had more trouble, with a check caused by enemy machine guns, but these were eventually overcome, though it meant that a night advance had to be carried out in order to finish taking the allocated objectives. By 8.24am, the headquarters of the 11th Suffolks was able to move forward, an indication of how concrete the success had been.

However, it wasn't quite as clear cut as this. At 7.20, Second Lieutenant H.A. Reed with Regimental Serjeant Major Tyrrell '*went out to reconnoitre the position and find a suitable situation for Battalion Headquarters.*' They succeeded, but when the battalion headquarters actually moved off they were held up in the German second line by an enemy barrage, and were split up, with two headquarters inadvertently being established for a time. This was eventually sorted out, but it became abruptly apparent that the trenches had not been so clear of enemy soldiers as had first been thought: '*Twenty German prisoners were captured by the five runners and the orderly room serjeant who together with the pigeon man and an R.E. Signaller comprised the 8 other ranks with Battalion Headquarters. The prisoners evinced no desire to fight in spite of the fact that they were more than two to one and there was an abundance of German hand grenades rifles lying about. They were sent back to our line in charge of two runners.*' At 9.30 they were able to move up to their position with the rest of the 11th Suffolks, laying claim to a German dug-out in the final objective.

At 12.15 the 11th Suffolks were able to report that '*two companies have consolidated and are garrisoning the trench fifty yards in front of the railway at the second objective* [and] *that two companies are in the Valley.*' The remainder of the first day of the assault was spent in consolidation and in recovering stragglers, ensuring that all troops were where they ought to be. It was also at this point that the more lightly wounded made their way to the Casualty Clearing Stations.

Arthur Gauge decided that '*as my shoulders ached, I thought I would get somebody to look at it and find out what it was. I told our officer I was going back, and we had gone so far that I thought I should never get back, but I did, and now I am in between the sheets in a nice little bed. They treated us well coming down in the hospital train.... We had very few killed, but a lot with only small wounds, so they could walk back.*'

The machine guns were moved forward at 1pm – these were the heavier ones, rather than the light Lewis guns which went forward with the attack – to prepare to defend against counter-attacks. No counter-attack was immediately forthcoming; indeed it seemed on initial reconnaissance '*the enemy could have been very easily driven back further Eastwards if fresh troops had been available and the weather conditions had allowed the more rapid improvement of communications.'* It was considered more prudent to hold what they had gained than to gamble on further success, which would be difficult as the troops were exhausted and the weather poor. If it failed it would damage British morale and encourage the enemy. Difficulty in following up an initial break in was to plague armies on both sides throughout the remainder of the war. The British Army in 1918 was able to consistently break in to the first few lines of the German trenches, and to do so consistently. But the loss of cavalry through its vulnerability to modern weapons, without its replacement by any fast moving alternative (tanks remained slow and prone to mechanical failures throughout the war), meant that there was no arm available for rapid exploitation.

The 11th Suffolks remained at the second objective around the railway cutting, while the 10th Lincolns and 15th Royal Scots pushed forward to the third objective. They were able to gain this, and by 3.30pm the troops were being moved forward in the third objective area to gain positions with good visibility and field of fire to defend against the expected counter-attack. The 15th Royal Scots had least difficulty in taking their objectives, despite the confusion that had occurred with units getting mixed up. Around fifty Germans came out to meet them with their hands up and holding white flags. The 10th Lincolns had a little more trouble in taking their objective as the wire had not been fully cut. However, wire cutters came forward and they continued advancing to find the German dugouts showing every signs of flight. The fires were still lit, cooked food stood on tables, and parcels from home were unopened – a great bounty for exhausted men who were undoubtedly cold and would have a long stretch of cold days ahead of them before relief.

Overnight, and continuing the following days, efforts were made to improve communications and to consolidate captured lines, rewiring in front of what was now the front line and preparing strongpoints for its defence. These had been selected beforehand and at least some of the work was given to men of the Royal Engineers, who were brought up to the front lines during the late afternoon of the day of the assault. The guns, too, were brought forward to a more advanced position in order to cover the new positions more effectively.

As the engineers were moving forwards, German prisoners were moving back. By 3pm, the number of prisoners which had passed through the Corps Prisoner Cages was 44 officers and 2,200 other ranks, a significant haul, especially when compared with similar information for 1 July. At home, this success was well reported in the newspapers. The *Cambridge Independent Press* told readers:

*'The great battle near Arras on Easter Monday is probably the most successful operation yet carried out by the British army.… In other days and other wars a battle fought upon such a scale – ending with the capture of over 12,000 prisoners and 150 guns – would have been decisive. But in the struggle of nations it is no more than the opening of a tremendous campaign whose duration cannot be predicted. The renewed British offensive has begun; for, indeed, the French and British Armies have been attacking the German forces on the Western line since July last.… The renewed offensive is a continuation of the attack, but it is also a development of the five months' battle of the Somme; for in the course of that campaign the Allied Armies learned a great deal from experience, by which they are now profiting. They learned so much indeed that they can now beat the German in every branch of warfare.'*

Perhaps not in every branch, but it certainly seems that lessons learned at the Somme were put to good use in both the planning and carrying out of the Arras offensive. And, after the battle, a number of reports were requested and issued on how the battle had gone and what could be improved. The British Army was determined to learn its lessons, though they would not always be applied either through the pressure of circumstance or through drawing poor conclusions from them, and the 'learning curve' was not so smooth as it might have been.

During the following days the captured lines were consolidated, communications improved and patrols pushed forward to gain ground towards Bailleul and Gavrelle. Over the three days immediately succeeding the assault the weather was very severe, the nights being particularly cold and snowstorms intermittent the whole time. This, added to the effects of the severe work in preparation to the assault, caused much exhaustion to the men, who also began to suffer from exposure and 'trench feet'.

By dawn on 10 April, *'trenches had been dug in the advanced positions beyond the third enemy line and the trenches in the third system had been consolidated and were in readiness for any counter-attack the enemy might make. During the night the enemy had been reported as preparing to advance but the attack never developed and the night passed quietly.'* The strongpoints in the area the 11th Suffolks were to hold had been completed by the evening and were garrisoned ready for the expected assault. During the day, patrols were sent out and the leading battalions did not find any enemy troops within half a mile of their current position – although as the experience of the 11th Suffolks' headquarters showed, not seeing German troops did not necessarily mean they weren't there!

During 10 April there was intermittent shelling on the new front line, but this caused few casualties. To add to the protection of the new positions, the trench mortars were brought up and integrated into the defences. Later that day, the 11th Suffolks were sent to the assistance of the 27th Northumberland Fusiliers, part of the Tyneside Irish Brigade. When they arrived, they discovered that the counter-attack was much weaker than feared and had been easily driven off, so they returned to their original position by 3am. The weather was getting worse, with heavy snowstorms and severe cold. The brigade war diary admitted that *'the general weather conditions were such as to try fresh troops, even more so fatigued troops, who for some weeks previous to the assault had been employed on the most arduous carrying duties.'*

There was more artillery fire from the Germans the following day, but on the whole it passed fairly quietly, without major incident. Patrols sent out by the forward battalions again found no sign of enemy troops, but conditions were such that moving forward would have been foolish. Although the Official History suggests that it is quite possible the men could have taken objectives significantly further in advance of those captured, thus perhaps saving heavy fighting further on, there were not men available to do this and, had they met opposition, it could have proved disastrous. On 13 April the 11th Suffolks moved up to the more advanced positions, swapping with the troops of the 10th Lincolns and 16th Royal Scots who had been there. During that night the shelling of the front lines decreased significantly and the weather began to improve, though the troops would still have been exhausted from the attack and consolidation.

The night of 13/14 saw the 11th Suffolks bombarded with gas shells, but the men pulled on their respirators and remained in their lines without panicking. Although gas was a terrible new weapon of warfare, after the shock of its first use it had lost much of its surprise value and the men on both sides of the lines were prepared for its use. It still made fighting more difficult and could cause casualties – especially if it wasn't spotted quickly. However, it was far from a war-winning weapon.

The division was relieved on 14 April, with the 11th Suffolks being the last body of troops to be relieved. *'During the day the weather conditions had improved and the comfort of the troops materially increased, but many men were in an extremely exhausted state and could hardly struggle back to their billets in ARRAS or to the embussing places.'* Even with the improvement in the weather, there had been no real shelter in the forward area and mud was ankle deep. It was an ominous precursor to conditions that would prevail later in the year, during the Battle of Passchendaele.

Captain Tuck later recalled of this time that:

*'Our job consisted in the taking of two objectives, the furthest of which was a wood known as Bois de la Maison Blanche. The attack was carried out according to programme and in scheduled time. The capture of prisoners was greater than expected: they almost marched themselves back in columns of fours. Three of our officers who had been wounded earlier in the attack carried on until the operations were complete, and were mentioned in Sir Douglas Haig's last despatch.'*

The men of the 11th Suffolks would have been glad to move into billets. Casualties had not been anywhere near as heavy as the last time they took part in a major assault. They had gone into action with a strength of 20 officers and 606 other ranks (this excluded those who were left behind to form a nucleus of a new battalion should the worst happen, or to be reinforcements as needed). When they left the trenches on 14 April, their strength was 12 officers and 465 other ranks, including some men who had been brought up during the battle as reinforcements.

Amongst those killed was Serjeant Leonard Pottrell, aged 22, who lived on Great Eastern Street in Cambridge. His captain wrote to his mother, saying:

17245 Lance Corporal Henry Alfred Cage of Ickleton. Awarded Distinguished Service Cross 11 September 1916. Wounded on 4 August 1916 with a gunshot wound to his right shoulder. Wounded again 8 April 1917 by shrapnel, leading to his discharge from service. (*Cambridge Weekly News* 13 April 1917)

8748 Serjeant Leonard Pottrell of Great Eastern Street, Cambridge. Killed in action 9 April 1917. (*Cambridge Weekly News* 11 May 1917)

'*It is my sad duty to write and tell you of the death of your son. He was killed in action on Easter Monday, 9 April, in the great attack on the German lines. You will have read of the British success on that day, and it was to fine fellows like your son that this success is due. As you know, he rose rapidly to a high position in this company, and I think all who knew him realised how worthy he was of the trust given him. I have never met anyone so truly a soldier as he, and had he lived he would doubtless have made a great name for himself in the Suffolk Regiment. As it is, he is numbered among the list of heroes who from Mons to the present day have given their best and their all for others. We have lost a faithful servant to the Battalion, and I have lost a personal friend. May it be some solace to you to know that your great sorrow is shared by many who knew and loved him.*'

16620 Lance Corporal Victor K. Pamment of Ely. Awarded Distinguished Conduct Medal for actions on 1 July 1916. Killed by a sniper 9 April 1917. (*Cambridge Weekly News* 11 May 1917)

Corporal Walter Jackson of Barton. Wounded 9 April 1917, and sent to a hospital in London. Right leg amputated after his parents had seen him doing well. He succumbed to his wounds on 14 May 1917. (*Cambridge Weekly News* 20 July 1917)

Born in 1895, he was young to have become a serjeant and to have gained such great respect. It is not entirely clear what he had done before the war – in 1911 he was an errand boy, but he is unlikely to have still been doing that in 1914. It is possible that he had enlisted in another battalion of the Suffolks before the war and was transferred to it; his regimental number is much lower than those of most men in the battalion, and much closer to some of the non-commissioned officers who had served in the 1st or 2nd Suffolks prior to the outbreak of war.

Another was Lance Corporal V. Pamment DCM, from Ely. He was killed by a sniper after having got some distance towards the final objective. He was one of the men who had volunteered at the start of the war, and received his DCM for his actions on 1 July. In a letter to his father, his officer said:

*'He was a fine fellow, very reliable, and we miss him greatly. Since rejoining us from the hospital he was attached to Company headquarters, and was in charge of the four Company guns.... I offer you my heartfelt sympathy in your overwhelming burden of grief, trusting that it will be alleviated by the thought that your dear son died doing his duty nobly, as he had always done bore.'*

## Chapter 14

# Analysing the Battle and Continuing the Attack

In the wake of the attack, commanders at all levels were requested to send in information about what had gone well and what could have been done better. The comments made indicate both how much had changed from the Somme and, after a subsequent assault on 28 April, that regardless of how well lessons might be known they were not always put into practice.

The main features identified were that the counter battery fire was successful in neutralising the fire of hostile artillery, something that had not happened effectively on 1 July, and that the artillery barrage was mostly excellent, leading to poor resistance from the enemy, although towards the end of the advance the creeping barrage became thinner and more ragged. The pace of the barrage seemed to be correct; instead of disappearing off into the distance, it remained close to where the men were – at times it held up the assault. In part, this would have been because the infantry was not held up by machine-gun fire. There was still no way to effectively communicate with the artillery in real time, but the pace had improved and was much more realistic than it had been.

Additional practical measures were requested. These included that the battalion stretcher-bearers come further forward, with the RAMC stretcher-bearers focusing on the front line areas and the battalion stretcher bearers thus freed to follow the assault more closely. More ominous was a request relating to stricter supervision of stragglers. *'It is suggested that Prisoner Posts [for captured Germans], under Military Police, be pushed forward as far as our front line and escorts from the front returned from there to their units. All battalions to be followed by selected non commissioned officers and men to search shell holes and drive forward shirkers.'* It is worth noting that this request came, if not from the bottom, then from battalion and company commanders. Clearly they were concerned about the problem of 'shirkers', perhaps fearing that the morale and drive of the battalion had declined with the introduction of more conscripts. It may also relate to the well known problems in the French Army, which saw front line troops mutiny after a failed offensive.

Although on the whole morale in the British Army remained high, the evidence of the near collapse of French morale, and the revolution in Russia, would have made all commanders more nervous. Part of the problem of stragglers was that there was a good deal of genuine confusion as to where men should be – the final portion of the attack was undertaken with far fewer troops than it should have been because large numbers of soldiers had become mixed together with other units and had lost cohesion. This was partially recognised, with the point being made that men needed reminding that when separated from their own unit, they came under the command of the nearest non-commissioned officer or officer.

Though the quantity of materials carried by assaulting troops seems to have been reduced already, it was recommended that it be reduced further still, with more use being made of carrying parties, following close on the assault, to bring in shovels and picks and other tools for consolidation. Yellow patches, to make men visible from the air and identify their unit, were believed to attract fire from snipers, men fell off steep bridges (for crossing trenches), and petrol tins had to be cleaned before being used – a good deal of unavoidable sickness was caused by neglecting this. Finally, rum was requested for the night before the assault, and tea and soup was much appreciated when battalions were returning from the trenches. An army, after all, marches on its stomach.

Relieved from the lines, refitting the division and integrating new men was the main priority. The division had lost thirty-one per cent of its trench strength during the assault and subsequent trench operations. Matters were made worse by the fact that the cold weather and poor conditions would have put a lot of men on the sick list. Between 15 and 21 April a large number of new men arrived, although battalions still only averaged a trench strength of about 520 men per battalion. In part this was because of the number of men who had been given other duties, or who might not be counted as the trench strength of the battalion while still being engaged on active service (such as the men chosen for trench mortar duty, who were on the strength of their battalion still, but would not have been available for trench duties in the way that those not in the trench mortar section were).

Training was carried out as far as possible, but *a great deal of the time was necessarily taken up by all regimental officers in refitting, and in replacing deficiencies in equipment and arms, including Lewis Guns, Stokes Mortars, etc.* The men who had arrived in the draft may not have had any more than three months basic training in England, and might not have been under fire before. Though the rest of the battalion was experienced, the decreasing number of men on the trench strength meant that nearly half would be new and that suddenly turned an experienced battalion into an inexperienced one. This was especially true with regard to junior officers, who might have been promoted from the ranks, and thus would have experience, or they might be fresh from cadet training with little real experience of the war.

Around this time one of their experienced officers was sent home, being too old to continue to withstand the rigours of active service. Lieutenant Colonel Kendrick wrote to his superior officers regarding his quartermaster, Lieutenant Daniel William Harper. *'I consider that owing to his age and previous service, he is not able to stand the strain of active service, and is therefore not able to carry out his duties to the best advantage of the battalion under my command, who are thereby suffering in consequence, this is especially noticeable now that we are on most active operations. I consider he would be able to carry out the duties of quartermaster at home.'* At this time, he was 52 years old, having previously served for twenty-one years in the Suffolk Regiment, retiring from the colours in 1906. In 1914 he re-enlisted and was commissioned in the 11th Suffolks on 30 October. Lieutenant Colonel Kendrick asked to swap him with a quartermaster currently with a training reserve brigade in England, who had been given permission to go on active service. This exchange was duly carried out, and Lieutenant Harper went on to join the RAF in early 1919.

The divisional war diary stated that *'owing to losses in good officers, non-commissioned officers and men in the first phase, the fighting value of the division even after five days' complete rest, could not be said to be anything approaching what it was on 9 April.'* Despite that, they would still be expected before the month was out to take part in another significant assault on the Chemical Works near Roeux.

During the night of 23 April, there seems to have been some sort of raid or operation, though there is no mention of this in the official documents.

However, Private Claude Newman, who was involved in it and wrote home about it, was definitely a member of the battalion. Moreover, since the operation was very small, apparently consisting of only five men, it might easily have been overlooked. Perhaps, too, it took place not on 23 April, but on the night of 24/25 April, when the battalion returned to the front lines. In any case, Private Claude Newman was with '*four others when they saw three Germans in a trench and went after them. On reaching the trench they found it was full of Germans and a desperate struggle took place, which resulted in the five being captured. They were taken into a German dug-out, and the enemy were about to kill them when one of their officers stopped them. The English men were thrown down and a blanket placed over them... they were left there until 25 April when a rescue party arrived. Private Newman had several bullets in his left arm, a fractured right leg, and to save his life his left leg was amputated.*' He was taken to the 13th General Hospital in France.

On the night of 24/25 April the 11th Suffolks, together with the rest of 34th Division, returned to the trenches. The 11th Suffolks were in the front lines, and would be leading troops in the assault to come, though the orders for this had not yet been issued down to battalion level. Enemy snipers were active in the trenches they took over, but the British gradually got the upper hand, though they were not able to entirely silence enemy snipers. On 25 April there was a heavy bombardment of the British front lines where the 11th Suffolks were, leading to the deaths of two men, with a further sixteen wounded. These casualties could be ill afforded, especially if they were experienced soldiers.

The operational order for the assault was issued on 27 April, at a conference of commanding officers. After that conference, they were issued down to company level at a second conference a few hours later. At 3am the following morning, all companies were in position and ready for the coming assault. The hastiness with which it was planned can be seen in the way the battalion level operation orders were scribbled on squared paper apparently torn from a notebook, rather than being typed up neatly.

Before the attack could take place, the battalion suffered at least one casualty from a German sniper. Private Ernest Frederick South was shot early in the morning. He had just been awarded the Military Medal, though official news of the award, for his bravery on 9 April, reached the

24738 Private Ernest F. South of Newmarket Road, Cambridge. Awarded Military Medal for actions on 9 April 1917. News of the award reached the battalion two days after he was killed in action on 28 April 1917. (Cambridge Weekly News *29 June 1917*)

battalion two days after his death. Private South had been a runner in the battalion, an essential but highly dangerous position, which meant that though news did not get back quickly, it did at least get back at some point, provided the runner was not killed doing his duties. Before enlisting, he worked for Lipton's Limited, where he was a porter in the grocery shop.

The assault was launched at 4.25am, under cover of a heavy bombardment. By 5am it was plain at battalion headquarters that the attack had failed. *'The attack was held up and driven back by the very considerable hostile machine gun fire from a trench which had been entirely missed by our barrage. What was left of our battalion formed up in our front line.'* This had been passed on to 101 Brigade headquarters, where it was reported at around 4.50. The left company of the 11th Suffolks had been driven back to the front line, while the remainder were engaged in heavy fighting near the Château Lesage grounds – nowhere near their objective. It took longer for the message to filter back to the brigade and division headquarters, though at 5.30 it was known that *'the right was held up at the beginning by at least six machine guns in the wood. Reported our men are trying to work round them.'* At 5.25am the artillery liaison officer with the right battalion reported that machine gun fire was *'very heavy from ROEUX village and ROEUX Wood. The centre seems to have got through. Some prisoners are being passed back. Chemical Works situation very obscure. Seems to be held up there.'*

One of the runners, who was probably killed while trying to take back information, or while returning to gather more information or give orders, was Private Ernest Oswald Howlett. A friend in the same battalion wrote home that his death was instantaneous. *'He will be missed by all of us, for he was always willing to do anything for anybody, and we all liked him. The runners of the company, of which he was one, send you their sympathy.'* Private Howlett was employed at the Leys School Farm, Histon Road, and joined up in November 1914. He had gone overseas with the rest of his battalion, and had been fortunate to have leave just before Christmas 1916.

Acting Captain John Norman Harmer was captured during the attack. After the war, when he was repatriated, the War Office asked him to give an account of how he was captured, so that they could decide whether or not he was to blame. He wrote to them as follows:

*'On 28 April 1917 my battalion was ordered to attack the Chemical Works at Roeux, near Arras. A Company, which I was commanding acted as support company and advanced about 100 yards behind the two leading companies. It was quite dark when the attack began, and my company had to be extended over about 700 yards, so that any control was impossible. I became separated from most of the company by some buildings, and eventually found myself in a shell hole with two men, a signaller and a runner, close to a very strong German position; apparently there was a big tunnel there, and the Germans had come out after the barrage passed. They fixed three machine guns on our shell hole and it was impossible to get either forward or backward. We held out for some hours firing as well as we could but the position was a hopeless one. The Germans were walking about on the top, I could see none of our men, and I knew the barrage for the next attack would wipe us out. The Germans eventually made signals for us to surrender, which we ignored for some time, continuing to fire, but our ammunition becoming exhausted, we had to give in.'*

Major Tuck made his way to the front lines to re-organise the defence and try and find out what was going on. He found 5 officers and around 300 other ranks, which included 2 officers and 60 other ranks from 16th Royal Scots, who were meant to work as moppers-up behind the advance. Instead, Major Tuck prepared them for possible counter-attack and ensured that the front lines at least were defended, even if the attack had failed. These men probably included the remaining members of the two companies of the 11th

Suffolks who made it briefly into the Chemical Works before being driven off by heavy machine-gun fire.

The forward observation officer (a member of the artillery who would have been as close to the front line as was considered safe, with good communications and a good view of what was going on) reported back at 6.50am that there had been no advance made in front of the Chemical Works, though there had been a slight advance elsewhere. The forward observation officer was not entirely popular – the after action report of the 11th Suffolks (probably composed by Major Tuck) stated that *'forward observation officers apparently think that their only work is to sit at Battalion Headquarters. They do not go up and observe things themselves and thereby get useful information for their Battery Commanders about the places that ought to be dealt with by artillery.'*

Because of the confusion as to where troops actually were, and the fact that this could not be adequately cleared up by anyone, never mind the unfortunate forward observation officers, it was decided at 7.15 that although the barrage had moved forwards onto the line of the final objective, the situation was not clear enough to bring it back to cover the position where the troops might actually be. At 11.55, though re-bombardment had been very carefully undertaken, the situation was still considered very obscure on 101 Brigade's front. The initial barrage had, however, failed to destroy the houses in the village or the wire in the hedges west of the château. This left ample hiding positions for machine guns and German soldiers, so it was little wonder that the men had been unable to advance.

It was just as well that Major Tuck had gone forward to reorganise the defence. Around 8am a counter-attack developed. Those British soldiers that had made it forward were driven back to the starting line. Around 200 German soldiers were able to penetrate the front line British trenches and open fire on the rear line. Bombing parties were organised by the 10th Lincolns and the 20th Northumberland Fusiliers, and a Stokes gun was also used to drive back the enemy.

Overnight, it became abundantly clear that nothing had been attained, and that in fact they were in a fairly dangerous position as regards possible further counter-attacks. The line of defence was organised on the original line from which the attack was made. The enemy was reported to be very nervous too, understandably so, expecting further British assaults (which did in fact occur). Snipers were active, little information could be gained about how far the attack might have got and whether there was an isolated party of troops somewhere in the German lines. The 11th Suffolks were briefly moved back from the front line to the support line, to enable a bombardment of the enemy position, before returning to the front lines to hold them and to provide guides for the two battalions of 102 (Tyneside Scottish) Brigade that had been ordered to attack the following morning.

That morning, Private Albert Isaacson died while he was sleeping in a shelter in the front line trench. *'His comrades did all that could possibly be done, and laid him to rest just in rear of the line. Your son was a brave and fearless soldier, and was liked by all his comrades and officers; the latter spoke very highly of him. He gave his life for a just and noble cause, and he will be greatly missed by all his company.'* The following day his brother was wounded in the face while in action; his mother, Mrs Shipp of Swaffham Bulbeck, received the news of both her sons in the same letter from Private E. Isaacson.

The attacks that took place overnight by 102 (Tyneside Scottish) Brigade were also unsuccessful. They were met by hostile fire and were unable to make any progress. The darkness hindered forming up together and isolated attempts to attack failed. By 9.20am it was clear that this attack, too, had been unsuccessful, and *'that the troops were practically in their original line.'* The front line during the following day *'was held by what remains of 23/NF and by Posts furnished by this battalion'* [11th Suffolks].

The Germans were too alert for any improvements to be made to the situation, or any further attacks to be ordered during the day, but overnight the RE and Pioneers were employed in improving defences. Patrols were pushed out during the night and found that the enemy was still holding his line and very alert. The stretcher-bearers of units were out all night collecting wounded, some of whom came from 51st Division and who had been lying out a week. No further attacks were made at this time and on 30 April the 11th Suffolks, and the rest of the division, were relieved.

The completely unsuccessful attack was analysed as much as the successful one had been and the key point brought up was the poor artillery fire, especially in the 11th Suffolks' report – a sharp contrast to the highly successful artillery work that preceded the operation on 9

April. The whole of 101 Brigade picked up on this, with a combined report stating that: *'The field gun barrage was quite ineffective against the machine guns. It is described as much thinner than on 9 April and with gaps in it. An officer states that it appeared to start in front of the houses and then to lift over them, the shells falling behind.'*

At divisional level, however, more emphasis was laid on:

*'The inefficiency of the training of the men and the lack of sufficient leaders told very severely during the operations of 28 and 29 April, when the task was a more difficult one than that set the division on the 9 April, in as much as the operations had to be carried out without the careful reconnaissance and preparation by all ranks necessary to ensure complete success, while the tactics to be employed were somewhat different from those required on the 9 April, for which the division had been specially trained. Added to this was the fact that a large proportion of the men had never been under fire. It was not possible to give the division a longer period for rest and training than 5 complete days after the first phase of the battle and this in a great measure, it is considered, was the cause of the failure of the division to carry out successfully the task it was entrusted with.'*

They did also mention that the artillery barrage had been weak, but the biggest focus was on the lack of time for training, the fact that specialised training based on the ground to be covered and tactics to be used could not be carried out (as it had been for the attack on 9 April). It was mentioned that the artillery barrage may have been weakened by the lack of time for planning. It seems like the different levels of the British Army picked out different causes for failure and learned slightly different 'lessons' from the operations they had undertaken.

Major General Nicholson wrote in an undated letter to a relative that the attack was against a difficult position, due to the village, river, railway cutting and a wood:

*'Wood, village and houses were all crammed with machine guns and the ground between the village and the river was swept by the machine guns from the further bank. We were rather hurried into the job without sufficient*

*time to reconnoitre and were rather tied down as to plan, unavoidably so perhaps as it was part of a bigger show. I believe we did actually hold the whole village for a time, but as no one who went into it has ever once come back it is difficult to say.'*

23971 Private James William Hepher of Swavesey. Killed in action 28 April 1917. (Cambridge Weekly News *22 June 1917*)

One of those who had joined the battalion shortly before the attack and would have had little, if any, time for training before he went into action, was Private James William Hepher. He was reported missing from 28 April; it was later revealed that he had died on this date, though his body was not identified and he is instead commemorated on the Arras Memorial. The son of Mr and Mrs Charles Hepher, Market Street, Swavesey, he went to France early in March 1917 and, after a period in a base camp, was transferred to the battalion with which he went into action – his first. He joined up on 24 January 1916, and served for a time in a garrison battalion in the UK. He was probably a conscript, or perhaps one of the final volunteers under Lord Derby's scheme.

The successful attack on 9 to 14 April led, within the division as a whole, to 132 officer casualties and 2,598 in other ranks. The unsuccessful one on 22 to 30 April led to marginally fewer: 106 officers and 2,538 other ranks, but these were suffered to no gain. On relief, the division was forty-eight per cent under strength. It would need time to recover before it was possible to go back into the battle, and on this occasion they were given that time.

The second attack had led to the loss not only of new men, but also of experienced soldiers whose loss could be ill afforded. Amongst them was Private William Flack. His company officer wrote to his mother, saying that he died instantly and could not have suffered any pain. He continued: *'He*

13670 Private William Flack of Hobart Road, Cambridge. Killed in action 28 April 1917. (Cambridge Weekly News *27 July 1917*)

15663 Serjeant Alfred Aaron Linford of Swavesey. Killed in action 28 April 1917. (Cambridge Weekly News *22 June 1917*)

*was one of the best men in my platoon … and I can only say he died doing his duty. The whole company and myself offer you our sincere sympathy.'* Private Flack had enlisted on 7 September 1914, while the battalion was training at the Melbourne Place Schools. Before the war he had worked for the Saxon Cement Company.

Another was Serjeant Alfred A. Linford, who joined in the early days of the war and went overseas with the battalion in January 1916. An officer telegrammed his father to say: *'I regret necessary delay in writing to tell you that your son, Serjeant A. Linford, was seriously wounded on 28 April, and that since then I have been unable to obtain any more news of him. You will shortly hear from the War Office an official report, and I trust you will write to me as soon as you do. Your son had been in my platoon since I joined the battalion in July last year, and I had always valued him as a very trusty non-commissioned officer. He was promoted serjeant a few days before our last action.'*

Some of those whose sons were reported missing in the attack got happy news a few days later. Amongst them was the mother of Private Alfred William Medcalf. Before the war he had been employed at Robinson's

Bicycle Showrooms, but he enlisted early in the war. He wrote a letter home to his mother to say that he was quite well, and was a prisoner in Germany. He encouraged her that *'there is nothing to worry about, because I am getting on as well as you could expect'*, and asked for as big a parcel as possible to be sent, full of cigarettes and food.

The parents of 19-year-old Private Frederick William Charles, also received news that their son was missing, but sadly the following week were told that he had been killed in action. He had enlisted at the beginning of the war, aged just 16, and was badly wounded on 1 July 1916. During the 1911 Census he had been at school, but by the time of his enlistment the local papers described him as a 'labourer' (they also claimed that he was born in 1895, not 1898 – he had evidently lied about his age to enlist).

16401 Private Frederick William Charles of Haslingfield. Killed in action 28 April 1917. (Cambridge Weekly News *29 June 1917*)

Second Lieutenant John William Reynolds Hunt was reported missing during the same attack and information about his fate took even longer to appear. His father wrote repeatedly to the War Office in an attempt to get news of him, first writing on 28 July, when he was told that no further information had been received and that they could only report him 'missing'. In December, he wrote again, and the reply was that *'it is regretted that no further information has been received... All repatriated Prisoners of War are being invited to give any evidence in their possession concerning the Missing and should any reliable information be received regarding this officer, it would be communicated to you immediately. So far, however, as the evidence in the possession of the Army Council goes, no officer has been a Prisoner of War for nearly so long a period as Second Lieutenant Hunt has been Missing without communicating with his relatives and it is feared that no information will now be forthcoming which would show him to be alive.'*

A few weeks later they wrote again to say that unofficial information had been received that Second Lieutenant Hunt had been killed. The postcard from Lance Corporal S. Ling giving the news has been preserved in Second Lieutenant Hunt's service record folder, along with the letter sent by his father and copies of the replies, at the National Archives. It reads:

'Dear Sir, I have just received your postcard about Lieutenant Hunt. Well Sir I will tell you all I know. Private A. Smith of D Company he was captured the same houre [sic] as myself and he told me the Mr Hunt was killed so will you kindly forward this on he was killed as Smith was banding [sic] one of his wounds up and then he got killed so if you can find A. Smith of the Suffolks Regiment he will tell you more he is a Prisoner of War but not in the same Camp as me I can't say where he is at all. Well I think I have said all I remain yours truly Samuel Ling Suffolk Reg C Coy No 5619 Langensalza Germany.'

Either Private A. Smith could not be traced (not surprising if that was the case – there must have been dozens) or he could give no further official information. In 1919, Second Lieutenant Hunt's father again wrote to the War Office, asking for a death certificate. The War Office was not able to supply one, as they couldn't say for certain that he had died. However, owing to the length of time since he was reported missing and the fact that no further information had been received:

'the Army Council are regretfully constrained to conclude, for official purposes, that Second Lieutenant Hunt is dead, and that his death occurred on, or since, 28 April 1917. I am to add that the Army Council have, unfortunately, no doubt as to the death of this officer, and to explain that their action, as set forth above, is notified to those concerned upon their application for a certificate of death, with a view to assisting them in dealing with the estates of officers whose deaths have not been reported to this department in a formal, individual, written statement. It is understood that these letters, which may be used in place of a formal certificate of death, are, as a rule, accepted for Probate and other purposes.'

Second Lieutenant John William Reynolds Hunt of Coton. The War Office was unable to fully confirm his death for some time afterwards, and could only conclude, a year later, that he died on or after 28 April 1917. Cambridge Weekly News 17 August 1917.

16427 Private Arthur Benstead of Long Stanton, wounded in the face 1 July 1916. Killed in action 28 April 1917. Cambridge Weekly News 4 August 1916.

16604 Private William Taylor of Harston. Killed in action 28 April 1917. Cambridge Weekly News 22 June 1917.

24766 Private Albert Shipp of Swaffham Bulbeck. Killed while sleeping in a front line shelter 26 April 1917. Cambridge Weekly News 22 June 1917.

14427 Lance Corporal Thomas Edwin Circus of Elsworth. Killed in action 28 April 1917. Cambridge Weekly News 29 June 1917.

14419 Private Harvey Askew of Willingham. Killed in action 28 April 1917. (Cambridge Weekly News *15 March 1918*)

13606 Private Wilfred Charles Pettitt of Horningsea. Killed in action 28 April 1917. (Cambridge Weekly News *10 May 1918*)

*Chapter 15*

# May–August 1917

After the failed attack on the Chemical Works, the battalion was pulled out of the line for a rest. A large focus of this training would have been bringing up to scratch the 114 other ranks who arrived as a draft from the base camp on 3 May. The battalion war diary refers to this training as *'preliminary training'*. This would not have been necessary for the men who had just come from battle, but for the new soldiers it would have been a vital introduction to the realities of war on the Western Front, particularly as those veterans who remained in the battalion could have given them valuable additional advice.

Once a few days of preliminary training had been completed, along with a move to a different training ground near Pernois, the battalion moved on to more difficult matters – company and squad drill, bayonet and shooting practice, and competitions with prizes awarded for the best rifle section, Lewis gun team, bombing section, signalling company, officer's charger (turnout) and transport team. As the month progressed, divisional training was introduced, with dummy attacks, parades and inspections.

June saw a return to the front lines, in the Gavrelle Sector. Here the 11th Suffolks alternated time in the line with time at 'rest', which, as well as meaning they got a chance to bathe, mostly meant working parties: laying wires, digging trenches and providing burial details. With the periods spent in the trenches being quieter, more routine information has sometimes been recorded than is usually the case. Thus, the procedure for relieving a battalion in the line is made much clearer than when the officer detailed to write the war diary evidently had dozens of important things to do, and plenty of other information to record. Most of the entries are very short, but perhaps to bulk them out, more details about how the trenches were handed over has been recorded. At noon on 7 June, the brigade sent out instructions for the relief of 20th Northumberland Fusiliers by the 11th

Suffolks that evening. At 6pm Lieutenant Colonel Kendrick went to the front line to investigate the situation; at the same time an officer from each company and one non-commissioned officer from each platoon went to the front line to take over the stores and find out the situation. At 8.15pm the rest of the battalion left their camp behind the lines and at 3am the relief was reported to be complete.

During this spell in the trenches, the 11th Suffolks were active in no man's land, pushing out parties each night to establish posts in advance of the front line. On the first night they went about 30 yards forward; the following night they were pushed even further out, to a distance of about 100 yards, with parties of men remaining hidden in shell holes during the day. They also continued to work on the front line defences.

One of those killed during the time in the line was Private Sidney George Lawrence, who had worked as part of the printing staff on the *Cambridge Independent Press* before the war. His wife received a letter from her cousin, Serjeant Harry Hobbs, who was a member of the same battalion, giving her the news. He wrote that her husband was killed in the trenches by a bullet on 1 June, the day that the 11th Suffolks returned to the line. '*It may be some consolation to you,*' the letter states, '*to know that he suffered no pain whatever, as his death was instantaneous. I was the first to reach him, and he was quite dead then. I shall miss him myself, for it was nice to have somebody you know. The rest of the chaps will miss him also, for although he had only been with us a short time, he was well liked by all who knew him. They all send their sympathy.*'

He had worked in the printing room of the *Cambridge Independent Press* for twenty-four years, having started out as an apprentice at the age of 14. He joined the army on 1 July 1916, presumably as a conscript, and first went to France in December 1916. He had been invalided home on 6 February (his birthday), and had only been out again a month before he was killed.

After their relief on 18 June, the 11th Suffolks once again spent time behind the lines training. This time the training programme survives (the previous month, the programme was 'attached', but seems to have disappeared in the almost 100 years since the war diary first being written and its current state in the National Archives). The programme included a rotation around the different companies, with each working on different skills. There was a focus on physical training, musketry, using the ground, and digging and patrolling trenches – all practical skills that some in the battalion would be past masters at, but in which many of the new men might require additional training.

It was added:

*'Company Commanders will lecture all officers and non-commissioned officers after each part of the programme has been carried out and should try and get ideas on patrolling etc from junior officers and non-commissioned officers who actually do the patrolling in the line – special attention being paid to bring to bear upon the men the fact of the importance of bringing in identifications of prisoners and if possible also to discourage the use of bombs and how much better it is to get a patrol as close as possible before challenging it and then of using the bayonet in preference to rifle fire or bombing.'*

Thus, although a lot of the training and the training programmes used would have come from the top down, room was made for experience to be passed up the chain of command too.

July proved much the same as June, with a mixture of trench warfare and periods of 'rest' which meant training and working parties. On the nights of 16 and 17 July, patrols in no man's land encountered hostile patrols and fighting ensued. On the first of the two nights, four enemy soldiers were reported to have been killed, while on the British side two officers were wounded, one other rank killed and three other ranks wounded. The following night the German patrols were driven off without reported casualties on either side, perhaps suggesting a mutual desire to avoid a second fierce confrontation. During training on 20 July, the battalion war diary proudly records that in an officers' shooting match against the 16th Royal Scots, the officers of the 11th Suffolks won by 100 points.

At the same time the newspapers marked the first anniversary of 1 July – the first day of the Battle of the Somme. 'In Memoriam' columns held dozens of notices relating to casualties. These often included short poems, such as that to Private R. Wilson, *'eldest and dearly beloved son of Mr and Mrs G. Wilson, of Trumpington, who was killed in action 1 July 1916.'*

*'Gone from us, but not forgotten,*
*Never shall his memory fade,*
*Fell while fighting for his country,*
*Lying in a soldier's grave.*
*– From his loving Mother,*
*Father, Sister and Brothers.'*

Or this one for 'Bert', Private B.W. Taylor, also killed in action on 1 July 1916:

*'He bravely answered his country's call,*
*He gave his life for one and all;*
*If we could have clasped his dying hands,*
*And heard his last farewell,*
*It would not have been so hard to part*
*With one we love so well.*
*Rest on, dear son, thy task is o'er,*
*Thy willing hands will fight no more;*
*A loving son, so true and kind,*
*No one on earth like thee we find.*
*– From his sorrowing Mother, Father,*
*Sisters and Brother.'*

There seem to have been too many notices sent in for one week, for the 'In Memoriam' notices for those killed on 1 July stretched across the whole of July. At the same time, some of the families who had been left wondering about the fate of their loved ones, gradually losing hope, were finally notified that the War Office now considered that, as nothing had been heard of them for a year, they must be dead.

Amongst these was Private A. Gilson, son of Mrs Gilson of 150 East Road. Private Gilson was formerly employed at the Star Brewery for several years. There was also Private Allen Tack, with the newspaper reporting: *'The Army Council have been regretfully constrained to conclude that Private Allen Tack, Suffolk Regiment, who has been missing since 1 July 1916, is dead, and that his death took place on that date. He was the son of Mr John Tack, foreman at Lolworth Grange, and prior to joining up was employed at Scotland Farm, Dry Drayton.'*

In response to this, there were calls for a local roll of honour. Many of the villages across the county had a Roll of Honour already, usually in the porch of the parish church or some other public place. Cambridge itself, however, did not have one, and the *Cambridge Independent Press* said that one should be established *'without delay'*, before people lost touch with the town or moved away, making it much more difficult to compile.

> *'The list should include, of course, not only men of the local battalions, but all men, whatever their rank or regiment, who have laid down their lives in the service of their country. No town of its size, probably, has suffered heavier losses in proportion to population than Cambridge, and we owe it to those who have made the great sacrifice to see that their memory is kept green. The matter is one, we think, for the Town Council.'*

From mid-August the 11th Suffolks began to train for their next offensive, which would take place on 26 August. The training areas were carefully laid out to resemble the trenches in which the men would soon be fighting. This method of training was successful, as the divisional war diary records: *'Great value was experienced from facsimile spitlocked trenches and short explanatory lectures on the ground by company and platoon commanders with aeroplane photographs. It was found during the attack that non-commissioned officers and men knew where they were from having followed the shape of the position in the spitlocked trenches.'* Training was also undertaken in consolidation and rapid wiring, not just in how to proceed during the attack.

A 'warning order' for the battle to come was issued on 8 August, stating that *'Operations for the capture of the high ground east of COLOGNE FARM and the enemy front trench southwards as far as the BUISSON RIDGE will be carried out by the Division during this month. The object of the operations is to drive the enemy off the high ground East of COLOGNE FARM and along the ridge East of VILLERET, depriving him of his present advantage in observation, and to obtain the best observation for ourselves into BUCKSHOT RAVINE and the low ground North of RUBY WOOD.'* Initially they were meant to attack on 21 August, but in the event they did not go over the top until 26

August; 101 Brigade was to take care of the first phase, while 103 Brigade moved forwards through the captured ground as soon as possible to capture the next portion of the objective. Because there were not sufficient assembly trenches close to the objective, the attack was to take place before dawn, under cover of a creeping barrage.

The night before the attack, one company of each battalion took over the front line of their battalion area, with another in the intermediate line and the remaining two further back in huts. *'This allowed each Battalion to reconnoitre the enemy's wire, peg out their assembly area, and make observations during H day.'* The assembly line pegs were joined up during the night and flanks were marked with luminous boards or heaps of chalk. Covering parties were arranged in no man's land to protect the forming up procedure, and all the men were issued with chewing gum. During practices, it had been noticed that there was a lot of coughing, easily discernible from a long way off and a sign to the Germans that an attack was about to take place. With the chewing gum, the coughing was largely eliminated.

Also on 25 August, *'a Chinese Barrage was opened on hostile trenches with a view to ascertaining, if possible, where the enemy barrage would come down. Roughly speaking, the enemy put down his barrage after six minutes on the Post line.'* Chinese Barrages were one of the many new tricks in the artillery's bag and involved a rehearsal of the barrage that would usually be placed down just before an attack, in order to see what the Germans would do when they suspected an attack would come. This would, in theory, enable the areas where the barrage came down heaviest to be avoided when the actual attack was launched, as well as giving a good idea of how long they had to cross open ground.

The remainder of the day was spent with the wire-cutting programme being undertaken by the artillery, with a half-hour pause at 2pm to enable the photography of hostile wire. Those parts which were observed to be still uncut could then be made the focus of the remaining time before the assault was to take place. At 11.30pm the 11th Suffolks moved up to their jumping off positions and suffered neither casualties nor interruptions. Their jumping off point was a sunken road, though this was unfortunately *'only sunken in parts* [so] *this was a difficult operation but was carried out without any incident. A covering party of two platoons went out about 120 yards in front, this party states it did not hear the Battalion forming up. The First Company was in position about 1 am and the whole Battalion about 2.30 am. It was a very cold night and therefore the men were very cold before starting off.'*

At 4.30am the creeping barrage and machine-gun barrage began and the attack was launched. By 4.50am the 11th Suffolks had gained all of their objectives and were beginning to consolidate. In this they followed their operation orders, which stated that *'after the capture of Objectives the erection of Obstacles will be priority.'* These obstacles were to be placed in various points along the new front line, with careful sighting of the trenches to be dug so that they joined up properly. These had all been planned out in advance with the help of detailed aerial surveillance photographs.

The barrage had also been carefully planned in advance. Seventeen minutes was allowed for the furthest advance, which was 750 yards. The 11th Suffolks, as the left battalion, had the longest advance up to the first objective. Ten minutes were allowed to capture this, at which point the barrage would move back 100 yards and then creep back at 50 yards a minute until it hit the second objective. There was a seventeen minute pause and then the barrage was to creep back again at the same speed to 300 yards distant, where it was to remain for thirty minutes. This was in order to protect the advance from possible counter-attacks. As it was not light enough to see even at thirty minutes after the attack, the barrage was continued until it was possible to see. *'The wire had been well cut and nowhere checked the advance. The creeping barrage was accurate and some Companies say they got closer under it than they did at Arras. There were hardly any complaints of short shooting.'* This would have made a huge difference to the chances of success.

As the attack moved off, Corporal Ernest George Ashman, according to a friend, was *'killed by a shell while going over the top. He died real game and like a man.'* His platoon serjeant also wrote home, saying:

*'I had known him for a long time, and a better fellow I have never met, always willing and thoughtful for everybody, and he will be missed sorely by the company. That he died shortly after being hit, suffering very little pain, may help you in your sorrow. He is being buried in a little village just behind our lines, and a cross will shortly be put up. On behalf of the non-*

*commissioned officers and men of the company I beg to tender you our very*
*sincere sympathy in your sad loss.'*

Ernest was 31 years of age at the time
and unmarried. He had joined the
Army in May 1915, and was one of
the men sent out to the front in the
wake of the attack on 1 July 1916 as a
replacement for battle casualties. He
was a member of St Philip's Church
on Mill Road, Romsey Town (now
largely swallowed up into Cambridge),
where he sang in the choir and was
part of the Men's Meeting. He
worked for the Co-operative Society
as a collector, and was well known in
the area.

Within the hour, the brigade had
been notified that all objectives had
been gained by the first part of the
attacking troops. The 11th Suffolks
had:

20345 Corporal Ernest George Ashman of
Romsey (Cambridge). Killed in action 26
August 1917. (Cambridge Weekly News *26
October 1917*)

*'encountered a certain amount of resistance at the junction of SUGAR and*
*MALAKOFF TRENCHES which ended in hand to hand fighting and*
*bombing. A machine gun there caused a few casualties but the crew were soon*
*killed. On arrival at the final objective it was noticed that TRIANGLE*
*TRENCH was strongly held. The Officer Commanding Right Company*
*decided to push on, which he did and thirty prisoners were captured from the*
*trench alone. This prompt action made all the difference to the operations*
*as it allowed MALAKOFF SUPPORT TRENCH to be consolidated*
*behind.'*

The killing of the machine-gun crew may very well have been done by
the battalion bombers. Corporal Charles Carlton, an instructor of bomb-

throwing and one of the battalion's bomb-throwers, received the Military Medal for his part in the attack. It was quite possible that his 'doing his duty' included dealing with this particular machine gun, especially as the battalion war diary mentions that a bombing party was detailed to deal with a machine gun that was causing trouble with consolidation.

It was for his actions on this day that Corporal Sidney James Day, who had originally been part of the 9th Suffolks before his transfer to the 11th Suffolks, possibly after being wounded on the Somme, was awarded the Victoria Cross. The citation read:

> 'Corporal Day was in command of a bombing section detailed to clear a maze of trenches still held by the enemy; this he did, killing two machine-gunners and taking four prisoners. On reaching a point where the trench had been levelled, he went alone and bombed his way through to the left, in order to gain touch with the neighbouring troops. Immediately on his return to his section a stick bomb fell into a trench occupied by two officers (one badly wounded) and three other ranks. Corporal Day seized the bomb and threw it over the trench, where it immediately exploded. This prompt action undoubtedly saved the lives of those in the trench. He afterwards completed the clearing of the trench, and establishing himself in an advanced position, remained for 66 hours at his post, which came under intense hostile shell and rifle-grenade fire. Throughout the whole operations his conduct was an inspiration to all.'

On the 11th Suffolks' new front:

> 'A trench was immediately started to join up TRIANGLE TRENCH and MALAKOFF SUPPORT. The Centre Company lost ground going through the Farm owing to the bad going, but as previously arranged the troops on either side of the Farm immediately bombed down MALAKOFF SUPPORT. The Left Company took all objectives up to time and established a block 30 yards North of junction of MALAKOFF TRENCH AND MALAKOFF SUPPORT.'

This was part of the defences that had been pre-arranged in order to protect the position from counter-attacks. It was, however, discovered that *'heavy made obstacles are too heavy to be carried, they take a long time to get up and are not much good.'*

Just after 5am hostile lights were observed being fired. These were probably the precursors to enemy counter-attacks, which were able to drive back the 15th Royal Scots from their most advanced position. However, the majority of the objective was held and, as it was discovered that good observation could be had from where they were, it was decided to accept the slightly shorter advance.

As the day went on, consolidation became increasingly difficult. The 11th Suffolks, together with a company of the 23rd Northumberland Fusiliers which had been attached to them in order to assist with consolidation, found *'consolidating and wiring difficult owing to shrapnel and machine gun fire.'* This was reported back to the division at around noon. Mid-afternoon, this difficulty was still ongoing. *'Wiring was interfered with by machine guns. All battalions captured both objectives with few casualties. Heavier casualties during the morning.'* The prediction prior to 1 July 1916, that consolidating and holding on to gains would prove more difficult than achieving them, was now proving true.

As well as interference with the laying of wire, there were repeated attempts at counter-attacks. Although the heaviest of these did not fall on the 11th Suffolks, they did still necessitate significant additional fighting. The attacks were generally driven off before they had really materialised, either by the artillery, if they were spotted in time, or beaten off with Lewis gun and rifle fire if they drew closer and had assembled more stealthily. In addition to this, heavy shelling caused significant casualties.

Lance Serjeant Albert Baxter was probably one of those killed during this period of consolidation. He was one of the original men in the battalion, having enlisted on 11 November 1914, and having gone overseas with the rest of the battalion in January 1916. He was home on leave in December, leaving the village of Stretham on Christmas Day 1916. Before the war he had been a teacher and was active in the Mission Hall, where he had conducted the service while home on leave. His brother, Corporal Frank Baxter, had been killed on 1 July 1916. Albert's officer wrote to his parents:

*'Your son Albert was in my platoon, and it is with the deepest regret that I have to inform you that he died doing his duty on Sunday last. He was doing an important piece of work, when a rifle bullet passed through his heart. A friend who was with him said he passed away instantly, and without any pain. I feel his loss very much myself, because he was one of the cheeriest men in the platoon, and he had a very good influence on the others. Moreover, he was one of my most trustworthy non-commissioned officers, and I could always rely upon him doing his level best in anything he undertook. I know it is a hard trial to lose so precious a son, but try and bear it bravely. If he can see us now he would expect us to be brave, and if he finds us allowing our sorrow at his leaving us to get the better of us it will mar the great happiness he has found.'*

The Royal Engineers, along with one platoon of infantry with each section, found many of the sites pre-selected for consolidation unsuitable, except where the 11th Suffolks had taken the trenches. The men who had gone through the assault were, by the night of 26 August, exhausted, and so the Royal Engineers and the infantry parties were found invaluable in assisting with consolidation and wiring.

At the end of the assault, the division had taken *'147 prisoners... 3 light machine guns, 1 Heavy machine gun, 5 Grenatenwerfer and 5 Minenwerfer... and many valuable documents.'* Two of the machine guns and three of the *grenatenwerfer* were captured by the 11th Suffolks. They had suffered, during the month (the war diary does not give a breakdown of figures as to which days casualties occurred) 2 officers killed, 5 wounded and 1 missing, plus 34 other ranks killed, 126 wounded, and 2 missing. These were low casualties for such a successful operation.

Consolidation took place between 27 and 29 August, though the weather deteriorated and made conditions in the trenches miserable, especially with additional digging going on churning up more mud. The battalion was relieved on the evening of 29 August and went into rest billets in Roisel.

After the battle, performance was again analysed. It was decided at the divisional level that the efforts to lighten the load of the infantryman had gone too far; not enough tools had been carried across for consolidation. It was also observed that *'after a dawn attack and continuous heavy shelling*

16321 Private Robert William Webster Toates of Haddenham. Died of wounds 8 May 1917. (Cambridge Weekly News *25 May 1917*)

20572 Private Ernest Thomas Freeman of Great Chesterford, Essex. Died of wounds 21 June 1917. (Cambridge Weekly News *27 July 1917*)

*throughout the day, the assaulting troops are incapable of digging and wiring at night, though capable of withstanding counter-attacks.'* It was therefore necessary to have RE and pioneers (infantry specifically tasked with assisting the RE) ready to go up at night and help with consolidation and wiring. Finally, *'there was a remarkable and satisfactory amount of initiative shown by all ranks, which had been fostered in all Battalions.'* It seems that the long period of rest and training had paid off.

At battalion level, similar things were observed. Although they might want to reduce how much the men had to carry, even at this level the number of picks and shovels taken over was not considered sufficient and, in addition, wire was needed much more quickly. It was hard to find a good balance between carrying too much to move swiftly and not carrying enough to hold on to what had been gained.

16587 Private Alfred Driver of Cambridge. Killed in action 11 June 1917. (Cambridge Weekly News *10 August 1917*)

43488 Private Herbert Hills of St Ives. Killed in action 26 August 1917. (Cambridge Weekly News *19 October 1917*)

The battalion had moved forward in sections; this *'proved to be the best way of moving in the dark, it stopped straggling also preventing the over zealous from running into the barrage.'* Moreover, the training, using a system of trenches designed to look as similar to the German ones as possible, was pointed out as a great advantage, as was allowing all ranks see maps and aeroplane photographs, in order to get the best possible idea, across all ranks, of what the conditions would be like in the attack.

## Chapter 16

# The End of 1917

After their battle on 26 August, the 11th Suffolks did not take part in any major operations for the rest of the year. However, conditions in the front lines gradually deteriorated, and they had to fight off enemy counter-attacks. In the wake of the battle, a number of decorations were presented to the men of the battalion, for excellent work and bravery during their operations.

The commander of III Corps, Lieutenant General Sir W.P. Pulteney KCB KCMG DSO, presenting the medals on 11 September told the battalion:

*'It is with great pleasure that I have come down this morning to give away Decorations – I am glad to say Decorations for so many branches of the division, both Artillery, Royal Engineers, Field Ambulances, Medical Services, and other services, besides the ordinary infantryman, who generally has to bear the brunt of the fighting but is dependent just as much as anybody else on those other services. When we congratulate ourselves on having captured a position we often forget the help we have had both from the Artillery and Machine Guns and all other sources. I cannot help but express to you how very pleased I am with the work you have done in the Division in these operations, and also for the way you have turned out after these arduous duties. I congratulate you all and wish you the best of fortune in the future.'*

Amongst those who received awards at this time were Captain R.V. Burrowes, Captain Wilfred Rodenhurst Hall and Major Andrew B. Wright, who all received the Military Cross, and several of the men in the battalion, including Private Charles Frederick Miller, Private B.C. Stocking and Private William Henry Rocke, received the Military Medal.

Lieutenant General Pulteney also reviewed the 11th Suffolks on parade, and addressed them, saying:

*'I have come down here to express to you the great satisfaction that you have given me in the work that you have done in these recent operations. You have shown that, although you had very hard fighting, with heavy casualties, at Arras and other points, it has not impaired your fighting efficiency and that good moral spirit that you had in the Somme fighting originally. I give you most hearty congratulations on it, as I have told you before. I want you, when drafts come to you, to instil that same spirit into them; and also just to give you one word of advice for the future, that is, that you must practice whenever you possibly can with your rifle; also the officers with their revolvers, and other units who carry revolvers. What we have got to look at in the future is, that we never know when the enemy will retire in front of us, as he did last year, and we must be prepared for these eventualities. The experience up north lately has been the immense value of fire discipline, and that every man trusted himself to his rifle and not to the bomb. After all, it is your weapons that you have with you, with the bayonet on it, that is going to win the war in the end.*

*Another thing I wish to speak about, this is to platoon commanders: When you take positions, remember that you must not put too many men in and crowd the trenches. It only interferes with the freedom of men in the trenches and it causes great casualties. Nobody knows better than myself, during an attack, the importance of numbers to carry out the attack and fighting programme. Still, after gaining a trench, there should be immediate thinning out, as once you are in this gives greater freedom of action.'*

The first part of September was spent rebuilding and working on newly captured trenches, and putting the line into a proper state of defence. The destruction of the enemy trenches by the British artillery had made it easier to capture them, but much harder to hold them after capture. The enemy was largely quiet, but there were problems with trench mortars and the battalion suffered a number of casualties from them.

They were congratulated on their hard work in this rebuilding work. Brigadier General R.C. Gore, commanding 101 Brigade asked their commander to *'convey to all ranks my appreciation of the really fine work done by your Battalion during their time in the newly captured trenches, in making the defences secure and the trenches habitable. The amount of salvage recovered is most creditable, I have never before seen trenches and the surroundings so clean and free from debris in such a short time after a battle.'*

Back in England, one of the officers who had been wounded on 1 July 1916, was preparing to return to his battalion. He had been commanding a cadet company in Cambridge after his recovery, until he was fully fit for service overseas. Captain John Wesley Wootton at this time evidently fell in love with Barbara Frances Adam, daughter of the late Dr James Adam of Emmanuel College. At the time she was studying at Newnham College. They married on 5 September at 2pm, in St Mark's Church, Barton Road Captain Wootton may have known Barbara before he was in Cambridge commanding a cadet company, as he studied history at Trinity College where he had been a keen sportsman and President of the Trinity Athletic Club. They had a quiet wedding and Captain Wootton would leave almost immediately afterwards for the front.

The battalion's second spell in the front lines in September saw higher casualties, with the enemy very active shelling and trench mortaring the front line trenches. The lines of approach were also continuously shelled, making it hard to carry stores forward to continue repairing the trenches, one of which was a new capture, taken on 11 September.

Amongst those killed was Private Charles Coe, who died of wounds received on 11 September. In a letter to Charles's wife, his platoon officer wrote:

*'It was with great sorrow I heard yesterday that your husband had died in hospital. I was his platoon officer, and although I knew him only for a short time, I had already found him to be one of the most reliable men. He will be missed by all of us. It was on the night of 11 September when we were holding a trench that had only that morning been captured from the Bosches that he was badly wounded.... He was taken down to the dressing station and was quickly got to the hospital. I was afraid from the start that he could not live, but only heard yesterday that he had passed away. The captain joins me in expressing our sympathy with you in your great bereavement.*

*He was as good a soldier as I would wish for, and he met his death cheerfully doing his duty.'*

Born in 1881, Charles had been a pathway mason, working for the Cambridge Corporation on the city's streets. He married his wife Mary Dorothy in 1905 and they had one child, Rosemond Dorothy, born in 1908.

Another who died on the same day was James Arnold, who left a wife and six children. He had been one of the first volunteers when war broke out and received the Military Medal for his actions on 28 April 1917. On that day he had risked his life to find the location of some machine guns which were causing heavy casualties amongst the 11th Suffolks. Despite surviving that attack, which was ostensibly more dangerous than improving trenches, he was killed on 12 September.

Charles Bradnam, of West Wickham, received news that his son Bennett Bradnam was killed by a shell on 13 September. Corporal Bradnam, with his

31955 Private Charles Arthur Coe of Thoday Street, Cambridge. Died of wounds 12 September 1917. (Cambridge Weekly News *5 July 1918*)

20436 Private James Cecil Arnold of Whittlesford. Awarded the Military Medal in May 1917. Killed in action 12 September 1917, leaving behind a wife and six children. (Cambridge Weekly News *12 October 1917*)

brother Albert, volunteered on 29 September 1914, receiving consecutive regimental numbers. Both brothers were wounded on 1 July 1916. Subsequently, Albert died of his wounds on 30 July, while Bennett recovered and returned to France in September 1916. His officer wrote home to give the news, saying:

> 'It is with the deepest sympathy that I write to inform you of the death of your son, Corporal B. Bradnam, who was killed in action by a shell on the night of 13 September. He was a fine lad, always willing to do anything that was asked of him in the most cheerful way, and I can assure you that I am much grieved to lose such a valuable non-commissioned officer. Everybody loved him in the platoon, and I am sure all join me in sending you our heartfelt sympathy in the sad loss of your dear son. He was buried by our clergyman in the British cemetery just behind the British lines. All his personal property will be forwarded to you as soon as possible. If there is anything further I can tell you concerning your son I shall be only too pleased to do so if possible.'

Bennett was the older of the two brothers by five years; in 1911 both had been working on a farm alongside their father.

On 22 September the battalion was warned of a probable enemy counter-attack, and so two companies of the 10th Lincolns were moved up into support, while C Company of the 11th Suffolks took up positions in shell holes just behind their current front line. The counter-attack duly occurred on 23 September. At 5am, the Germans attempted to take Farm Trench, under cover of a heavy barrage which began with whizz-bangs and soon increased in intensity. The early morning mist made it difficult to see the Germans approaching, but as soon as they were seen the SOS signal was fired and within three minutes the British artillery was in full swing. Before the artillery was in full action, the 11th Suffolks held the German infantry off with rifle and Lewis gun fire. The Germans were observed:

> 'to have great difficulty in crossing No Man's Land. One party attempted to get round our right flank but they were dealt with by the Lewis Guns in TURNIP LANE, which it is thought inflicted casualties on the enemy.

*When it got lighter little groups of Boches could be seen trying to get back to their own lines, they had packs and rifles slung, these parties were dealt with by rifle and Lewis Gun fire, which it is thought inflicted heavy casualties. The enemy's barrage was principally over our front line, CART TRENCH coming in for more severe treatment than FARM TRENCH, most of the Minenwerfer shells fell on our left. Considering the intensity of the enemy's barrage there were very few direct hits on our front line and our wire was not seriously damaged.'*

Despite the thinness of the British wire, it was still sufficient to help stop the German attack, emphasising yet again the importance of cutting wire in the attack, and of strong wire in maintaining a defence. By 6.15am it was all over and things were quiet again, though the battalion snipers remained busy shooting at isolated Germans who were trying to return to their own lines. The British casualties from the attack were light, with seven other ranks wounded. The German casualties would have been far heavier from this failed attack.

Private W. Pratt from Barton was awarded the Distinguished Conduct Medal for his actions that day. He was the first man of his village to receive such an award, and had been one of the first three lads from the village to enlist in Kitchener's Army. He had seen significant prior action with the 11th Suffolks, coming through 1 July 1916 unwounded, though he was later wounded in the foot. The citation for his award read: *'during a raid on 25 September 1917, by his courage and devotion to duty, Private Pratt saved what might have been a critical situation. Lying on the parapet, in spite of the heavy enemy barrage, he shot down the trench and kept back a party of the enemy who were endeavouring to work round to our flank.'*

The battalion came out of the line on 25 September and moved to Peronne by bus. There they spent some time resting and bathing and two days later received a draft of 266 other ranks to replace recent casualties. They then travelled on, by train this time, to Bienvillers–au–Bois. Rest, bathing and training continued until 9 October, when they moved to Soult and Leipsig Camp. Here, they did much heavy work on rebuilding roads, and suffered comparatively high casualties, with two of their officers dying of wounds and six other ranks also killed in the three days they did this work. Forty-two others were wounded too.

One of the officers who died was Captain John Wesley Wootton, who had married his sweetheart shortly before returning to the 11th Suffolks, having been wounded on 1 July. His wife of little over a month received the news that he had died of wounds. His loss to the battalion would have been significant; not only had he experience in France prior to his being wounded, but he had also spent time training cadets and so would have been valuable to the battalion in integrating new cadets. He had been a colour serjeant in the OTC before the war.

The other officer who died was Second Lieutenant Clement Percy Joscelyne. He had attended Bishop's Stortford College in Hertfordshire from 1895 to 1901. Before the war he worked in furniture retail in Buenos Aires, Argentina, but returned to England to enlist.

Among the men, William Charles Barrett, who died on 9 October, had married Lily Sutton at the start of the year. He was probably a conscript, judging by his service number (45185). Another was John Richard Collen, the 25-year-old son of John and Emma Collen of Newmarket. Like most in the battalion, prior to enlistment he was a farm labourer.

The corps commander acknowledged the good work that had been done by the battalion in improving the roads, saying, '*I am glad to add my appreciation of the way this very important work has been carried out in spite of casualties, and the excellent spirit with which all ranks have tackled the job*' – the local RE commander had also congratulated them.

On 18 October, the battalion moved to a new camp near Stray Farm. Overnight, the camp was bombed with gas shells and the whole battalion was slightly gassed. Lieutenant F. Ashworth and Serjeant Boggis, together with about twenty others, were more seriously affected and became casualties. Private J. Wilderspin from Old Chesterton, who had been one of the first from the village to enlist on 12 September 1914, wrote home to say that he was in hospital in Brighton, suffering from gas poisoning and trench feet. He wrote: '*I have no use in my feet at all, and my voice has also gone – due to the gas, I expect – but I hope to be feeling better again shortly. I received my lot at the beginning of last week.*' He also lost a lot of the use of his hands. Before the war he had worked at Trinity Hall Boathouse, before being employed by the confectioner William Christmas, on Sidney Street, Cambridge. He enjoyed sport in his spare time, belonging to the Old Chesterton Cricket

Club, the Granta Football Club and the Old Chesterton Institute Cross-Country Team.

Despite being gassed the previous day, on the night of the 19/20 October they went into the front lines to relieve the 20th Northumberland Fusiliers. The relief was completed without incident but they found conditions '*very wretched*'. No telephone lines or other means of communications were available, so the battalion was completely reliant on runners. Pill boxes all looked alike, especially in the dark, so doubtless these runners occasionally (or not so occasionally) got lost. There was only a single duckboard track to the battalion headquarters, from there onwards it was a case of '*good luck and enjoy the mud*'. The front line companies were in shell holes, largely free of water, but they suffered from near continuous shelling.

In the *Cambridge Independent Press* it was admitted that:

> '*Not the least trying of these conditions is the mud which seems an inevitable concomitant of modern warfare. It is much the same on whichever part of the line one may be, and whether the mud of Picardy is muddier than the mud of Flanders is a point that will doubtless form the subject of many a heated argument in days to come. Personally, having been well bemired with each, I should say that the characteristic quality of the mud of both districts is its extreme muddiness. The story of Christian's plight in the Slough of Despond will henceforth have a new meaning for every man who has soldiered on the Western front.*

On the night of 21/22 October, part of the battalion (A and D Companies) were moved up into close support of the 15th and 16th Royal Scots, who were to take part in an attack that day. The battalion headquarters had quite a scare on 22 October when '*a shell from a 4.3 gun landed a foot above the doorway of NORTABEN FARM Pill Box, the door facing the enemy had it been a foot lower it would have come right inside of the Pill Box and killed the whole Battalion Headquarters.*'

At 5am that day, the 15th and 16th Royal Scots attacked with the 35th Division on the left and 102 Brigade on the right. '*The attack was not a success*', and so during the night B and C Companies of the 11th Suffolks came forward to relieve them in the original front line. '*Owing to disorganisation of the 15 and 16/R Scots no guides were available and companies had to make the best of their way on their own.'*

The report on this attack made many of the same points which had been made in past analyses of failed (and successful) attacks. Over a third of attacking troops were *'partially trained reinforcements lately arrived from the Base'*. Enemy aeroplanes were active constantly during the day, locating the positions of attacking troops and firing into shell holes – aircraft were beginning to play an increasingly important part in warfare, and the experiences of the 15th and 16th Royal Scots on this occasion merely served to highlight this. As on 1 July 1916, the enemy artillery had not been adequately dealt with and so during forming up both battalions suffered heavy casualties. The British artillery barrage opened up behind the British front line, so the front companies had to move back immediately before the attack, and then struggle forward over a longer section of ground. Heavy machine-gun fire was encountered, though one company got through to their objective and were consolidating. No other troops were able to get forward, so the company that had succeeded was forced to fall back to the original front line shell holes. The ground was waterlogged and that, combined with heavy losses before the attack had even started, from both artillery and intense machine gun fire, made it impossible to succeed.

The report concluded:

*'Considering the large proportion of recent reinforcements in both battalions that had no training whatever with their units since their arrival in France, great credit is due to the Company Commanders, Platoon Commanders and non-commissioned officers of the 15 and 16/R Scots in the handling of*

12461 Private Joseph Perry of Newmarket. Died of wounds 18 September 1917. (Cambridge Weekly News *5 October 1917*)

*their Companies, Platoons and Sections, both in forming up and during the attack, and to those of the 10th Lincolns and 11th Suffolks in taking over the line without a hitch on the night of 22/23, without guides, in darkness, and under harassing shell fire.'*

On 23 October, the 11th Suffolks found that they were not entirely sure where the front line was meant to be, and that neither B nor C Company had been able to occupy the frontages they were meant to take over, and this could not be corrected during the day. It was hard, too, to evacuate stretcher cases, *'of whom there were a great number'*.

The following day saw the division withdrawn completely from the line, to 'rest' once more. On 30 October, they were addressed by Major General C.L. Nicholson, the divisional commander. He told them:

16588 Private William Morley of Fen Ditton. Killed in action 22 October 1917. (Cambridge Weekly News *11 January 1918*)

17141 Private William Webster Bannister of Hildersham. Died 4 December 1917. (Cambridge Weekly News *1 March 1918*)

20150 Private Henry George (Harry) Rider of Little Shelford. Died of wounds 20 October 1917. (Cambridge Weekly News *5 April 1918*)

16641 Lance Corporal Edwin George Cracknell. Killed in action 17 October 1917. (Cambridge Weekly News *10 May 1918*)

'I had you out here this morning just to see how you looked after this last rather strenuous time in the trenches, or rather shell-holes. I am very glad to see how well you look. You have been through a very great deal and have done it extraordinarily well.... The behaviour of the two attacking battalions, as brought out in the detailed report which has been sent to me, is beyond all praise, and as regards the 10th Lincolns and 11th Suffolks, although they had no actual attacking to do, I always look upon a relief on the night of an action, under most unfavourable circumstances, a very difficult operation, and on this particular night the difficulties were increased a hundredfold. Now, this Brigade has been over the top four times this year. Everything you had to do has been done to the utmost of your ability. On two occasions out of the four you have done everything you were asked to do, and done it well, and the failure on the remaining two occasions was no fault of yours in either case. I can say nothing more, except to congratulate you again on your magnificent behaviour and to say that I am more than proud to have such a brigade under my command.'

The first half of November was spent in training, football and games more generally. On 12 November they returned to the lines and were mostly engaged in working parties and carrying parties for the Royal Engineers. However, this meant that when they went into the front line four days later they discovered that the trenches were good, and though there was '*a moderate amount of trench mortaring*', it was generally quiet. The pattern continued for the remainder of the year.

One of those killed in November was Private Jack Mansfield, who died on 23 November, a year to the day since he had first gone to France. He worked in his father's coal business, and was a highly respected and well-known Histon man. '*He was a regular attendant at the Wesleyan Church. Private Mansfield leaves a widow and one child, and it is pathetic to note that the latter he has never seen, the child having been born since his leaving with the Colours.*'

*Chapter 17*

# Early 1918

The year 1918 dawned fraught with anxiety, for though America had joined the war on the Allies' side, prospects still looked poor in France. The Russian Revolution of 1917 still held a prominent place in many people's minds, and made it clear that the 'Russian Juggernaut' of which so much had been expected in the early part of the war was not going to come steamrollering to the assistance of the Allies in the west. The Germans were able to muster 192 divisions, compared to the French and British total of 156, though this numerical advantage was not going to last for long. Everyone expected an attack, and soon.

The first edition that year of the *Cambridge Independent Press* (and *Cambridge Weekly News*, the two papers having merged in late 1917) proclaimed:

*'Courage and determination are the qualities with which experience bids us meet the New Year which opened on Tuesday. Cause for anxiety there must be as long as the heavy cloud of the war hangs over the world, but there has not been, and we do not think there can be, any return of the torturing anxiety of the first days of the war when everything was in doubt. If we do not know the precise terms on which the struggle will end, we have a reasonable certainty that the peril which menaced civilisation has been averted.*

*The Central Powers cannot win, and the recent peace offer was one of many indications that they know it.... The historian, it is pretty certain, will fix upon two principal events in the past year – the entry of America to the war and the Revolution in Russia. The meaning of the first of these events we think we can see, though he would be a bold man who attempted an estimate of the scope of its influence. As to the second, we can do little more than wait upon events. The Russian Revolution is still "in process of becoming". It will not cut itself off sharp at the end of a year to enable us to examine it.... Happily, there is no sign of a faltering purpose among the Allies. Nor is there anything in the facts we have to review that should depress our hopes.'*

There were also increasing concerns about morale at home, let alone in the trenches. The editor of the *Cambridge Independent Press*, having spoken to some of the local soldiers claimed that:

*'For Pacifists the men at the front have the utmost contempt, and they did not hesitate to express it. "If the Government makes peace with the Boche before we've smashed him," said a Cambridge lad who was wearing the Distinguished Conduct Medal ribbon and two wound stripes, "I'll never call myself an Englishman again." Even more bitter is the feeling against labour agitators and strikers. "If they want to strike," said a Battalion humorist, "let 'em come out here and strike the Boche."'*

Cheery words, but in France, the official prognosis was rather more gloomy. On 18 January, a policy document was circulated (very cautiously, one assumes), which stated:

*'The outstanding feature of the present military situation is that the initiative has passed from the Allies to the enemy and no prospect can be seen of regaining it for several months.... We must expect that Germany will push on with preparations for an offensive campaign this year; that she will strike as soon as she is ready; and that her object will be to force the Entente to give her favourable terms this year.... A successful blow straight towards Paris from the North-east, falling on the junction between the two Armies, throwing the French armies southwards and the British armies westward, placing the Germans in a position to throw their weight alternately against the flank of one or the other once a gap might be made, and opening the direct roads to the Capital, must present very great attractions to the enemy....*

*Such an enterprise as the above, if the enemy could make the first break through rapidly by weight of numbers and regardless of loss, might have most serious, perhaps disastrous, results for the Allies.... Further south an advance could be made earlier; and in addition to the growth of the American Armies, the enemy is no doubt aware that the British troops require rest. He will also doubtless learn of the reorganisation of our troops about to be undertaken, and will not fail to realise its temporary effects on the readiness of the divisions for action.... The first step for us, therefore, is to do all that is possible to defeat the first onset, by developing our defences everywhere to the utmost.'*

This strike, aiming to separate the British and French armies, was in fact what would happen. However, despite their predictions, the British Army was ill-prepared to meet it as the event turned out.

An acute shortage of manpower led to the reorganisation of the Army, with many battalions being disbanded. Divisions went from having twelve battalions to only nine. This decision was pushed through by the Cabinet, against the wishes of the professional soldiers on the War Council. Lloyd George feared that if he gave more manpower to Haig the men would be wasted in futile assaults. There were also concerns that many of the remaining drafts to send overseas were 'boys', soldiers between 18 and 19 who were old enough to serve in England and to undergo training, but who were not meant to be sent to the front until they turned 19. The War Council warned:

*'There is every prospect of heavy fighting on the Western Front from February onwards, and the result may well be that even if the divisions successfully withstand the shock of the earlier attack, they may become so exhausted and attenuated as to be incapable of continuing the struggle until the Americans can effectually intervene. In short, the Council would regard the acceptance of the recommendations in the draft report, without further effort to provide the men they consider necessary for the maintenance of the forces in the field during 1918, as taking an unreasonably grave risk of losing the War and sacrificing to no purpose the British Army on the Western Front.'*

The Cabinet was not moved. The reorganisation had to go ahead.

This reorganisation was not a simple matter of removing one battalion from each brigade and using the men thus freed to fill up the remaining battalions.

A policy was put in place that no Regular or First Line Territorial battalion would be broken up, and that newer battalions were to be broken up first. This led to a considerable movement of troops between divisions, with forty-seven being affected by troop movements. While the changes were taking place, between 29 January and finally being completed on 4 March, work on the defences was interrupted and the fighting capability of the army was severely impaired. Fortunately, the anticipated German attack did not fall while the British Expeditionary Force was in the throes of reorganisation.

The shortage of manpower was worsened by the fact that Haig anticipated that the German attack would fall further north, and thus left the Fifth Army in the south weak. He had also determined that they could afford to lose more ground there than they could in, for instance, the Ypres section, which would have let the Germans get within striking distance of the coast with only a small advance.

With the expectation of a German attack, not only was the structure of the British Army being altered, but its defensive tactics too. Instead of a strongly held front line, there would be a series of outposts, and a 'battle zone'. There were meant to be inter-connected machine-gun posts and bunkers, each covering the other. The Forward Zone should be lightly held, intended only to delay any attacks and to stake a claim on the territory. The Battle Zone was the area where the fighting was meant to take place, but many commanders did not fully understand, or trust, the new tactics and placed up to a third of their manpower in the Forward Zone. The British troops were all experienced in hard fighting, save the newest drafts, but instruction had focused on the problems facing troops on the offensive, and on how to dig and maintain trenches, not on how to prepare for defence.

Lack of time meant that the Rear Zone, all too often, was not constructed at all, or was only partially constructed. There was much work to be done across all the projected zones of defence. With the focus on the offensive, defensive arrangements had been neglected, and in many cases defences were sited at the furthest point reached by an offensive, rather than taking into account the lie of the land and the best tactical position available.

The German Spring Offensive was widely expected everywhere, with some trepidation. After commenting on the early signs of Spring, the editor of the *Cambridge Chronicle* wrote:

'In normal times these evidences of the reawakening of Nature and the approaching of the Vernal Equinox would be unreservedly welcomed, but in the presence of the cataclysm of the great war our joy is chastened by a realisation of the nearness of the "spring offensive" and the terrible clashing of arms that must occur this year. We are not afraid – one meets with no signs of fear go where he may in this country – but we cannot forget what we shall have to bear. The wooden crosses as well as the Victoria Crosses, which will be gained by our dear ones in the course of the next few months, the loneliness of the little cemeteries on a foreign soil as well as the admiring crowds at Buckingham Palace. Now more than ever it is necessary that we should concentrate all our thoughts and energies upon the war and the winning of it.... Sacrifices have been made which may be lost if we are not thorough to the end.... During the remainder of this fourth year of the war our motto should be "The war, the whole war, and nothing but the war."'

With this in view, it is little surprise that the 11th Suffolks spent much of January, February, and early March working on the trenches. Matters were made worse by the spring thaw, the first signs of which were reported on 7 January. During their second spell in the front lines of the new year, the 11th Suffolks reported that *'trenches started to get in bad condition'*. Matters continued to deteriorate. A few days later, they found *'trenches falling in considerably, dugouts and shelters collapsed as the result of rain following thaw, conditions miserable. Enemy very quiet.'* Doubtless the Germans were struggling just as much with the poor weather conditions, although the German dugouts and trenches were generally dug deeper and more sturdily than their British equivalents.

During the next week the battalion spent nearly all their time working on reforming and draining these trenches, with the assistance of the Royal Engineers. Some wire was put out too, but although there were great plans for new defensive lines and a new defensive scheme, this would take a lot of digging and a lot of work to complete. Something had to be available for use in the meantime, and so before work could be started on the new defences, the existing ones needed to be at least prevented from collapsing and put into a state resembling readiness.

At this time, the battalion was able to send fifty men back each night to the transport lines to get dry clothes. However, this was only fifty out of a strength of what was probably around 400-500 effective men. With casualties and the probable high incidence of sickness given the conditions (although this is not explicitly reported), there was no way that the battalion would reach its supposed strength of around 1,100 men, let alone its initial establishment of 1,500. The remainder of the battalion would have to remain shivering in wet clothes for the night, though for those who did get back for dry clothes it would have been a welcome relief.

On 25 January, the commander of 34th Division sent a message to 101 Brigade, aimed particularly at the 11th Suffolks. He said that he had *'heard with pleasure of the good work performed by the 11th Suffolks in draining the trenches during the recent thaw and congratulates the Battalion accordingly.'* Perhaps for fen-land farm labourers this task was not all that different to what they would have been doing in peacetime. From this date the battalion was able to shift its focus towards building the new support posts, which would have criss-crossing fields of fire in order to be mutually supporting and thus stop any German attack in its tracks. In theory, at any rate.

The East Anglian units, including the 11th Suffolks, had once again proved their worth not only in fighting, but in *'work at which no other troops can touch them – turning the soil. At tunnelling they are possibly inferior to the troops from mining districts, but at digging trenches and levelling roads they are unequalled. Time after time they have been specially thanked by the powers-that-be for the way they have carried out work of this kind.'* This praise from the editor of the *Cambridge Independent Press* would seem to be borne out by the number of times the battalion war diary records them digging new trenches and repairing existing ones.

A few months later, the *Cambridge Chronicle* had a small feature article entitled *'They Also Serve'*, by a Subaltern in France. He wrote:

> *'One day there will be a memorial erected to those who fell, not gloriously in action, but obscurely; those who never experienced the magic of adventure in the turmoil of No Man's Land; those who were sniped as they went about their work, or were hit when with working parties behind the line. They are as much a part of the war as those to whom it was given to die*

*more adventurously. For they die with the same purpose at heart, waiting patiently.'*

While most of the battalion was busy in France rebuilding trenches all but destroyed by the weather, Private Joseph Howlett MM, had been fortunate enough to get leave. He took advantage of this to have a quiet wedding to his fiancé Miss H. Northfield, from Cherry Hinton. The bride wore a navy blue costume with matching hat and Private Howlett would have worn his uniform. Corporal L. Howlett, probably his brother or cousin, and another member of the Suffolks had leave at the same time and was able to act as best man. Joseph had enlisted on 13 November 1914. He was discharged on 8 August 1918, with wounds severe enough to render him unfit for further service, but there is no record of what those wounds were as only his Silver War Badge record and not his full service record survives.

At the end of January the battalion was withdrawn from the front lines and moved to a training ground. They found the enemy very active in bombing this area from the air due to the brightness of the moon, but fortunately little damage was done and no casualties were suffered. The month had not been a particularly pleasant one, but the battalion suffered few casualties. Two men were killed, one died of his wounds and another four were wounded.

One of these men, Serjeant William John Honeywood MM, was likely one of the battalion's original members. It is not clear in what circumstances he died, but his loss would have been sorely felt both at home and in the battalion. There were increasingly few of the original men left in the battalion, but the way in which training had taken place meant that much of its original character had been retained. He had been born in Sudbury in 1896 and worked on a local farm before enlisting.

February was largely spent training, although a few working parties had to be provided. On 5 February, a draft of fifteen officers and 300 other ranks arrived from the 9th Suffolks, which had been disbanded as part of the shift from a twelve battalion per division system to a nine battalion one. One of these men was Private Joshua Barritt, who had enlisted (or, judging by the date, probably been conscripted) on 11 February 1916. He was only 5 feet 1½ inches tall when he enlisted, so in the early stages of the war he would have been rejected as too short to go overseas on active service. (This assumes his form is accurately filled in and that it's not the case that an extra ten inches have been blurred off the paper by the passage of time!) However, with the desperate need for manpower this was no longer the issue that it had been. He had been lightly wounded in November 1917, but not severely enough to require hospitalisation. Eventually demobilised in November 1919, he is probably typical of this draft of 300 men and fifteen officers. On the whole, they would have been men with some active service experience, perhaps a lot, and so while they would need to be integrated with their new battalion they would not have needed quite such in-depth training as drafts from England.

On 16 February, the battalion also received a new commanding officer, Lieutenant Colonel Morris Ernald Richardson DSO. A pre-war officer who had had experience in the Boer War before he commanded a battalion of the Northumberland Fusiliers in the First World War, he had married Olive Katherine Soames in 1905. The description of their wedding makes it clear that both were from wealthy families. The bride wore a gown of *'soft white satin, trimmed with old Venetian lace and pearl embroidery, with a Court train of silver tissue, over white chiffon. She wore a diamond pendant, the gift of her father, and carried a bouquet of orange blossom, lilac and lilies of the valley, the gift of the bridegroom.'* They then proceeded to honeymoon on the Riviera. Morris Richardson was also personally brave. The citation for his Distinguished Service Order which was awarded in August 1916 reads: *'For conspicuous gallantry in action. When he had received three wounds in the attack he refused to go back till he had given orders to his successor. He remained two hours in a dangerous spot, and then walked back to Brigade Headquarters and personally reported the situation.'*

Sometime in February, a journalist for the *Cambridge Independent Press* was invited by the War Office to go over to France and see the conditions there. This seems to have been part of a wider policy by the War Office of releasing more details than ever before about the lives of the soldiers overseas in order to boost morale on the home front. A number of those taken overseas were trade unionists (including my great-grandfather, who wrote an account of his own trip round the trenches and who was a trade unionist in the printing industry).

The account of the *Cambridge Independent Press* gives some interesting details about what life was like behind the lines, as well as details of former actions that the 11th Suffolks – and other East Anglian units – had been part of:

'*In areas where troops are camped behind the lines in rest billets, great pains are taken to relieve what would otherwise be a very monotonous time. "Cinema" is a notice one frequently sees painted outside a large improvised structure in the midst of utter desolation. Here may be seen the latest films, from educational to comic. Every division, too, has its own Pierrot troupe, composed for the most part of professional performers. Some of these are really excellent. I've seen many an inferior entertainment at first-class music halls at home to one I attended within sound of the guns in France.*

*Equally welcome are the lectures that are frequently arranged on all kinds of subjects, scientific, literary and historical. Men of repute like Dr Holland Rose have made frequent tours of the front, and only last week a party of University men left Cambridge on a similar mission in response to a War Office invitation.*

*Competition football may be dead in England, but it is very much alive in France, and the chances of this or that battalion in the divisional final are discussed as earnestly as the prospects of the next push. We happened to arrive at one part of the line just as one of these classic contests was proceeding. There was a great "gate", and the general commanding himself set the ball rolling. I have never seen a more enthusiastic crowd even at the Crystal Palace.*'

He was also able to report in more detail the following week on some of the actions that the battalion had taken part in, and the state in which it was found at the end of February 1918.

'*The character of the Battalion is still much the same, though its personnel is sadly changed, for no Battalion has seen more deadly fighting. One of the first faces I met as I dropped into the burrow was that of P.C. Crissal, of the Cambridge Borough Police Force and Band, who is the Regimental Serjeant-Major. He was the first Cambridge policeman to volunteer, and went out with the Battalion in January 1916. He was wounded at*

*Bazentin-le-Petit, in the Somme offensive, on 4 August, but was soon back again, and is now one of about a hundred who are left of the original crowd, almost every one of whom has been wounded either once or twice. A good fifty per cent of the Battalion, Crissal told me, are still East Anglians; the rest are a mixed lot, including Londoners and even Scots.'*

During February the battalion suffered no casualties at all, though at the end of the month they began a return to the front, taking up positions in the front line on 1 March. They were in the lines near Croiselles, close to Arras. It wasn't just the 11th Suffolks that had a quiet time in January and February. The official reports of both the British and French armies made it clear that matters were quiet across the Western Front. In summarising them in early February, the *Ely Standard* reported:

*'The Southern British Army on the Western front has taken over more of the line from the French, and our front now extends to just south of St Quentin. The extension of our front, which was carried out very quietly under cover of the anti-fighting weather which has prevailed, was only discovered by the Germans when they attempted a raid, as they believed, against the French. There has been little news of importance in the British and French reports. Artillery activity at various points has been recorded, and a few raids.'*

The brigade war diary carries a report on the state of the defences:

*'Except on the extreme left of the Sector, the front and support line consisted of the recently captured Hindenberg Line, sited on the forward slopes of two spurs and astride the Valley of the Sensee in front of Fontaine Lez Croiselles. The front and support lines were held as thinly as was consistent with safety, the Reserve Line being the main line of resistance and rallying point for troops who might be forced to evacuate the front and support lines. It was from this line that counter-attack to recapture any part of the front or support line that had been lost would be made. The front, support and reserve lines constituted the Forward System or First System. In rear of this, defence was organised in a series of 'systems' and switch trenches, wired and prepared for all round defence.'*

This system apparently followed the theory that had been laid down. The 11th Suffolks reported on 2 March that the sector they had taken over seemed very quiet, but they were expecting an attack form the enemy any moment. A lot of this expectation now stemmed not from hypothesising about what was likely to happen, but from statements from captured enemy prisoners and deserters. One in particular said that the attack would be on 13 March, but subsequent information suggested that it would fall some time later. This turned out to be the case. However, to be on the safe side all the battle positions on 101 Brigade's front were manned and the artillery fired 'counter-preparation' barrages at various times during the night. Patrols were also sent out to wait in no man's land for any early indication of an attack, but to no avail. The night passed off quietly.

The 11th Suffolks were in the line on 12 March and overnight. They found things very quiet, though the trenches still needed a great deal of repair and reorganisation. Things were perhaps not quite so well prepared as those at brigade headquarters liked to think.

It wasn't just in the British Army that an attack was expected. The same expectations were high in England too. The editor of the *Ely Standard* wrote:

'*Germany's peace arrangements with Russia… are significant events in the history of the war, but, in spite of their importance, the centre of interest is tending to shift once more to the West. In spite of stormy weather, growing activity is reported from the Western Front. There is also great activity amongst those who discuss the enemy's plans and prophecy his action. Forecasts of the possible German offensive in the West are as profitless as predictions of this kind must always be, and, unless the possibilities of the situation are carefully weighed, it is likely to breed more illusions than it dissipates. It is perfectly true, of course, that Hindenburg has an opportunity of placing more effectives upon the Western Front than he could command last year, at the time of the retreat to the famous line which bears his name…. It is quite a gratuitous assumption that the initiative will rest with the enemy. It may be that the Allies will choose to wait for, and to break, a German offensive, but, if this decision is taken; it will not be a concession of inferiority, but a strategy designed to defeat the enemy.*'

The General Staff did not quite share his confidence – they had admitted long since that the initiative rested with the Germans in the beginning of 1918, and were just hoping that they could defeat the likely attack and use it to their advantage, though they were by no means completely confident about that.

Around this time, Drummer Arthur Wilson was wounded in action, while returning with a company from taking rations to the trenches, *'when a German shell burst near by; he was wounded slightly in both shoulders, in the hip, and also somewhat seriously in both legs; he is now in hospital, and appears to be going on satisfactorily.'* He was better known as 'Rugby' Wilson in his home town of Histon, where he had been one of the 'stars' of the Institute Football eleven, and had had a great deal to do with its success when it became one of the best in the county.

Despite concerns at home about the morale of the army, the editor who went abroad found the men he spoke to largely positive. He wrote:

*'If we do not win the war the fault will lie with the people at home, not with the men at the front. The Army in France is sound from top to bottom. I have talked out there with men of every rank from General to Private, and without a single exception they have declared in effect that rather than the Allies should accept a premature or unsatisfactory peace, they are prepared to hold on until relieved by a generation yet unborn…. Not only could I discover no trace of gloom or despondency, but on the contrary, a spirit of cheerfulness and dogged determination that was like a tonic after the grousing and grumbling to which one had grown accustomed in England. The discomforts and dangers, the privations and perils, are accepted as part of the great game.*

*I have visited battalions both in rest-billets and in the trenches. I have marched with them along the roads and I have dined with them in their dug-outs, and never in my life have I met more positive cheerfulness, infectious good humour or a keener zest in life. To say that they are enjoying the war would be absurd. But they are facing it with a spirit that makes one ashamed to complain about the comparatively petty inconveniences one has to put up with as a stay-at-home civilian. They march along to take their places in the front line trenches as though on a field-day – joking, laughing, and singing – though they know they may never return. These men have looked death in the face and they are not afraid. They are anxious for the war to end, of course, but only on terms that will ensure a lasting peace.'*

On 20 March, Lieutenant Colonel Richardson left the battalion, having been promoted to command 175 Brigade. Major G.L.J. Tuck, who had joined the battalion in its early days in Cambridge and who was a former member of the CUOTC, took over command of the battalion, just in time for the German attack. His promotion was reported in the *London Gazette* on 17 May, but was effective from 9 April.

23511 Serjeant Arthur Pammenter of Coronation Street, Cambridge. Died of wounds 17 January 1918. (*Cambridge Weekly News 7 June 1918*)

Promotions were not always put through as quickly as officers might like and it was not uncommon for men to hold two or three ranks simultaneously.

Around the same time, someone back home published a poem questioning the basis of the war and asking whether it was worth it. No answer is given, though the implication does seem to be that it was, or should be, worth it in the end. As the war ended, and as the peace that followed proved disappointing to many, these questions would become more bitter and in some cases grew to have the answer 'no'.

### 'WHAT THINK YE?

What are we fighting for, men of my race?
And the best of us dying for?
For wealth? Or profit? Or power? Or fame?
Or a statesman's bust? Or a Monarch's name?
Or for aught that the sons of our sons could blame,
Did we throw the dice of war?

Why are ye weeping, sisters of mine,
With a mien so proud and brave?
Do ye weep because of the utter woe?
Are ye proud because ye would have it so,
Though Fate should have dealt you this final blow--
--And there's nothing to mark the grave?

What are we fighting for, women and men,
And the best of us dying for?
It was just because we had signed our name,
and the creed of the Briton's to honour the same,
It was only that, and our own fair fame,
We took up the gage of war.

Was it worth it? What think ye, women and men
Of the race which scorns a lie?
Dead things we can worship – live things we must rue,
The life that is false – or the death that was true--?
When the great bell peals through the pillars of blue,
To ring in Eternity?

                                                    W.A.B.'

## Chapter 18

# The German Spring Offensive (1)

On 21 March, at 4.15am, the Germans opposite Bullecourt opened up an intensive bombardment. This initially fell along the front of 9 Brigade, before moving across to include that of 101 Brigade too. The bombardment did a lot of damage to the front line which the 11th Suffolks had spent so much time improving, but less damage was done to the wire itself and the bombardment caused few casualties. This was followed around 7am with a creeping barrage on the right hand portion of 101 Brigade's front (the 11th Suffolks were on the left), but no infantry assault followed in their sector. In the front of the battalion on the left, a party of Germans did manage to get in, but were driven out and killed, leaving some of their bodies in the trenches.

The 59th Division, on the other side of the 11th Suffolks, suffered a severe attack, which quickly broke through their defences. The 7th Sherwood Foresters were overwhelmed and the Germans began working along the front, intending to attack the 34th Division in the flank. Shortly after noon the Germans were in complete possession of the whole Forward Zone of the 59th Division and the battalions in that division had suffered severe casualties.

Much labour had been expended by Major General Nicholson during the previous weeks in preparing flank defences. This meant that when he became aware of the breach in the 59th Division front (though not, initially, how serious that breach was), the 22nd Northumberland Fusiliers formed a defensive flank, making use of carefully pre-sited Lewis and machine guns. According to the British History, *'when, about 11.30 am the enemy, after renewed heavy bombardment, attacked the 34th Division both in front and flank, from the direction of Bullecourt, the preliminary measures taken proved sufficient to hold the advance for some two hours. Then a further extension of the north-*

*westerly movement from Ecoust, now in enemy hands, enabled the Germans to work round the right of the right flank battalion.'*

At 1.30pm, Major General Nicholson heard that the Germans had made it as far as Écoust, and at once he strengthened his flank defences on the right hand side by sending up 103 Brigade. From that time onward, the flank was gradually pushed back north-westward. Counter-attacks slowed the German progress, and the fighting was often hand-to-hand, but the Germans were able to make steady progress on that side of the 34th Division defences.

At the same time, according to the 11th Suffolks' war diary, nothing much was apparently happening. However, in both this and later German offensives the war diaries could not be kept accurate and up-to-date – everyone was too busy fighting. These offensives are harder to piece together than any of the other battles the battalion took part in as many of the sources give conflicting times and descriptions. The attack may also have been perceived differently from where the 11th Suffolks were to where the rest of their division was, as the Germans were attacking from the flank, not head on.

The bombardment the 11th Suffolks were under gradually died down, and it looked like, perhaps, the German assault was not so terrible as it could have been. At 12 noon, the men across 101 Brigade were ordered to stand down. The brigade war diary stated that *'The situation at this point appeared to be that the enemy had penetrated the line south of Bullecourt, but it was reported that he was well held.'*

The comparative quiet did not last and it soon became clear that the 11th Suffolks were in for a day of hard fighting. At 3pm an intense bombardment was opened on the front of the 11th Suffolks and their neighbouring brigade. It ceased half an hour later and at that point the Germans attacked, primarily onto the front of the left company of the 11th Suffolks and the neighbouring brigade. The Germans came in *'wave after wave'*, advancing from south to north. The north-east portion of the company on the left (C Company) was involved in the attack. Contact was lost temporarily between part of this company and its headquarters.

This was almost a separate struggle to the one going on at the flank of the 34th Division, where it met the 59th. The Germans attacking the 11th Suffolks were met by heavy fire, over open sights, from two batteries of

160 Brigade Royal Field Artillery. The Official History adds some interesting details about this artillery battle, something which can often seem quite removed from the infantry struggle. However, in this case the men of these two batteries, when forced to abandon their guns, *'fell back about two hundred yards to the trench which now became the front line, and fought with rifles and Lewis guns until dusk, when they crept out, covered by rifle fire, and man-handled their guns back to the waiting teams. Both batteries were again in action in the early hours of the next morning.'*

The Germans did not have things all their own way. C Company at close range, with battalion headquarters troops and B Company at a 1,000 yards range, were able to get into a position of enfilading fire on the enemy attack – firing along it lengthwise – and caused considerable casualties. This was one of the things that had caused such heavy casualties to the British forces attacking on the Somme. Where one portion of the line was able to hold out, those troops could cause serious trouble for those advancing on either side.

However, despite this the Germans were able to break in between the 15th Royal Scots and the 11th Suffolks. Parts of the line were blown in accordance with pre-made plans, but the Germans continued to advance, getting nearly 1,000 yards into the British lines. However, defensive flanks were formed and the German advance checked. By 6pm, the 11th Suffolks had counter-attacked and regained the lost ground in the front line.

No less than three attacks were attempted by the enemy, all of which were repelled, and heavy fighting continued all along the Sensee River until nightfall. By 6pm the front had stabilised, as far as the 11th Suffolks were concerned, and a bombing block formed to prevent the Germans extending lodgements in the British lines sideways. Twice they attempted to get through, and twice they were beaten back.

The method of creating a bombing block was to send sappers (Royal Engineers), or other troops if they were unavailable, to create a 'double block' system of defence. A bombing party, followed by a barricade party with the stores needed, *'should be sent up that trench as far as possible until stopped by fire down the trench, when a barricade should be constructed round the nearest corner. A length of 30 or 40 yards straight should then be left and a second barricade with a loophole in it and if possible a small passage round which can be readily blocked by a portable obstacle. The barricade is then held by a party of riflemen established at the loopholed block, which is practically a loopholed traverse. The length of 30 or 40 yards between prevents it being possible for the enemy to bomb this party out of their trench without venturing out of the first block into the 30 or 40 yards of straight trench which, being covered by rifle fire, is rendered untenable.'*

Not only did the Germans try to attack, but the 11th Suffolks also attempted to regain some of the lost trench by attacking from the bombing block. They, too, were unsuccessful. It's quite likely that the Germans had set up a similar block, in which case they could be almost impossible to storm, especially if there was ongoing hostile fire.

The 11th Suffolks were also attacked by German aircraft during the afternoon, two of them strafing Shaft Trench. The garrison, however, fired back, and were able to bring down one of the aircraft with machine-gun and rifle fire – an impressive feat if it was accurately reported. Often aircraft which looked to have been destroyed or damaged turned out to have simply moved away for areas of the front where they were going to have fewer bullets whistling through the canvas and wooden frames. Considering their flimsy appearance, First World War aircraft could often take a surprising amount of damage before they were destroyed, provided there was no fire involved.

The early newspaper reports were surprisingly close to this account of the attack, although the 11th Suffolks were on a section of the line that seems to have avoided the brunt of the German attack. The *Cambridge Independent Press* reported:

*'At 8am a powerful infantry attack was launched by the enemy on a front of over 50 miles, extending from the River Oise, in the neighbourhood of La Fere, to the Sensee River about Croiselles.... The attack, which for some time past was known to be in course of preparation, has been pressed with the greatest vigour and determination throughout the day.... In the course of the fighting the enemy broke through our outpost positions and succeeded in penetrating into our battle positions in certain parts of the front. The attacks were delivered in large masses and have been extremely costly to the hostile troops engaged, whose losses have been exceptionally heavy. Severe fighting continues along the whole front. Large numbers of hostile reinforcing troops have been observed during the day moving forward behind the enemy's lines.'*

At 6.45 that evening, the battalion received a warning order from 101 Brigade that there would probably be an order to withdraw to the second system of defences on Henin Hill under cover at darkness. All company commanders duly assembled at Battalion Headquarters by 7.30pm, and some of the preliminary orders were sent out. These orders were confirmed by the brigade at 8pm, and only slight alterations were needed to the drafted orders that had been prepared.

B Company straight away sent a platoon forward to help cover the withdrawal. D Company, which had been in reserve, was already where it needed to be. A Company covered its withdrawal using three Lewis Gun teams to form a rearguard. As they withdrew, the bombing block was attacked twice more. B Company covered the second part of the withdrawal, and then D Company and one platoon of B Company covered the final withdrawal of B Company to their new positions. By 1am this manoeuvre was complete, A and C companies in the front line of the second system of trenches, and all wounded had been evacuated from the front system.

That same day, Private Robinson Mitham was awarded a Military Medal for his actions. Although the citations for the Military Medal do not usually survive, in this case it was reported (some time later) in the local press, and so it is possible to know the details:

> 'On 22 March two of the other stretcher-bearers belonging to Private Mitham's company had become casualties, and the third, who had gone to the dressing station, was unable owing to heavy enemy shell-fire to return to the trench. Private Mitham had therefore to attend single-handed to the very numerous casualties of the whole company for several hours during which the Germans were deluging the trench with shells of all descriptions.'

Robinson Mitham had enlisted on 10 December 1915, but his enlistment was deferred until 10 April 1916, at which point he joined the Suffolk Yeomanry. After going to France in September 1916 he was transferred to the 11th Suffolks. He was wounded by a bullet in the foot on 28 April 1918 and sent home to England before discharge as unfit for further war service.

The battalion was not done fighting. From 5am on 23 March, an intermittent bombardment was opened up on their new headquarters, being particularly heavy on the reverse slope of the position, around battalion headquarters. At 8.45, a strong enemy party advanced towards the new position, apparently along the communication trenches that had connected the two systems together. They were driven off by Captain George Frederick Reid, who was wounded during the fight. He was awarded the Military Cross for his actions during this battle. The citation reads:

> '*For conspicuous gallantry and devotion to duty. He showed great coolness and skill in commanding his company under very heavy fire. At one time, he dashed out with some of the company headquarters personnel and routed the enemy, being wounded seriously.*'

44036 Private Robinson Mitham of Swavesey. Awarded Military Medal for actions on 21 and 22 March 1918. Wounded in ankle 28 April 1918. (Cambridge Weekly News *13 September 1918*)

Another two attacks were made on the same part of the line, with the enemy attacking to the north-west from Croisilles. The attacks were beaten off with a combination of rifle, Lewis and machine-gun fire.

At 9am, the battalion's pioneer serjeant, who had been at Ipswich Dump, reported that troops to the right were retiring and the enemy advancing. Almost immediately afterwards parties of troops from the right were seen retreating towards battalion headquarters. They were stopped by headquarters officers and made to form a defensive flank along with headquarters personnel.

After the troops to the right had retired. Captain W.E. Harrison, commanding A Company, sent a platoon to form a defensive flank to cover his position. At the same time, Captain L.H. Redwell, commanding B Company, found a party of 150 Germans forming up on his right, between the two companies. He adjusted his line in order to meet up with Captain Harrison's men and form a firmer defence.

At 11am, B Company was forced to take up alternative positions in shell holes, as the British artillery was shelling the front line. This maintained contact between the right of D Company and the left of A Company, giving them a better view of a valley which was not easily visible from the first line of the second system. The Germans tried to take advantage of this by putting in small parties, but were prevented from doing so by rifle fire. More enemy troops were seen moving forward, and at 11am hostile shelling made the position almost untenable.

Between noon and 1pm, low flying aeroplanes twice attacked the battalion, this time they were not able to shoot any down. Troops to the right of the battalion were seen retiring westwards in large numbers, leaving their right undefended. Battalion headquarters was moved to a slightly less heavily shelled spot, and at 2.30 the Intelligence Officer, Second Lieutenant Edward Trevor Bolton, went over to the right to try and find out what was going on. He found a small party under an officer who explained that he was going to continue withdrawing, and stated that they were the last party to leave.

Lieutenant D.E. Johnson, the Signalling Officer, went to the companies in front of Henin Hill and found them still in the same position as they had held before the troops on the right had retired. Earlier in the attack he had helped to maintain an exposed wire connecting battalion headquarters with a buried cable and thus the brigade headquarters. He was awarded the Military Cross for his actions both in maintaining the cable and in going forward to reconnoitre the position 'under very heavy shell fire.'

Despite Lieutenant Johnson's efforts in maintaining the connection with the rear via telephone cable, the 11th Suffolks were unable to stop the shelling of their lines by their own artillery, and so at 4pm B Company withdrew into A Company's area and Hind Avenue. As this was going on, the enemy tried to work along the trench to attack the right of A Company in the first line of the second system. This was the result of the troops on the left retiring and leaving the flanks exposed. Lieutenant W.R. Hall, who had already received the Military Cross for his actions during the attack on 26 August 1917, formed a block and repulsed several of these enemy attacks. He was wounded, but continued fighting 'with great coolness and determination' before he was killed. Captain W.E. Harrison sent a platoon to the right of battalion HQ personnel, which was reinforced with a platoon of D Company, to try and strengthen the flank position.

Around 5.15pm, with the enemy advancing in considerable numbers from the south, D Company withdrew into Hind Avenue, and at 6pm an assault was launched from the south against the right of the battalion. They were engaged with rifles, Lewis guns and with Vickers guns from the 34th Machine Gun Battalion. The enemy suffered considerable casualties, but were able to work round the defensive flank formed by battalion headquarters and two platoons of A Company. These were forced to withdraw under heavy machine-gun fire from the south and west of Henin Hill.

As this party passed the battalion headquarters, the officers, runners and signallers left their dugout and formed up behind the bank. They brought down heavy fire on parties of the enemy who were attacking C Company and the remainder of A Company, and were also able to fire on the enemy as they attempted to advance westwards from the south and west of Henin Hill.

By 7pm, C Company and the remainder of A Company had been almost entirely surrounded, and so began to withdraw, completing this withdrawal by 8.30pm. Their withdrawal was covered by some of B Company with a Lewis gun, and Lieutenant C.H. Woods, whose *exceptional gallantry contributed largely to the success of the withdrawal.* He was killed in covering the withdrawal.

Private William George Barker, a rifle bomber who had been in A Company, was taken prisoner during this action. It is likely he was separated from the rest of his company when the Germans managed to work round the edge of the headquarters company and part of A Company. He had originally joined the Territorial battalion and went to France in 1915. After being wounded, he was transferred to the 11th Suffolks. He was initially reported missing from 21 March, but his parents subsequently received a letter from Chaplain Roberts, of Cassell Camp, Germany, to say that he had died of wounds and was buried on 15 April.

The 11th Suffolks, less the battalion headquarters and two platoons of A Company, assisted the 3rd Division in holding Hind Avenue, facing south. The headquarters and the two platoons of A Company moved back at 8.15 to a position in the third system, in front of Coyelles. They left behind a small party under Captain J.H. Brett, the battalion's adjutant, to cover their withdrawal; he was subsequently ordered by the commander of 9 Brigade to remain and cover the withdrawal of the brigade to Henin, staying until 2.30am.

As evidence of how close to surrounded the whole battalion had become, when Captain C.V. Canning led C Company headquarters back to Hind Avenue at 8pm, they came across a party of eight Germans, with five British prisoners. They killed all the Germans, released the prisoners and *'brought them in'* – which seems to imply these prisoners might very well have surrendered to the Germans and may not have been quite so keen on being 'rescued' as might be thought. Captain Canning was awarded a Bar to his Military Cross for his actions on this day. The citation read: *'While in command of his company he established a bombing block and drove off four determined enemy attacks. He rescued five prisoners from the enemy. He showed great tenacity and skill in handling his company under most trying circumstances.'*

At midnight, orders received via the 3rd Division were carried out and the battalion was relieved by a battalion of the 31st Division and moved back to Armagh Camp near Hamelincourt. At midnight the remainder of the battalion in Hind Support received orders through 3rd Division to withdraw and rejoin their battalion.

In summing up the whole of the day and a half of fierce fighting, the brigade war diary stated that:

*'Though no general attack had taken part on the front of this Brigade front the whole of the Brigade subsequently became involved in the operations which had started on its right flank and was actively engaged on its entire front for the remainder of the day of the 21 and the whole of the 22, sustaining heavy casualties, vacating their positions only in the face of overwhelming odds or when ordered to do so to conform with the direction of the line on its flanks.'*

On 23 April, the battalion marched to Ayette and bivouaced in 'artillery formation'; in other words, they spread out to minimise any casualties from hostile shelling, so that one shell would not kill too many people. This was especially important when camping on open ground, without the shelter of trenches which were dug in zig-zag patterns to avoid shrapnel from a single shell travelling too far down the trench.

Congratulations were in order from various levels of commanders.

The Commander of the Third Army, General J. Byng, wrote:

'*I cannot allow the 34th Division to leave the Third Army without expressing my appreciation of their splendid conduct during the first stages of the great battle now in progress. By their devotion and courage they have broken up overwhelming attacks and prevented the enemy gaining his object, namely, a decisive victory. I wish them every possible good luck.*'

GOC VI Corps, also wrote to the battalion as follows:

'*The heavy loss the 34th Division has suffered and the trying work that has fallen upon it during the last three days, makes it unavoidable that it should leave the VIth Corps. Will you please thank all ranks for their work during the opening stage of the great battle now in progress. The task that they had to carry out was not an easy one, and I fear that their losses have been great.*'

C.L. Nicholson, the Divisional Commander, added to this while addressing the men, having just read out the Army and Corps Commanders' words:

'*On my own behalf, I wish to record my high appreciation of the gallantry and the stubborn power of resistance shown by all ranks and arms of the Division on the 21 and 22 March. When the full story of those days is known, the gallant fight of 102 Brigade and part of 101 Brigade on the 21 March when outflanked and almost surrounded, the stubborn and protracted resistance of the 11th Suffolks on the left of the Division on the 21 and 22 March, and the steady disciplined gallantry of 103 Brigade on the 21 and 22 March, will go down to history among the greatest achievements of the war.... As admirable as the gallantry displayed in action, has been the high standard of discipline, endurance and cheerfulness shown by all during the days which have elapsed since the Division was withdrawn from the line.*'

He also sent separate congratulatory orders to the Divisional Artillery and complimented the 34th Machine Gun Battalion, a new formation. He stated that they '*laid during the 21 and 22 March, the foundation of a tradition of its own. No higher praise can be given to it than to say that the orders issued to the Battalion, that each gun was to be fought to the last man and the last round of ammunition, were carried out in all cases, in the spirit of the order and in many cases, to the letter of the order.*'

For their actions on that day, the 11th Suffolks received one Bar to Distinguished Service Order, one Bar to Military Cross, five Military Crosses, four Distinguished Conduct Medals, one Bar to Military Medal and eleven Military Medals. At a Territorial Force Association Meeting, shortly after the news was received, it was resolved that:

*'The County Association offers to the commanding officer, officers and non-commissioned officers and men of the battalion their hearty congratulations on the long list of honours conferred on the battalion for distinguished and gallant services in the field. The bravery of this battalion is a source of the greatest pride to the county.'*

At home, the newspapers tried to put an optimistic slant on things. The *Cambridge Chronicle*'s editor, for instance, wrote:

*'The initial rush of large bodies of troops in close formation, backed up by an unprecedentedly great concentration of artillery, was sufficiently powerful to sweep back our lines for several miles. This advance was made at a prodigious sacrifice, the loss of men according to all accounts being colossal. Our casualties are no doubt heavy, and unfortunately many of the more severely wounded must necessarily have been left behind in the retreat and remain as prisoners of war in the hands of the enemy. Our loses in guns and material are also high, but in spite of the huge effort she has made, Germany has not succeeded in breaking our line or inserting a wedge between us and our allies.*

*The rush of the first few days has not been maintained, and as our reserves and those of the French have come upon the scenes, the pace has slowed down very considerably, and we quite hope in a few days to hear that the forward tide has been altogether stemmed…. There is not the slightest reason to be anxious about the ultimate result of this movement, though it is quite possible we may have to retreat still further in certain sections of the line. No army can continue to advance rapidly if its effectives are being put out of action at the pace that the Germans have been doing the last few days. On the whole the outlook is distinctly bright, not only as to the holding of the German advance, but as to the ultimate collapse of the German Empire.'*

Private Elias Hankin of Girton was killed during the German attack and his body was not found. He is commemorated instead on the Arras Memorial. He left a widow and three children, having married Lily in 1906. Before the war, like many of the battalion, he was an agricultural labourer. His service number (23687) suggests that he joined up sometime in 1915, perhaps taking his time to decide whether his duty to his family was best served by staying at home to care for and provide for them, or by going overseas to protect them from the possible evils of a German invasion.

In contrast, Private William Renshaw, also killed on 22 April, was 20. He had joined up soon after the outbreak of the war, aged 16. He was wounded in the shoulder on 1 July 1916, and then sent home again in early 1917 suffering from frozen feet. He lived in Oakington with his family before the war, where he worked on one of the local farms.

14425 Private Herbert Webster Driver of Elsworth. Awarded Military Medal for actions on 21 and 22 March 1918. (Cambridge Weekly News *5 July 1918*)

15618 Company Serjeant Major Stanley William Mead of Foxton. Awarded Military Medal and Distinguished Conduct Medal in 1918. (Cambridge Weekly News *12 July 1918*)

*Chapter 19*

# The German Spring Offensive (2)

After the battle the 11th Suffolks went into rest and training for a short spell, before returning again to the front lines in the Houplines sector on 30 March. On their way, they had a little more excitement. Near Auxi-le-Château an over-excited dispatch rider came dashing up to General Nicholson and told him that the Third Army had completely broken and was in full flight. General Nicholson was not convinced, so had the man put in the guardroom for spreading false rumours. But, just in case it did prove true, he directed his brigades to take up positions covering the town and to prepare for battle. *'The troops, though tired, were very cheery, and took up their positions readily, quite keen at the thought of another battle.'* Or at least, that was the impression the writer of the Divisional History, J. Shakespear, got from them. The matter resolved itself into a few tractors and a couple of British cavalry troops who had been mistaken for Uhlans and the march to the rest area continued.

On 1 April it was reported that the situation was as follows: *'Normal trench warfare, quiet sector, front line untenable owing to water. Support reserve lines held.'* The heavy casualties that 101 Brigade had suffered in March had been made good, but the writer of the brigade war diary was concerned that *'no opportunity had been possible of training or ascertaining the abilities of these reinforcements'*. There was some shelling and trench mortar activity during the day, and on 4 April patrols failed to find any trace at all of enemy movement. It looked like the Germans had also abandoned their front line and not just the British. And, once again, the 11th Suffolks had to put a lot of effort into improving the defences of the sector they were holding.

The plan of defence was as follows: *'The defensive system consisted of the Front, Support, Intermediate and Subsidiary Line, the front line being a series of posts garrisoned by day, and vacated at night, the front being protected by vigilant patrols.'* The brigade war diary continued: *'In view of the fact that there was no Brigade in Divisional Reserve (the Reserve Brigade being liable to reinforce any part of the Corps Front) it was essential that the positions held should be defended as stubbornly as possible.'*

On 5 April the 11th Suffolks were relieved and were able to spend some time bathing, resting and refitting. They then began more intensive training two days later. This training was made more difficult by the need to stand to from 5am on 7 April until told to stand down as the danger had not materialised. That same night there was an intensive gas shell bombardment, which mainly hit artillery units, causing a large number of casualties from gassing. Many thousands of gas shells, and some high explosive shells, had been dropped, but no infantry action followed the bombardment and the following day went quietly. At this time Frank Hayden Hornsey arrived to join his new unit. He had been conscripted into the Army on 19 November 1917. After training with the 3rd Suffolks in England, he was sent overseas to join the 11th Suffolks. Contrary to regulations, he kept a brief diary in a small pocketbook throughout his service. The entry for that night reads: *'Arrive to front all night bombardment & Gas. no sleep.'*

From 6 April onwards, there had been increasing signs that the quiet sector they had moved to was not going to remain that way for long. Two deserters captured on the right of the corps sector stated that there was going to be an attack. Trench mortars were said to have been put in place, along with new emplacements. Officers and non-commissioned officers were reported to have been seen from other divisions, with their insignia covered, and some of them were suspected to have come straight from the Eastern front. The corps circulated this information from the prisoners, but it was taken with a pinch of salt as deserters from the same division had been proven by events to have made false statements. However, there was evidence from other observers that the Germans were working on roads and railways, and so observation was to be carefully maintained.

Erquinghem began to be shelled on 9 April and so the 11th Suffolks were turned out of bed (the shelling began at 4am), got in front of the village, and waited for an anticipated attack. This also meant that, as they were in artillery formation in the fields and trenches, they would be less vulnerable to hostile shelling. At 10am the shelling became more intense, and at 11.15 the battalion was ordered to move back to Bac Saint-Maur. Barely had they began to move when the order was cancelled and the 11th Suffolks ordered *'to form up facing Fleurbaix and get in touch with 103 Brigade on left and 16/R Scots on right.'* Three companies were put in the front line and one in reserve, and by 3pm the line was established and in touch with both flanks. *'For the remainder of the day enemy attempts to advance were repulsed.'*

The following morning, about 7am, there was another attack and the Germans were able to break through between the right of the 12th Suffolks and the left of the 16th Royal Scots. The 12th Suffolks fell back and the Reserve Company of the 11th Suffolks was despatched to counter-attack. Just over an hour and a half later, they had succeeded in driving back the enemy forces and filling in the gap between the right of the 11th Suffolks and the left of the 16th Royal Scots. During the heavy fighting, the Germans were believed to have suffered heavy casualties, but part of the 16th Royal Scots became entirely cut off and fought until surrounded, commanded by Major A.E. Warr who was afterwards reported missing. He, along with six or seven others, was in fact captured.

Moving up the support company left the 11th Suffolks without any reserves at all, except for the battalion headquarters personnel who had dug in just west of La Rolanderie Farm. The area is today the site of the Suffolk Cemetery, maintained by the Commonwealth War Graves Commission. Two companies of the 4th Duke of Wellington's (West Riding Regiment) were ordered forward, but had not arrived before 3pm, when orders were given to withdraw. Throughout the morning the right of the battalion had been slowly pushed back, but they were able to maintain contact with the troops on their right. Further along on the brigade front, however, a gap had opened up due to a retreat north of the river, leaving the 16th Royal Scots with their right flank exposed. There were not sufficient troops to properly defend the western part of Erquinghem, but only a small number of Germans trickled through.

At 2pm a particularly heavy attack took place across the whole front of the 11th Suffolks, with the exception of the left company, and the Germans were able to gain a lodgement in the centre of the lines, creating a gap. The two right companies were forced to withdraw to conform to movements of troops to their right, under the cover of outposts, and were finally able to get in touch with the part of the 4th Duke of Wellington's that had been sent forward to assist. Battalion headquarters personnel acted as reinforcements for the centre part of the line, where the Germans had got in, and were able to force them back out. By about 3pm, the line was held and the whole brigade front was re-established.

However, at 12.45 orders had been received from the division that they would withdraw to the left bank of the Lys, and this commenced at 3pm. Holding out, and regaining the ground that they had lost, must have seemed futile when it was then given up. Frank Haydn Hornsey wrote: '*German breaks through but new position retreat terrible 2-30 blow up Armentiers bridge all kit lost. stand in wheatfield all night raining hard.*'

Brigade troops remained in position to cover the withdrawal of other British soldiers, '*meeting and repulsing in the meantime several attempts of the enemy to break through their positions. Enemy machine gun activity during this period was very severe but no part of the line held was conceded until the order for withdrawal was given. The withdrawal of troops of this Brigade to the left bank of the river was executed in good order, though somewhat harassed and hampered by hostile machine gun fire.*'

The 11th Suffolks did not receive the orders to withdraw until 3.20pm, at which time the officer commanding the 9th Northumberland Fusiliers (to the battalion's left) stated that he would need about two hours to withdraw his forward troops. '*The battalion held off repeated attacks of the enemy until about 5 pm when the troops on the left had withdrawn and the Left Company were heavily engaged from three sides, while the centre of the battalion was heavily pressed by the enemy with numerous machine guns.*' They had come close to being surrounded and a number of men were taken prisoner at this time.

It is probable that it was for his actions here that Lieutenant Cyril Lemmer Bryant won his Military Cross. The citation reads:

'*For conspicuous gallantry and devotion to duty. After the company commander had become a casualty, this officer took command and drove back repeated attacks by the enemy. When the battalion was ordered to withdraw, he covered it with the remnants of the company until completely surrounded, and then cut his way out at the point of the bayonet.*'

At 9.05 orders were received that the line was to be held as a picket and that further movement of the enemy to the north-east was to be prevented. Now

101 Brigade were ordered to occupy parts of the railway line, withdrawing still further, and they completed the move by 5.30am on 11 April, the 11th Suffolks moving back last to provide a cover for the rest of the brigade forces. Patrols and outposts were pushed forward and, interestingly, from this point on brigade orders are scribbled on bits of paper apparently torn from a notebook, instead of being typed out. Clearly something happened to either the typewriter or the typist.

It was on this day that Field Marshal Sir Douglas Haig issued his famous 'backs to the wall' order to all ranks of the British Army in France and Flanders:

> 'There is no other course open to us but to fight it out. Every position must be held to the last man: there must be no retirement. With our backs to the wall and believing in the justice of our cause each one of us must fight on to the end. The safety of our homes and the Freedom of mankind alike depend upon the conduct of each one of us at this critical moment.'

The battalion certainly did their best to follow these orders, although little mention of this now famous order was made in either the battalion or brigade war diary.

Lieutenant Edward Trevor Bolton, of Liverpool, died on 10 April. He had been the battalion's intelligence officer and, unlike many of his fellow officers, had studied at Oxford, not Cambridge. He had married Eliza Josephine Nisbett in 1910, and the two then moved to London where he was a solicitor. He was buried at the Suffolk Cemetery, La Rolanderie Farm, Erquinghem–Lys – so although he was reported as killed in action, he may have actually made it at least part way back from the front lines before he died, or he may have been killed by a shell further back from the lines. The bodies of many of the other men who died on these days were not recovered and they are instead commemorated on the Ploegsteert Memorial.

The following day, 11 April was, briefly, a quieter one for parts of the brigade; 103 Brigade was heavily attacked, but the 11th Suffolks were not drawn into this fight. About 6pm, the battalion received orders for a withdrawal at 7.30pm. The line they were meant to withdraw along proved impossible, as it was already in the hands of the enemy, and so the battalion was forced to move cross country in order to reach their new position, where they were billeted as part of the reserve in a farm near La Blanche Maison.

The following morning, the situation was rather unclear. Officers' patrols were sent out to try and find where the Germans and the British were. They returned to report that the 31st Division was returning and the enemy advancing. Enemy patrols tried to push forward and take ground held by the 11th Suffolks, and two companies of the battalion, sent to form a defensive flank and connect with the 16th Royal Scots and the 29th Division, were able to stop and reform most of the 31st Division which had been retreating. Of course, no unit engaged in defending against the German advance was willing to admit that they had fallen back first. Every battalion and every unit diary I have seen so far claims that the unit only fell back in accordance with movement on either side, and only with orders to do so.

The minor attacks of the morning were followed around 5pm by a much more determined attack, forcing back the front line *'slightly'*. A new line was taken up, in touch with both flanks. There was a constant concern in the British Army to maintain a continuous line – they feared the Germans would do to them what they had hoped to do in all of their advances, which was to get inside the front line defences and then attack the rest of the defences side on, where the defenders would not be as well prepared. German cavalry was spotted in the outskirts of Bailleul and the situation around the town continued to be confused. Part of 103 Brigade was sent as a garrison, and part of the 3rd Division was on the outskirts of the town blocking the approaches to the enemy – though not, it seems, well enough to prevent a cavalry patrol penetrating their lines. Frank Haydn Hornsey wrote that they *'hold the Germans after retreating 6 miles Farmhouse burning cattle bellowing we let all cattle & sheep pigs loose guard at night'*.

The night and most of the following day passed quietly until 3.30pm when, after a very heavy bombardment, the Germans attacked again. *'The attack developed in considerable force and after severe fighting... the Left Forward company was withdrawn and was placed in line with the Reserve Company.'* By 6pm this had become a solid front line once again. Meanwhile, the right forward company held its ground, being heavily engaged *'by considerably superior forces from all sides, they did not withdraw to conform with the movements of the neighbouring troops. The stand of this company under Captain*

*L.H. Redwell enabled the right of the Brigade and 174th Brigade to form a line between this Battalion and the Steam Mill.'*

At 11.40pm a warning order went out that there was to be a further withdrawal that night, which commenced at 2am on 14 April. Before the withdrawal could be carried out, Brigadier General Robert Clements Gore was killed by a shell, along with his Brigade Signalling Officer, while the Brigade Major, Captain Gilbey, was also wounded. The loss of their senior officers would have made matters even more complex for the troops under his command, especially as Brigadier General Gore had been allowed a good deal of latitude as the 'man on the spot' to co-ordinate the response to the German attacks.

During 14 April there was very heavy shell fire, but no further infantry attacks. In the evening the battalion was withdrawn to go into the reserve, the relief being complete at 5am the following day. However, despite the heavy fighting they had seen, moving into the reserve did not mean a rest – the battalion spent the day digging on the new trench system, so they probably remained well within range of enemy fire. By this time the 11th Suffolks were barely a separate unit. Casualties had been heavy across the brigade, so the battalion now contained, as well as its own remaining troops, the remnants of both the 18th Northumberland Fusiliers and the 15th West Yorkshires.

The battalion did not even get a full day of the rather dubious 'rest' they had enjoyed in reserve. By 9pm, they were once again the front line through a continued enemy advance. Troops of the 59th Division had begun falling back from around 5.30pm, in response to a heavy German attack. At 9.40, Lieutenant Colonel Tuck sent a report back to Brigade HQ that *'Position in front is very serious. Officer Commanding 2/6/North Staffs in person reports his battalion, and probably the whole brigade broken. I have patrols out in front. Stragglers coming through freely, mostly without arms or equipment.'* An order was sent back that they were to hold the line at all costs in order to allow the 59th Division to reform in rear of them.

Further digging and wiring was carried out in what was now the front line on 16 April and an attack in the afternoon was driven off. There was heavy shelling the following day and further attempts by the enemy to advance, but they too were driven off. On the night of 17/18 April the battalion was relieved, moving into reserve positions. Here, things remained quiet, and on 21 April they were relieved by the 133rd French Division and marched back to bivouacs well out of the firing line. The official casualties given in the war diary are 8 officers and 42 other ranks killed or died of wounds, 10 officers and 157 other ranks wounded, and 5 officers and 272 other ranks missing, a total of 471. Unlike on the Somme, though, when hopes were expressed that many of these men might be prisoners and not actually killed, a number were.

One of those who became a prisoner was Private Joseph Chapman, who wrote home to his parents in May to tell them that he was now a prisoner of war in Germany. He had been reported missing since 9 April. He was one of the original members of the battalion, having enlisted in October 1914, along with his brother who died on 1 July 1916.

There were two Joseph Chapmans in the battalion, and the newspaper report did not give his regimental number. However, he is one of the soldiers for whom the full service record, and not just the medal index card, survives. (Many of the service records of First World War soldiers were destroyed during the Blitz. Some survived, to become the 'burnt documents', while some additional service records survived by being filed as part of the Ministry of Pensions' records. This record, fortunately, has not been too badly damaged – some of the service records are badly charred at the edges, or have holes in the middle of pages where an ember must have landed on them.) He had been admitted to hospital in late January 1916, shortly after going overseas with his battalion, but the reason is not recorded, and he was only away from the battalion for three days. He was then hospitalised again with scabies in late March 1916, before being wounded during the Battle of the Somme on either 1 or 2 July, with a machine-gun bullet in the abdomen and a wound to his wrist too. After being treated at Chichester, he remained in England for a while until he could be rated A1 and fit for active service overseas again.

Before returning overseas, he came under military discipline for overstaying his pass, being given six days confinement to barracks and having three days of pay docked. He rejoined the 11th Suffolks on 19 May 1917 and was wounded again on 14 June that year. This time the wound was not serious – he was not returned to the UK, but treated in Etaples. After rejoining his battalion in September, he was again hospitalised, this time with tonsillitis, for nine days. Rejoining his battalion on 21 January 1918, he would have fought unwounded through the early part of German Spring Offensive, but was captured later on 10 April.

Congratulations to the battalion, the brigade and division, were once again in order. General Nicholson addressed the men, on 23 April, saying:

*'I am not going to keep you here very long. I only had you out this morning just to give you a message which I have been told by the Army and Corps Commanders to give you. The message is this – There is no question of thanks or congratulations from the Higher Commanders for the performance which the Brigade and Division has put up during the fighting which lasted without cessation from the 9 to 21 April. What they say about it is this. They want to express their admiration for gallantry and tenacity with which all ranks have carried out their duties, and have held on to positions which have been given to them. It is a fact that throughout the whole of the operations the front of the Division was never broken, nor did any single unit retire from its position until it was ordered to do so, and it is for this purpose that the Army Commander General Sir Herbert Plummer and the Corps Commander Lieut General Sir A Hamilton-Gordon have told me to express to you their admiration. I can add nothing to this. I have always been proud of this division, but not until recently did I realise quite how good it was. There is no question that it has been a great performance and carried out by all ranks in a way worthy of the highest traditions of the British Army, and there is no higher praise than that.'*

For a change, too, more details were given to the press about what units had taken part in the attacks and what had happened. Perhaps the complaints from the press and public about their desire to know more of the specific doings of their men were making an impact, particularly with the need to reassure the public in the wake of the German advances, or perhaps it was decided that as the Germans had taken a number of prisoners they had to know what units were where anyway. Regardless, an extract from *The Nation* published on 27 April was copied out into the battalion war diary.

*'It is interesting to know that it was the 34th Division which made so stout a fight against von Below at CROISELLES. The subsequent appearance at ARMENTIERES won tribute from the German staff. It was almost surrounded when the order to evacuate ARMENTIERES was given, and a part of it was cut off and fought against overwhelming odds in the ruined city. Such deeds as these are our best insurance against a German victory.'*

For all that the division was congratulated, words could not change the fact that it was woefully under-manned. A War Office report into the fighting state of divisions gave the following details: *'34th Division: Heavily engaged on SOMME Battle front. Moved to First Army and relieved 38th Division in ARMENTIERES sector on 29 March. Heavily engaged in ARMENTIERES sector. Relieved by portion of 59th and 33rd Divisions on night 15/16 April. Of very little fighting value. Casualties since 21 March – 244 officers, 7,155 OR'*

17240 Private Charles Hubbard of Grantchester. Wounded 1 July 1916. Killed in action 15 April 1918. (Cambridge Weekly News *11 August 1916*)

15324 Private Arthur Bunting of Great Abington. Killed in action 19 April 1918. (Cambridge Weekly News *2 August 1918*)

43878 Private Howard Charles Howlett of Swavesey. Initially reported wounded and taken prisoner, later known to have died between 9 and 19 April 1918. (Cambridge Weekly News *30 August 1918*)

18367 Private Arthur Missen of Newmarket Road, Cambridge. Killed in action 28 April 1917. (Cambridge Weekly News *27 September 1918*)

Matters during this fighting were so confused and hectic that most casualties of the battalion during this period are not given a definite date of death, but are rather said to have died between 9 and 19 April 1918.

The Higher Command was growing seriously concerned about their prospects. A secret document circulated on 26 April stated:

*Provided the enemy continues his operations on the same scale as he has done for the past five weeks, it is evident that by the end of May only some 43 British divisions will be available on the British front. Of these a considerable proportion would be greatly exhausted by continuous fighting and therefore unfit for battle. … the state of training will not permit of the American battalions going into battle at once on arrival... I am forced to come to the conclusion that it will inevitably be necessary sooner or later to shorten the British front by a deliberate withdrawal to the line BETHUNE*

43747 SIGNALLER FRED HILLS, A. Co., 11th Suffolks, only son of Mrs. Hills, Cemetery-lane, Linton. Reported missing since April 9th, 1918. If any returned prisoner of war could give any information concerning him Mrs. Hills would be very grateful.

16600 Serjeant Clarence Thomas Mabbutt of Mawson Road, Cambridge. Military Medal awarded July 1918. Gassed September 1917, wounded March 1918. (Cambridge Weekly News *4 October 1918*)

43747 Signaller Fred Hills, A Company. He had been reported missing, and his family published this appeal for any information on him from returned prisoners of war. Sadly he had been killed in action on 19 April 1918. (Cambridge Weekly News *7 March 1919*)

*– ST OMER – DUNKIRK, and I am taking the necessary precautions to meet this eventuality.'*

Eventually, the report continued, it might prove necessary to either abandon the Channel Ports, or become separated from the French, and it was considered that the best of the two options was to abandon the Channel Ports and remain with the French.

*Chapter 20*

# Leaving the 34th Division

A fter the battle was over (for the 34th Division at any rate), they began training again, but, once again, their 'rest' did not last. After a few days for bathing and refitting, it was back to digging new lines of defence, under intermittent shelling and which led to several casualties. While they were digging on the Brandhoer Line from 28 April to 30 April, eight men were killed.

One of these men was Lance Corporal Arthur James Mason. He had enlisted at the start of the war and was one of only three men from Chippenham who came through 1 July 1916 without being wounded. A memorial service was held in Chippenham in June, when news of his death – and the deaths of three other local men – had been received. 'O Rest in the Lord' by Mendelsson was played at the start of the service, suitable prayers were read, and the service ended with 'I know that my Redeemer liveth'. In 1911 Arthur Mason had been an apprentice carpenter; by the time war broke out he had probably finished his apprenticeship, and could have continued in his trade for at least part of the war. He would probably have been making better money than he would get in the Army, but evidently with him, as with so many other young men, patriotism and a sense of adventure outweighed personal profit and he enlisted under age at 17 or 18 years old.

Private Albert Edward Morfee died on the same day. He was born a year after Arthur Mason, in 1897, but his regimental number shows that he was conscripted when he was officially old enough to serve. Born in Hastings, in 1911 he lived at home with his widowed mother and was attending school. He was the youngest and only surviving son of his mother, and died of wounds received on the day of his death.

There is no mention in the war diary of drafts having arrived, but they were going into the line as a working party rather than to hold the line, so the fact that they were massively under strength may not have been considered an immediate problem, nor a bar to the work they were doing.

The early part of May was occupied with further digging on the new defensive lines, until 12 May when they were moved back from the lines into reserve and rest. Worth mentioning as part of this, if only for the fact that it features repeatedly in both the brigade war diary and in the brief notes that Frank Haydn Hornsey kept, was the demolition of Goedmoet Mill. On 30 April the brigade requested permission to destroy the mill, which was being used as a marker by enemy artillery. On 1 May, permission was granted, units warned, and at 9.30 the brigade war diary reports *'GOEDMOET MILL demolished.'* Or, in the words of Frank Haydn Hornsey: *'Big Windmill blown up by our R.E. Farm house blowed up.'* The severe damage to the French countryside was not solely the fault of the Germans – both sides caused huge destruction both in trying to kill their enemy and break his lines, and in cases like this where destruction was to protect the lives of their own soldiers by removing a convenient aiming point.

By this point in the war artillery techniques had improved enormously. Accurate weather forecasts and careful testing of the characteristics of every individual gun, with allowances made for wear and tear, enabled more accurate shooting. Together with the work of the Royal Flying Corps and Royal Naval Air Service (after 1 April 1918 these were amalgamated into the RAF) which led to massively improved accurate maps this created the ability to shoot at a target 'from the map'. In other words, without the ranging shots normally necessary to hit anything accurately. However, aiming points were still a useful addition to the new techniques, as shown in this incident.

Having left on 12 May, the 11th Suffolks arrived in Brunembert two days later, after a combination of bussing and route marching. Here, according to the war diary, *'battalion trained and refitted as far as possible. Bathing and games.'* On 16 May orders were received that the battalion, still significantly under strength, was to be broken down into a training cadre, to train up new American soldiers. These American soldiers were finally beginning to arrive in strength, but it would take still more time before they were fully ready to go into the lines. Matters were not helped by the fact that the American officers believed the French and British had grown overly timid through trench warfare, and what was needed was a vigorous frontal attack, a gallant and glorious charge which would overwhelm the German defences. Unfortunately this was exactly what the French, in red and blue uniforms, had proven futile in the early days of the war, and the Americans suffered huge casualties through their commanders' refusal to learn from the French and British. Preparations were begun to decide which officers and men would remain in the training cadre and which would be sent to other units. It looked like the 11th Suffolks' reward for their hard work in stopping the German Spring Offensive was to be broken up.

In the event, this did not come to pass. On 19 May news was received that the battalion would not in fact be broken up and just under a week later this was confirmed by orders to move to the 61st Division. Before they left, General Nicholson gave a speech praising the work they had done, saying:

*'Colonel Tuck, Officers, non-commissioned officers and men of the 11th Suffolks – I have had you out this morning for what will probably be the last time I shall be able to speak to you. As you may know, it is probable that you will shortly be leaving this and going to another division. It is very sad to me and I hope it is for you; but you might have had a worse fate.*

*I have always looked upon this battalion as one of the best if not the best in the division. Wherever I have known the battalion to be in action I have always felt confident of their success. Ever since I have commanded the division, this battalion has always been absolutely reliable, and looking back over the fighting of the last eighteen months I cannot recall a single instance when the 11th Suffolks did not carry out everything that was expected of it. It was so throughout the fighting at Arras early last year, it was so at Hargicourt, and in particular on 21 and 22 March at Henin Hill, when no troops in the world could have done more.*

*You now have a number of young men who have not been out long, and are only recently joined. I can tell them that this battalion has a reputation second to none in the British Army.*

*I shall follow the career of this battalion with the greatest interest, and I have no doubt that you will always do your duty as thoroughly as you have done while under my command.*

*I wish you the best of luck – and God bless you.'*

According to the war diary, May saw only two men killed. However, the record of *Soldiers Died in the Great War* for the Suffolk Regiment and the Commonwealth War Graves Commission, report five soldiers killed during the month. Three of these died of wounds, so it may be that they are included under the twenty wounded soldiers (though none were mentioned as having died of wounds in the casualty figures given by the war diary), or that their deaths were not reported back to the battalion, as they would have (probably) been removed from the battalion's roll when they were wounded.

At least two of these five soldiers were original members of the battalion – Frank Predam Bailey, who joined in November 1914, and Harry Martin, who enlisted in January 1915.

Frank Bailey was the son of William Needham and Maud Mary Bailey. He was at school in 1911, and living with the family were two lodgers who were students in the university and candidates for holy orders. His mother ran the family home as a lodging house for students and his father worked for the college in the 'gyp' or kitchen. One of the lodgers shared the family surname, but as he was from Lancashire and is listed as a 'boarder' in the census it's unlikely that they were related. His mother was a resident of Montreal, Canada, so it's surprising that Frank didn't take advantage of that connection to enlist in the Canadian forces as a number of others with tenuous links to the colonies did. One wonders how much the lodging students had to do with the young lad in the same house, and whether they helped him with his homework, or if they lived completely separate lives. Probably as there were only a handful of lodgers in the house they would have more to do with the family than in a place where there were a number of students.

Harry Martin was an older soldier, 27 at the time of his death and married. He had lived in Chatteris with his wife, whom he married some time after 1911 as he was single in the census. He had been a horsekeeper during the census, and probably continued in the same or similar profession. He died at the 44th Casualty Clearing Station, so he would barely have been moved back from the lines where he was wounded before he succumbed.

One of the other casualties was John George Langhorn Burrell, who may have been an original member of the battalion, though when he received his Distinguished Conduct Medal the citation states that he was in the 2nd

Suffolks. Interestingly, although the citation gives the date of the award as 11 March 1916, his family was not notified of the award until after his death, and it was not reported in the local press until October 1918. This perhaps suggests that the award should be dated 11 March 1918, although the 11th Suffolks were not attacked until 20 March. The circumstances of the award do not quite match up with March 1918 either. The citation states that: *'After an attack on an enemy trench, Private Burrell remained in the open, under heavy fire, collecting and bandaging the wounded and working so close to the enemy parapet that he was continually being bombed while doing so.'* The 2nd Suffolks were in action around 2 March 1916, and again on 27 March 1916, so this may have been part of a 'line straightening' operation or a more minor attack. It just seems peculiar that it would have taken so long for the award to be reported at home.

Before his death he had been wounded four times, so he may well have served in multiple battalions of the Suffolk Regiment. Although wounded soldiers generally seem to have returned to their own unit, if they came to England to recover they might be sent to a different battalion in the same regiment, or another regiment altogether. It's not entirely clear what the logic behind the decision was, though presumably it depended on where casualties had been heaviest. He had only been out at the front around six weeks after recovering from his last wound before he died, and so he would have seen action in April and possibly March defending against the German advance. Prior to enlisting, he worked for Mr Swann, a contractor on East Road, Cambridge.

On 26 May the 11th Suffolks formally came under the orders of General Officer Commanding 61st Division, at Molinghem. With the decision not to disband the battalion came new drafts, 200 men arriving on 28 May, while the battalion was in rest. One of those who joined on this date was Thomas William Bryant. He had attested to join the Army on 25 September 1916, but was not called up until 2 March 1917 when he was old enough to serve. His medical record states that when he attested he was 5 foot 7 ins, weighed 112lbs, and had a cleft palate and hare lip. According to his service record, he initially served in the '7th Cycle Regiment (Left Wing)', possibly part of the VTC, before transferring to the 2/1st Suffolk Yeomanry. As part of this unit he was hospitalised with ringworm in November 1917, then on

14 April 1918 he was transferred to the Suffolk Regiment, embarking for France the same day. He spent some time in a training base overseas for final training, perhaps at the notorious 'Bullring', though his service record does not give the precise place. On 28 May he joined the battalion in the field. He had been a farm worker before the war, but evidently was not considered so essential to the agricultural side of the war effort that he couldn't be spared.

For a change, the rest period this time was occupied solely with training, absorbing the new draft, and, one hopes, actually resting too. Frank Haydn Hornsey describes the week of 19 to 25 May as *'Parades till 1. played football in evenings [?] hear the big air raid on St Omer on Whit Sunday night,'* and the rest of the month as having the *'usual parades'*, with the exception of a move by train. He makes no mention of the change of division, probably because the size of a division meant that to most ordinary soldiers it would seem distant. They might occasionally see their divisional general, but for the most part it was their immediate companions, their section, platoon and company officers that they saw the most of, with even the battalion commanding officer a figure of somewhat distant authority. The 61st Division had a poor fighting reputation after a disastrous first action on the Somme on 19 July 1916, and was composed of Second Line Territorial units from the Birmingham area. This reputation was probably not deserved – the division seems to have been no worse and no better than any other, and had fought well during the German Spring Offensive though with heavy casualties.

The division's commanding officer, Major General John Duncan, was himself new to the division, replacing the quietly efficient Major General Colin Mackenzie at the end of May 1918, just as the 11th Suffolks arrived for service with their new division. After the war he went on to command the Shanghai Defence Corps, and had, when he died in 1948, served for over fifty years with the Colours.

There was no digging of new defensive lines and as May moved into June the training began to take on a somewhat different nature. They were now training for 'open warfare' and 'offensive action'. The battalion signallers trained with 42 Squadron RAF in signalling with a new 'Popham' panel. These were square patches of ground outlined with white stones, with white canvas strips being placed out in the centre to pass on information according to what shape the strips were put in. Five of the officers were sent on a course of instruction where they saw a demonstration with tanks. The British Army was gradually moving to a more integrated system of fighting, or 'all arms' attack. However, they still lacked an effective method of exploitation – cavalry was generally too vulnerable to be used to sweep ahead of the infantry once the lines had been broken and turn a minor defeat into a rout, while the tanks were still mechanically unreliable, slow, and also vulnerable, though not quite so vulnerable as horses.

June 9 saw a return to the trenches, although five officers and 107 other ranks went to a camp for further training under J.H. Brett. The sector of trench that they took over, in the St Floris sector near the Lys Canal, was quiet. Hard work was done on defences and a good deal of active patrolling overnight, though movement by day was restricted, probably by how close the lines were together. At this point, Frank Haydn Hornsey left to go on a course, and after 13 June there are no more entries in his diary. On that day, when a draft of nine new men arrived (they seem to have been returning casualties), there was an inter-company relief and it was reported that there were *'patrols locating enemy posts and defences'* and *'our command of no man's land good'*.

The remainder of the month passed off quietly, spent doing a combination of front line stints, working parties and time in reserve. The section they took over from 21 June, in the same general area, was even more exposed than previously, so nothing could be done during the day, but at night active patrolling continued fairly successfully.

According to the war diary, two other ranks died during the month and seventeen were wounded, along with two officers being wounded. Again, however, the Roll of Honour and the Commonwealth War Graves Commission give a slightly higher total of three men killed.

One of them was Thomas Charles Custance, of Kingston, who was 24 years old and left a wife and child. He was one of the original members of the battalion and had been wounded in the arm on 1 July 1916. A memorial service was held at Kingston Church on 30 June 1918. He was the second son that his parents had lost, though the other son who died was not in the 11th Suffolks. He had another brother, William, who remained in the battalion, and who survived the war.

June was quiet across most of the Western Front, until on 15 July the Germans tried another major attack on the Marne. However, this time the Allies were ready and counter-attacked, inflicting a significant defeat on the Germans. It was significant not just for its actual immediate results, but for the fact that it marked the point at which the Allies were ready to take back the initiative. The counter-attack was a French one, launched by General Mangin's French Tenth Army, including at that time the 1st and 2nd US divisions. British and Italian forces were also involved in the fighting, although the 11th Suffolks remained in a quiet area.

For the 11th Suffolks, July continued much the same as June. At home, people remembered those they had lost in the 'Great Push' of 1916. Although on 5 July the Germans sent up a large number of parachute lights and there were large scale raids by battalions on either side, the 11th Suffolks spent the first part of the month in active patrolling and working on the lines. There were risks even in this though, and one member of the battalion, Private Christy Graham Burden, suffered an accidental wound with a pick. Before the war he had been a telegraphist clerk, so he lacked the same familiarity with digging the soil that the farm labourers on the battalion would have had. Perhaps that contributed to his injury – in any case he suffered a wound in his right hand and wrist, which left him with limited movement of his right index finger when it eventually healed. The wound was considered serious enough for him to receive a thirty per cent disability pension after his discharge.

Returned prisoners of war grouped on Parker's Piece for photo. (Cambridge Chronicle *22 January 1919*)

Returned prisoners of war lead by band processing through Cambridge. (Cambridge Chronicle *22 January 1919*)

View of procession of returned prisoners of war in Cambridge. (Cambridge Chronicle *22 January 1919*)

View of procession of returned prisoners of war in Cambridge. (Cambridge Chronicle *22 January 1919*)

At the end of the month the divisional war diary recorded:

> *'Training has not gone on as well as might have been desired, owing to frequent changes in locations, and to the fact that commanders of formations and units had to carry out a good deal of reconnaissance while in the XV Corps area. Training facilities in the XV Corps area were good, but in the XI Corps area there is no ground suitable for manoeuvring near the ST HILAIRE Brigade. The Divisional Artillery did no training in the XV Corps area, as they were employed on work in the forward area.'*

It would have to be enough; the 11th Suffolks would soon go into action again.

According to the war diary the battalion suffered another two men killed during the month. Again the actual number of those who died was higher – seven men in total; however, only two of these were killed in action. Two were recorded in the casualty records as having simply 'died', which suggests that they may have died of the Spanish Flu. The remaining three died in Germany as prisoners of war.

Amongst the casualties during the Spring Offensives had been a number who were taken prisoner. It took some time for information to filter back to England, and conditions in

Tea for ex prisoners of war, held in the Corn Exchange. (Cambridge Chronicle *22 January 1919*)

the prisoner of war camps could be atrocious. Several men of the battalion died in captivity, some of wounds, some, perhaps, from poor treatment and exposure.

Private William Pratt DCM, of Barton, was one of those taken prisoner during the early part of the Spring Offensive. He had enlisted in October 1914 and was wounded in the foot on 6 July 1916. He returned to the front

Crowd following procession of returned prisoners of war in Cambridge. (Cambridge Chronicle *22 January 1919*)

Laurel wreath memorial draped with Union Jack, hung in Guildhall. (Cambridge Chronicle *22 January 1919*)

lines, and was awarded the Distinguished Conduct Medal for his actions during a raid on 25 September 1917, the citation reading *'by his courage and devotion to duty, Private Pratt saved what might have been a critical situation. Lying on the parapet, in spite of the heavy enemy barrage, he shot down the trench and kept back a party of the enemy who were endeavouring to work round to our flank.'*

On 3 May 1918, it was reported in the *Cambridge Independent Press* that *'Official information has been received by Mr and Mrs D. Pratt that their son, William Pratt, DCM, Suffolk Regiment, is amongst the missing. Mr and Mrs Pratt have already lost one son Samuel, and have another son Frederick in France.'* It was not until June that his parents were informed that he was now known to be a prisoner of war in Germany, one of many from the battalion who were taken prisoner on those two days. Given the nature of the fighting and the fact that large chunks of the battalion were reported to have been very nearly cut off, it's not surprising. Before the war, Private Pratt had worked on one of the local farms as an agricultural labourer, and he gave his age on enlisting as being 19. However, he was actually born two years later in 1897.

One of those who died as a prisoner of war was Claude Lynn, who had lived with his wife at 55 Beche Road, Cambridge. He was reported to have been taken prisoner and to be wounded at the end of May. He had enlisted in April 1916, possibly as part of the Derby Scheme which meant that as a married man he would theoretically be called up later than the single men who volunteered for deferred service or service when they were needed, or possibly as a conscript. Five months later, in October, he was reported to have died on 2 July. News about prisoners of war could take a long time to make it back to England – it had to pass through various agencies, and after the Spring Offensive there were large numbers of British prisoners of war about whom information was awaited by families.

After the war was over, Private Arthur R. Kidd wrote to the secretary of the Cambridgeshire and Isle of Ely Prisoners of War Help Committee describing the conditions they had been kept in. He stated that although they were given the name of a place where they were to be sent and where they should have parcels and letter sent, they never went there and so no parcels were received. He continued:

'*Taken prisoners at Erquingam (Armentières), we were taken to Fort Macdonal in Lille. About 5,000 British and Portuguese troops were there, and we were put into cells, 250 in each. The accommodation should only have been 50 at most. The ventilation was a window about two feet square. We were allowed out into the air for five minutes each day, in which time we had to draw our food, which was a quarter of a loaf of black bread and a bowl of thin soup or cabbage water. Sometimes we had to wait for 36 hours for this meal, and some of the fellows, being so weak, fainted as they got into the air. Even water was denied us. For seven weeks we tolerated this agony. Boots and different articles were exchanged with the German sentries for potatoes and bread. The verminous condition, too, was almost unbearable, as no one had a wash or a shave during the whole seven weeks, and beards were numerous amongst us lads of 20. I think this treatment is one of the most horrible events of the war, and ought to be brought to the notice of the right authorities. It was reported to an officer in France, and I believe the number of the camp Commandant was also taken.*

*From there we were split into smaller parties and taken to camps just behind the lines to work, principally at shell carrying. We left Lille three days before our troops occupied it, and were marching practically every day until we eventually arrived at a village called Wambeek (50 kilometres from Brussels). Work from there was carried on. We were up at 4.30 in the morning and had to walk 12 to 15 kilometres to work, some fellows in bare feet. Wooden clogs were very numerous. Working till three o'clock in the afternoon, we were again marched back to our billet, to our one meal a day.*

*The Belgian people were very good to us, and I fully believe more deaths would have occurred if it had not been for their kindness in giving us bread and potatoes. After liberation from this camp, where we were when the armistice was signed, we all started off together and arrived at Courtrai in batches of twos and threes. Several poor fellows died on the road through exhaustion and exposure.*'

One of those for whom the journey home was too much was Private R.E. Lee of March.

*'He was practically starved and had no wash for seven months, being made to do heavy work, such as carrying ammunition. He collapsed on reaching the British lines, and his wife was telegraphed for. Pneumonia and dysentery set in, and though everything possible was done for him, Private Lee died shortly after his wife reached him.'*

The official service records also back up this information. Private Joseph Pope of York Street, Cambridge, claimed a pension after his discharge for rheumatism. He had been a cook in the 11th Suffolks, but during the German Spring Offensive had evidently been drafted in to fight. He was captured and kept in a prison cage *'for one month with no shelter to sleep under'*. He was treated in Mons Hospital for six months while a prisoner.

*Chapter 21*

# Victory

From 8 August 1918, the British Army launched a series of offensives which became known as the 'Hundred Days', though at the time no one knew how long this would take. Indeed, many leading military figures were planning for a much longer campaign and began drawing up plans for the 1919 offensives. However, General Haig insisted that it would be possible to break the Germans in 1918, and this time he was correct.

The 11th Suffolks were involved in this campaign throughout its duration, albeit not constantly. On 8 August the British Army would go on the offensive in the area around Amiens, with the 11th Suffolks taking part in this, though not in the area where the greatest advance was made.

After spending the first week of August training, on 7 August company commanders went up to the lines where they would attack to reconnoitre the ground. The following day, at 2am, the 11th Suffolks went into the line and a few hours later the battalion proceeded over the top *'to get in touch with the enemy'*. They moved through the 16th Royal Warwicks, and found that Loxton Farm was occupied by the Germans, too strongly for an attack without artillery assistance. *'Touch was kept with enemy throughout the day but he did not retire further.'* The 11th Suffolks were on the very edge of the Amiens battle – elsewhere the Germans were forced to retreat, lost over 100 guns and 7,000 prisoners, retreating in places up to seven miles. It was reported the following day in the *Cambridge Independent Press* as *'a brilliant victory'*, but *'it was possible that the Germans, on account of the previous attacks, had intended to retire, but this attack had come as a complete surprise, and had upset whatever plans they had formed.'*

The losses of guns and so many prisoners (450 guns and 12,000 prisoners in actuality, a change from reporting on the Somme where gains were often over-reported) indicated how significant the defeat was. After the war, Ludendorff would call 8 August 'the black day of the German army', and at the time he offered his resignation to the Kaiser and apparently had a complete collapse of morale.

Although the local press reported it as being 18 August, it was actually 8 August, during this attack, that Private Joe Utteridge was killed in action. According to the letter sent home by the chaplain:

> *'Our battalion was acting as an advanced guard for the whole division, and the Germans were retiring. There were snipers about, and your dear brother-in-law was killed instantly by a shot from one of them. Immediately after the advance our battalion was relieved, but his body was in such a dangerous spot that it could not be recovered. But the Germans are sure to retire further, so that his body will be recovered.... Your brother-in-law was always cheerful, even under the most adverse circumstances, and he was a general favourite among the other men in his company.'*

One of his friends also wrote home to Joe's sister-in-law, saying: *'He was a very good pal, and a very good and brave soldier. I am sorry to lose him. He only lived two minutes after he was hit; I was with him till he died. The only words he uttered were: "I'm hit and done for" – he was hit in the stomach. The boys are sorry to lose him.'*

On 9 August the 11th Suffolks carried out active patrolling, finding that the enemy still occupied posts at Flagon Farm and Loxton House, before being relieved at midnight and going into reserve to rest, bathe and continue training. Five days later they were back in the line, though in support this time for a few days, where it was mostly quiet.

On 20 August they moved up to the front lines, the relief being completed at 1am. Later in the day, the Germans

24789 Private Joseph Utteridge of Cambridge Place, Cambridge. Killed by a sniper 8 August 1918. (Cambridge Weekly News *4 October 1918*)

were found retiring to shorten their line. Patrols went out and followed closely on the heels of the German retreat, harassing their movements. They had advanced 1,000 yards by 8.30am, and patrols were established out to a further 1,500 yards in front of that.

On 21 August there was a further advance – the battalion was ordered to act as an advanced guard to the brigade. D and C Companies were caught in a heavy gas shell and high explosive barrage on their way to forming up, suffering many casualties. During the month, 7 officers and 227 other ranks were wounded by gas shells, though as the battalion came under gas bombardment at one other point during the month it's impossible to be sure how many were suffered on each occasion.

Two men died on that day, Private Arthur Cyril Standen who had been conscripted into the Army and couldn't have been overseas long as he was born in 1899. He would have been 19 when he died, barely old enough to serve overseas. It's possible that he was gassed earlier in the year as well; an 'A Standen' of Kent was reported in the *Kent and Sussex Courier* as being gassed, however the cap badge in the photo supplied does not appear to be that of the Suffolk Regiment, so it could easily be another Private A. Standen. Born in 1876, Corporal Henry Worley, who died on the same day, was at the opposite end of the men brought in to fill a desperate manpower shortage. He lived in Norwich with his wife, Charlotte and, until he was called up, he worked on the tramway as an engine man.

Despite the early casualties from gas, the 11th Suffolks began to advance at 3.30pm. They did not have things all their own way – heavy machine-gun and rifle fire was encountered across the whole of the front line from strong enemy rearguards, and it is possible that the two men killed on 21 August were killed by this rather than the gas. By 9pm they had secured an advance of 2,500 yards on the left and 1,000 yards on the right, a stark contrast to their much more costly, and much less significant in terms of distance, advance on 1 July 1916. Both the British and the German armies had come a long way since then. The British Army had grown in strength and experience, with its higher commanders learning their trade, albeit not always consistently. Considering the amount of effort it took just to move so many men around, let alone keep them fed and supplied (even without taking into account that this was often done on roads ill-suited to the task, or on hopelessly overburdened railways, and that they then had to go into battles which required great quantities of ammunition, services for casualties, etc) it had come a huge way from the six division expeditionary force of 1914.

On 22 August the 11th Suffolks were relieved and moved into brigade reserve, but later that same day A Company had to come forward again to secure the junction of forces between the 1st East Lancashire Regiment and the 9th Northumberland Fusiliers. The following day, the brigade was ordered to move forward again, but opposition was particularly strong and the division to the left did not get very far forward. The advance was only slight, but it was part of a general pushing back of the German army. It wasn't yet anything like a rout, but it was a promising start.

At home, the newspapers warned against speculation on how much longer the war would last. The editor of the *Cambridge Independent Press* wrote:

> '*The brilliant successes of our arms on the Western Front are necessarily reviving speculation on the length of the war, and it is desirable that we should keep continually before us the facts which must govern a settlement. The capture of prisoners and guns, the advance over miles of territory – all these things are excellent. What we require, however, is such a victory as will make Central Europe, which is, for all practical purposes, Berlin, powerless to carry out designs that are fatal to the free life of the rest of the world. There must be no foolish concentration of vision either on the West or on the East. It is the world situation that matters.*'

The rest of August proved quiet for the 11th Suffolks, with a draft of six new officers and 309 other ranks arriving on 28 August. Salvaging operations, to try and rescue what was possible of crops damaged by shelling and the fighting, were undertaken too. Many of the original men of the battalion that were left would have found this work similar to that which they would have been undertaking at home, if they hadn't been at war.

September saw the battalion withdrawn to divisional reserve, where they did route march exercises, practised attacks and listened to lectures. On 7 September, however, they moved back to the front lines and were heavily shelled through the following evening. C Company attempted an advance the following day, but were forced to withdraw under heavy machine-gun fire.

The next day, A Company was able to advance to the flank of Erquinghem. This was the place they had first gone into the trenches in February 1916, while attached to an experienced battalion to learn the ropes. It was also the place where they had been attacked and driven out in April 1918. Now they were back, though they were not able to take it immediately.

The following day, D Company was ordered forward to advance on Erquinghem. Setting off at 3am on a night/early dawn attack they were unsuccessful, being forced to retire by superior numbers of enemy troops. The attempt was 'reviewed' at 2pm, and two new forward posts were established 200 yards in front of the main line. They were relieved at midnight, so did not have to continue in the attempt to take the town.

After a period of training, they returned to the front lines on 21 September. The remainder of the month, both in and out of the lines, was quiet save for some action in the air, shelling and a few occasions when gas was released. On 23 September the 11th Suffolks were forced to watch helplessly as a British observation aircraft was set upon by German fighters and was seen to fall in flames. October began in much the same way as September, with a spell of training undertaken, focusing on open warfare exercises and the battalion going into GHQ reserve.

On 24 October they returned to the lines, once again attacking the German trenches. They attacked at 4am over the River Écaillon to secure the high ground. Objectives were taken by 5.45am, and two officers, ninety-eight other ranks, two trench mortars and seven machine guns were captured. This was, however, a much more difficult assault than some of their previous ones had been. Captain George Frederick Rimell Baguley was awarded a Bar to his Military Cross for his part in this action. The citation reads:

*'He led a company near Vendegies on 24 October, 1918, with great dash. He succeeded in getting them across the River Ecaillon very quickly in spite of heavy fire. Later he was severely wounded while leading his company to the attack of a crest strongly held by machine gunners. He continued to cheer his company forward until the crest had been captured and the machine gunners dealt with. His courage and determination were an inspiration to all under his command.'*

Acting Captain Sydney Ward Turner was in command of the reserve company.

> *'When all the officers and many of the non-commissioned officers of one of the assaulting companies had become casualties he took command of the two companies, reorganised them, and continued the advance, although he was himself badly wounded in the leg. After he had been wounded in the other leg he sat up in the open and continued to direct his command until compelled by faintness to desist.'*

Company Quartermaster Serjeant Harry Mann also had to take over command of his company when all the officers became casualties. After he did so, he reorganised the company and *'what remained of his company succeeded in overpowering the stubborn resistance of three machine guns and their teams, capturing a number of prisoners and taking his company objectives. Throughout the operation he showed great courage and determination and fine powers of leadership.'*

However, at 6.15am there was a heavy counter-attack on the left rear of B Company which was in the lead. Acting Captain Henry James Percival *'commanded an assaulting company near Vendigies on 24 October 1918, with great dash and determination. He crossed the River Ecaillon under considerable fire, and then reorganised his company and advanced against and overcame very strong resistance by enemy machine-gunners. Later, he was severely wounded whilst repelling a strong enemy counter-attack, but remained at duty.'*

The 11th Suffolks were forced to form a defensive flank, as the left of the brigade had been held up by heavy fighting and was unable to enter Vendigies. After *'three company commanders had become casualties,* [Lieutenant George Turner] *took command of remnants of the four companies and organised with great skill a defensive flank and brought fire to bear on enemy posts.'*

Warrant Officer Charles H. Causton won the Distinguished Conduct Medal for the same action:

> *'During the attack on Vendigies on 24 October 1918, when his company was severely counter-attacked from the rear, he fearlessly walked about the field under very heavy machine-gun and trench mortar fire, cheering and*

Victory Swimming Sports at Soham in 1919. (*Cambridgeshire Collection, Cambridge Central Library. Y.SOH K19 18625*)

Victory Parade 1919, St Andrew's Street. (*Cambridgeshire Collection, Cambridge Central Library. S.1919 13506*)

*encouraging the men; and assisted greatly in rallying and reorganising his company after his company commander had been severely wounded. His gallantry and determination were of very great value at a critical time.'*

Touch was gained with the left flank about 1900 hours and overnight the Germans withdrew from Vendigies. Even at this late stage at the war the Germans were able to put up localised heavy resistance and cause significant casualties – the 11th Suffolks lost thirty-three men killed on that day. This was far more than the ten killed on the attack of 8 August, and for less initial result than the former attack.

Among those who died was Thomas George Bovingdon, who left a wife and at least three children. Before being conscripted he worked as a tailor and lived in Woodford, Northamptonshire. Another was Ben Mingay, born in 1886, and who married Margaret Smith in Newmarket in 1912. Before the war he worked as a farm labourer and, though it's not certain, his service number strongly suggests that he enlisted in the first few months of the war.

A few days later, on 27 October, the 11th Suffolks went into action again, this time with orders to find out what the enemy strength was on the River Rhonelle, and to attempt to force passage across and form a bridgehead. They found the enemy in strength on both banks of the river, the northern bank being strongly held by machine guns. A Company managed, around 7am, to get a section across, but all were killed or driven back before this could be exploited and their original position was assumed again at 7.30am. A German counter-attack at 1pm was beaten off with artillery, but there was heavy gas shelling overnight.

Temporary Lieutenant George Gentle, who had taken command of his company during the action four days earlier when his company commander became a casualty, was awarded the Military Cross for his actions on 24 October and during this attack. He *'was ordered to attack a bridge near Maresches, and, though wounded, led a reconnoitring patrol down to the bridge and then led the company to the attack'*. George Gentle was a farmer in civil life. Born in 1897, he joined the Cambridgeshire Regiment on 2 February 1917. He was then discharged to a commission after being part of the 2nd Officer Cadet Battalion at Pembroke College, Cambridge. He went overseas on 20 July 1917, joining the 11th Suffolks in the field. Less than a month later he was wounded but remained at duty, and then, a few days after that, was wounded again with a gunshot wound in his right leg. He was later informed by the War Office that as the wound on 20 August was accidental, he was not entitled to wear a gold braid wound stripe for the injury.

They were withdrawn to support on 28 October, and then the following day suffered a direct hit on battalion headquarters. Two men were killed and eight injured, fortunately it seems none of the battalion officers were killed. A shell striking battalion headquarters could, and at times did, put a whole unit out of action for days while the battalion was reorganised. The Company of Royal Engineers raised in Cambridgeshire (the 203rd) suffered just that fate.

With the exception of supporting the 9th Northumberland Fusiliers in a successful attack where they were barely needed, except to carry supplies, that was the end of the fighting for the 11th Suffolks. They were ordered to march to billets in reserve on 1 November, arriving the following day, and on 3 November received a draft of 167 other ranks and began training for another attack. Rumours were rife everywhere of a possible Armistice, but rumours of an Armistice were common fare in France. However, these rumours were strong enough that the *Cambridge Independent Press* printed a denial on 8 November: '*Rumours were very rife yesterday afternoon and evening that an armistice had been signed with Germany that afternoon. Inquiries at the Foreign Office, Downing-street and the American Embassy, however, failed to elicit any of this.*'

This time, however, the rumours would prove to be correct. On 11 November, the battalion war diary reports:

'*Training continued. Battalion attack scheme. Telegram from Advance XVII Corps "Hostilities will cease 1100 hours today Nov 11th aaa Troops will stand fast on line reached at that hour which will be reported by wire to Corps HQ aaa Defensive precautions will be maintained aaa There will be no intercourse of any description with the enemy aaa."*'

A congratulatory telegram was received from the Lord Lieutenant of Cambridgeshire, Charles Adeane, and was published to all ranks. '*On behalf of the County and Isle Hearty Congratulations on the Glorious Victory to*

Return of Prisoners of War to Cambridge in 1919. (*Cambridgeshire Collection, Cambridge Central Library. S.1919 25817*)

Peace Celebrations, group photo taken on Parker's Piece. (*Cambridgeshire Collection, Cambridge Central Library. S.1919 28816*)

*which you have contributed so much.'* Tuck replied: *'CAMBRIDGESHIRE BATTALION SUFFOLK REGIMENT much appreciate your message and Battalion is proud to have represented COUNTY and ISLE in last smashing blow.'*

The war was over, though it would be some time before the men were able to return home to their families. Training continued despite the Armistice, although the focus switched on 13 November to ceremonial drill for the victory parades that were sure to come.

The *Cambridge Independent Press* reported on 15 November, its first issue since the Armistice:

> *"'You are entitled to rejoice. The people of this country and the people of the Dominions and our Allies have own such a victory for freedom as the world has never seen." So said the Prime Minister to the crowd assembled in Downing-street on Monday. It was the greatest day in history that any of us are likely to be permitted to see. The signing of an armistice is not the actual signing of peace, but no one doubts that the end of the worldwide conflict has come…. The Allied prisoners of war come home; the German prisoners remain…. More crushing, more humiliating terms have never been imposed on a defeated great Power. There is, as the Premier has said, real cause for rejoicing, because we have triumphed in a good cause, but in our rejoicing let us not forget those who have made victory possible, the millions of brave soldiers and sailors and airmen who have given their lives in the great cause, or who have come home maimed and suffering. Let us spare a thought, too, for the widow and the orphans, and all others who have been bereaved.'*

The 11th Suffolks remained in France for a time after the signing of the Armistice. In February they were presented with their colours, the ceremony taking place in a small French village in the Somme valley, near where they had suffered their greatest casualties in the whole of the war.

> *'The scene of the ceremony was some open country about eight miles from the historic town of Abbeville. It was a bright morning, but there was a vicious snap of cold in the air as the troops marched on to the impromptu parade*

*ground – a large stubble field, which provided just enough room for the impressive ceremonial of the presentation. Unfortunately, the battalion was not at full strength. Demobilisation had reduced its numbers appreciably and removed from the ranks many of those who had borne the brunt of the hard campaigns of the last four years. But the old discipline and parade ground smartness for which the 11th Suffolks are noted remained, and it was a stirring sight as the men with arms sloped took up their position.*

*It was just on mid-day when a sharp word of command from the Commanding Officer (Lieutenant-Colonel G L J Tuck, DSO) brought the battalion to attention. On the Abbeville-road to the left – outlined as all French national roads by a double line of tall, slender trees – a grey-covered car was drawing to a standstill. Out of the car stepped two men, whose red and gold caps distinguished them, even at that distance, as "brass hats."*

*They were Major-General F J Duncan, CB, CMG, DSO, commanding the 61st Division, and Brigadier-General B L Auley, CMG, DSO, of the 183rd Brigade – the 11th Suffolks Brigade. As the two Generals walked*

Officers of the 11th Suffolks at the Presentation of Colours to the battalion in France, 1919. (Cambridge Weekly News *21 February 1919*)

*across the fields the battalion which was drawn up in line, sloped arms. It was a fine piece of work. The long line of bayonets flashed in the sun as the rifles were brought to the slope, and the battalion made the movement as one man.*

*The General drew near. The Colonel's voice rang out. "11th Suffolks, General Salute: Present Arms." The men came to the "present" with a wonderful precision, the line of officers in front saluted, and the drums behind struck up.... The battalion was formed up for the dual ceremony of Consecration and Presentation of the Colours. The formation was that of three sides of a square. In the centre the flag was placed against piled drums. The chaplain stepped forward and read the short, simple and dignified consecration service. This was the prelude – and a fitting prelude – to the Presentation.*

*Major G West (acting second in command of the Battalion) stepped forward and handing the Colours to General Duncan, General Duncan in turn gave the Colours to the Senior Subaltern (Lieutenant H Williamson),*

Ceremony of the Proclamation of Peace. (Cambridge Weekly News *11 July 1919*)

Victory Parade in Cambridge outside Freeman, Hardy and Willis after signing of Armistice. (*Cambridgeshire Collection, Cambridge Central Library. S.1918 21181*)

Victory Parade in Cambridge, on signing of Armistice. (*Cambridgeshire Collection, Cambridge Central Library. S1918 12742*)

*who received them on bended knee. Rising, he stood at attention, his back to the Battalion, while the General addressed the troops.*

*The General's speech was brief and admirably suited to the occasion. He explained that the Presentation would have taken place much earlier, but for the fact that its Commanding Officer was on leave and desired to be present at the ceremony. In view of all that Colonel Tuck had done for the Battalion and his long association with it, it was felt that the ceremony ought to be postponed to enable him to attend. Of course that meant that some of those who had fought for the Flag were not there, but those who were left were receiving it on their behalf. The General reminded them of all that the Flag signified – the great ideals of King and Country it embodied. He urged them to remember the Empire it represented, the freedom so dearly bought, the sacrifice of life so freely made.*

*Colonel Tuck replied very briefly, expressing the Battalion's gratitude to the General for the presentation as the King's representative, and mentioned that some 200 officers and 4,500 other ranks had served in the Battalion, of whom over 40 officers and 900 other ranks had laid down their lives on the field of battle. He then called for three cheers for the General, which were lustily given.*

*This brought the ceremony to its most impressive and final stage. The Battalion was re-formed into line and sloped arms. As the Senior Subaltern turned round and marched slowly to his place in the centre of the line the Battalion presented arms, every officer saluted, and the drums struck up the National Anthem.'*

Returned soldiers from Fulbourn with wives and mothers. (*Cambridgeshire Collection, Cambridge Central Library. Y.FUL.K19 23941*)

Armistice Day in Wisbech, with the band of the London Scottish who were quartered in the town, at the market place. (*Cambridgeshire Collection, Cambridge Central Library. 6575*)

Scene at Cambridge Station when the cadre of the 11th Suffolks arrived home. (Cambridge
Weekly News *21 November 1919*)

Scene at Cambridge Station when the cadre of the 11th Suffolks arrived home. (Cambridge
Weekly News *21 November 1919*)

It was not until November 1919 that the remaining cadre of the 11th Suffolks came home to Cambridge where they were greeted by the Lord Lieutenant and their raiser, Charles Adeane, the Mayor, the Vice-Chancellor, and various other representatives of the town, county and university. There was a good crowd of townsfolk too, and many more would have watched as they paraded from the station to the Lion Hotel, where the returning soldiers were treated to a dinner. During a speech, Adeane promised the battalion would enjoy 'undying fame'. Sadly over the years the battalion has been largely forgotten, perhaps because of the Cambridgeshire Regiment's much clearer connection with the county, perhaps because of the way the men were scattered throughout small villages rather than being collected in one town or city. With the centenary commemorations under way, perhaps that will change.

# Chapter Notes

Sources used throughout. Unless otherwise stated in individual chapter notes, all information is from the following sources:

Information about the raising and individual members of the Cambridgeshire Kitcheners has been collected from the *Cambridge Independent Press, Cambridge Weekly News, Cambridge Daily News, Cambridge Chronicle, Herts and Cambs Reporter, Newmarket Journal* and *Wisbech Standard* August 1914 – March 1919. These newspapers have considerable overlap in the printing of official announcements about the battalion, but there are some variations. All are available on microfilm at the Cambridgeshire Collection, Cambridge Central Library, and most of the *Cambridge Independent Press* has been digitised.

In March 1918 a journalist from the *Cambridge Independent Press* was allowed to visit the front lines and speak with men of the Cambridgeshire Kitcheners. His report, spread over several weeks, gives an additional personal account of the battalion's activities, and from incidental details it is almost certain that the account was given by Gerald Tuck.

**War diaries** – these often contain similar or overlapping information at the various levels of command and have been used to supply the details of where the battalion was and some information about the fighting.

Battalion War Diary: WO 95/2458 and WO 95/3062
Brigade War Diary (101 Brigade): WO 95/2455 and WO 95/2456
Brigade War Diary (183 Brigade): WO 95/3059
Division War Diary (34th Division): WO 95/2432, WO 95/2433, WO 95/2434, WO 95/2434, WO 95/2435 and WO 95/2436
Division War Diary (61st Division): WO 95/3035 and WO 95/3036
J. Shakespear, *The Thirty-Fourth Division 1915-1919. The Story of Its Career from Ripon to the Rhine* (London, 2009) gives a good overview of the division's work.

**Private Letters/Documents**
Sidney Beeton's letters and an account of his service were shared by Tony Beeton, as was information about Arthur Elborne.
Bernard Hammond's family history was shared by Paul Hammond.

Oliver Hopkin's letters are available at Bury St Edmund's Record Office.

Private Papers of Private W.J. Senescall. Imperial War Museum London, Documents. 15087. Although every effort has been made, it has not been possible to contact the copyright holder.

Private Papers of Major General Sir (Cecil) Lothian Nicholson KCB CMG. Imperial War Museum, Documents. 9975. Used with permission of Michael Nicholson.

Frank Haydn Hornsey's journal is in the Bury St Edmund's Record Office.

Isaac Alexander Mack's letters are available freely as an ebook at Project Gutenberg.

Information from the 1911 Census, Distinguished Conduct Medal Citations, and Service Records, have been accessed through Lives of the First World War and are Crown Copyright.

Citations for the Military Cross and Victoria Cross can be found in the *London Gazette* which is searchable online. Tony Beeton has put all of these citations onto his website at www.curme.co.uk/102.htm#Cambs%20Suffolks%20Resource%20 Guide

Additional material used in each chapter has been noted below:

### Chapter 1
The controversy over Charles Adeane's letter to the King was printed in the *Cambridge Chronicle* February 1916.

Territorial Force Association Minutes, Cambridgeshire Archives, Shire Hill.

The Journal of William John Brand was compiled by O.C. Mayo, and published as *Journal from a Small Village: The diary of Pampisford's Postmaster William John Brand 1914-1918* (Cambridge, 2002)

Information on Balsham shared by Tony Beeton.

Later reflection on enlistment *Cambridge Independent Press* 1 March 1918.

A community has been created on Lives of the First World War to show the history of the nine men of Elsworth who enlisted together.

### Chapter 2
Additional information about Charles Adeane and Madeline Adeane and their family can be found in Claudia Renton's *Those Wild Wyndhams: Three Sisters at the Heart of Power* (London, 2014)

Mother's Union, *To British Mothers: How they Can Help Enlistment* (London, 1914)

*London Standard, How to Help Lord Kitchener* (London, 1914)

Allen Broman, *A Short Course of Physical Training for the New Armies* (London, 1914)

**Chapter 3**

Lord Esher on the Officer Training Corps in the *Yorkshire Evening Post* 18 July 1913

CUOTC's programme *Cambridge Independent Press* 17 January 1913, 24 January 1913, 7 March 1913.

The Marching Song was published in *Cambridge Weekly News* 1 January 1915.

**Chapter 4**

The full story of General Fitton's career can be found on Lives of the First World War.

Captain B.C. Lake, *Knowledge For War: Every Officer's Handbooks for the Front: Based on the War Office Syllabus of Training* (London, 1915)

CDS 383: Extract from *'Notes on the minor tactics of trench warfare'*. Imperial War Museum EPH 1484.

Edgar Wallace, *Kitchener's Army and the Territorial Forces: The Full Story of a Great Achievement No. 3* (London, 1915 or 1916)

Captain Basil Williams, *Raising and Training the New Armies* (London, 1918)

Information on football matches during training from Jack Alexander, *McCrae's Battalion: The Story of the 16th Royal Scots* (Edinburgh, 2003)

Additional information on Major General Ingouville-Williams can be found on Lives of the First World War. The account of the incident on New Year's Day was widely reported, this account principally from the *Derby Daily Telegraph* 4 January 1912.

Rudyard Kipling's description of signaller's training in *The New Army in Training* (London, 1915)

102 Brigade Orders (1915). The only copy I have found is in the Imperial War Museum, London, shelf reference 02(41).42 [ 102 Bde.]/3

Officer, *The New Army in the Making* (London, 1915)

A paper by the General Staff on the Future Conduct of the War 16/12/15, accessed online at http://leoklein.com/itp/somme/texts/future_conduct.html

**Chapter 5**

Report of death of Ian Duncan Claughton, the *Cheltenham Chronicle*, 18 March1916.

**Chapter 6**

CDS 383: Extract from *'Notes on the minor tactics of trench warfare'*, Imperial War Museum EPH 1484.

Compiled by J.E. Edmunds, *Military Operations: France and Belgium* (1922-1947), Fourth Army Tactical Notes are in the 1916 Appendix. Additional information from 1916 Volume I.

WO 158/327 Battle of the Somme: Summary of Operations, Raids and Patrols on Night 29th/30th.

## Chapter 7

Account of 1 July 1916 is put together from battalion, brigade and division war
diaries and WO 158/327 Fourth Army Summary of Operations, 1/7/16.

All other information is from local newspapers, except:

Letter from Maxwell-Lawford, reproduced in *In Memory of Osbert Harold Brown*.

## Chapter 8

All information from local newspapers and census records, except that on Sidney
Beeton which was supplied by Tony Beeton. To find out more about the individual
soldiers, please see their pages on Lives of the First World War.

## Chapter 9

Poem 'The Dying Bugler Boy' published in the *Ely Standard* 21 July 1916.

## Chapter 10

Letters to Captain Brown's parents published in In Memoriam book

Account of British soldier bathing in a shell hole next to a dead German from
Captain Tuck's account.

## Chapter 11

*SS 408: Some of the many Questions a Platoon Commander should ask himself on
taking over a Trench, and at frequent intervals afterwards,* Imperial War Museum
K 13/429.

## Chapter 12

Letters to Captain Osbert Harold Brown's family from *In Memory of Osbert Harold
Brown.*

Poem/Song 'Do Your Bit' printed in the *Cambridge Independent Press* 19 January
1917.

*SS 143 Instructions for the Training of Platoons for Offensive Action, February 1917.*
Imperial War Museum EPH 1558.

Letters to Alec Bailey's parents in the *Bury Free Press* 14 April 1917

Information on Royal Flying Corps operations from WO 158/320, Third Army
Summary of Operations, April 1917.

## Chapter 13

Compiled by J.E. Edmunds, *Military operations: France and Belgium* (1922-1947),
1917 Volume 1.

Lieutenant Daniel William Harper, Officers' Service Records, WO 339/108363.

John Norman Harmer's account of his capture, Officer's Documents, J.N. Harmer,
WO 339/5453.

Second Lieutenant John William Reynolds Hunt Officer's Documents, W.R. Hunt,
WO 339/41825.

## Chapter 17
War Office Document looking at the likely future progress of the War WO 158/20, 146 Note on the Present Situation.

Compiled by J.E. Edmunds, *Military operations: France and Belgium* (1922-1947), 1918 Volume I contains the warning to the Cabinet.

'What Think Ye?' Published in the *Cambridge Independent Press* 15 March 1918.

## Chapter 18
Compiled by J.E. Edmunds, *Military operations: France and Belgium* (1922-1947), 1918 Volume 1 contains details of the wider German attack an account of the 160th Brigade Royal Field Artillery's actions during it.

Instructions on how to create a bombing block *CDS 383*: Extract from *Notes on the minor Tactics of Trench Warfare*, IWM.

## Chapter 19
Information on Edward Trevor Bolton from the *Liverpool Echo* 23 April 1918.

Fighting State of Divisions WO 158/20.

The full text of General Haig's 'backs to the wall' order can be found here: http://www.firstworldwar.com/source/backstothewall.htm

## Chapter 20
Account of Arthur James Mason's memorial service: *Bury Free Press* 15 June 1918.

Information on Albert Edward Morfee's death in the *Hastings and St Leonards Observer* 11 May 1918.

Information about the 61st Division and their fighting record found in MA in First World War Studies, University of Birmingham, http://clevelode-battletours.com/wp-content/uploads/2012/10/61st-Division-in-WW1-UNIVERSITY-OF-BIRMINGHAM.pdf

Account of Major General John Duncan's death in the *Yorkshire Evening Post* 20 September 1948.

## Chapter 21
Ludendorff's statement about 8 August 1918 and his collapse of morale: Gary Sheffield, *Forgotten Victory The First World War: Myths and Realities* (Kindle Edition, 2014) Loc 4250.

Possible report of Private A. Standen being gassed the *Kent & Sussex Courier* 10 May 1918.

George Gentle Citation for Military Cross *London Gazette* 3 October 1919, and Officers' Service Records, WO 339/79355.

Account of Presentation of Colours Cambridge Daily News 20 February 1919 – cutting in Territorial Force Association Records.

# Suggested Further Reading

## The 34th Division

J. Shakespear, *The Thirty-Fourth Division 1915-1919. The Story of Its Career from Ripon to the Rhine* (2009)

John Sheen, *Tyneside Irish: 24th, 25th, 26th and 27th (Service) Battalions of Northumberland Fusiliers* (2013)

John Sheen, *Tyneside Scottish: 20th, 21st, 22nd and 23rd (Service) Battalions of the Northumberland Fusiliers* (2014)

Jack Alexander, *McCrae's Battalion: The Story of the 16th Royal Scots* (2003)

Peter Bryant, *Grimsby Chums: The Story of the 10th Lincolnshires in the Great War* (1991)

## Other Books

Tony Ashworth, *Trench Warfare 1914-1918: The Live and Let Live System* (Basingstoke, 1980)

Jeremy Black, *The Great War and the Making of the Modern World* (London, 2011)

Caroline Dakers, *The Countryside at War 1914-1918* (London, 1987)

Richard van Emdan, *Boy Soldiers of the Great War* (London, 2005)

Richard van Emden, *The Quick and the Dead: Fallen Soldiers and Their Families in the Great War* (London, 2011)

Victor Wallace Germains, *The Kitchener Armies: Story of a National Achievement* (London, 1930)

Adrian Gregory, *The Last Great War: British Society and the First World War* (Cambridge, 2008)

Paddy Griffith, *Battle Tactics of the Western Front: The British Army's Art of Attack, 1916-18* (London, 1994)

Charles Messenger, *Call to Arms: The British Army 1914-1918* (London, 2005)

Martin Middlebrook, *The First Day on the Somme: 1 July 1916* (London, 1971)

Johnathon Nicholls, *Cheerful Sacrifice: The Battle of Arras, 1917* (1990)

William Philpott, *Attrition: Fighting the First World War* (London, 2014)

William Philpott, *Bloody Victory: The Sacrifice on the Somme and the Making of the Twentieth Century* (London, 2009)

Claudia Renton, *Those Wild Wyndhams: Three Sisters at the Heart of Power* (2014)

Gary Sheffield, *Forgotten Victory – The First World War: Myths and Realities* (London, 2002)

**Kitchener's New Armies**

Peter Simkins, *Kitchener's Army: The Raising of the New Armies 1914–1916* (Manchester, 1988)

Tim Travers, *How the War Was Won: Command and Technology in the British Army on the Western Front, 1917–1918* (London, 1992)

Roni Wilkinson, *Pals on the Somme 1916* (Barnsley, 2006)

*Appendix*

# List of All Men Mentioned in Book, with Service Numbers

All the men of the battalion mentioned in this book are listed below, together with their service numbers. To find out more information about them (where this is available), they can be easily searched for on the Lives of the First World War site. Using the service number and 'Suffolk' tends to be the easiest way to do this. Officers do not have service numbers, however, so a search for surname and battalion usually works. They are all also in a community entitled 11th Suffolk Regiment, and all the men who died on 1 July 1916 are in an additional community.

13662 Private Harry Adams
15813 Lance Corporal George Allgood
14429 Private Harold Allgood
15887 Private Sidney Alsop
15885 Private William Alsop
20436 Private James Cecil Arnold MM
20345 Corporal Ernest George Ashman
Lieutenant Frederick Ashworth
14419 Private Harvey Askew
Major General B.L. Auley CMG DSO
Lieutenant Nicholas Beauchamp Bagenal
Captain George Frederick Rimell Baguley MC and Bar
15911 Private Alec Bailey
16414 Corporal Frank Predam Bailey
17141 Private William Webster Bannister
16910 Serjeant Charles Walter Barber
13777 Serjeant Reginald George Bareham
16349 Private William George Barker
45185 Private William Charles Barrett
28615 Private Joshua Barritt
17512 Private Walter Fred Barton
16315 Lance Serjeant Albert Baxter
15766 Private Sidney Edward Beeton
16427 Private Arthur Benstead
43603 Second Lieutenant (formerly Serjeant) Sidney James Ward Boggis
Lieutenant Edward Trevor Bolton

43030 Private Thomas George Bovingdon
15471 Private Albert Bradnam
15472 Corporal Bennett Bradnam
14434 William Henry Braybrooke
Captain J.H. Brett
3/9896 Company Serjeant Major William George Brooks
16301 Private George Brown
16603 Lance Corporal Leonard James Brown
Captain Osbert Harold Brown DSO MC
Lieutenant Cyril Lemmer Bryant MC
49950 Thomas William Bryant
8060 Corporal William Ernest Buck MM
15324 Private Arthur Bunting
49536 Christy Graham Burden
17667 Private John George Langhorn Burrell DCM
Captain Robert Vivian Burrowes MC
17245 Lance Corporal Henry Alfred Cage DCM
Captain Cyril Victor Canning MC and Bar
3/10337 Corporal Charles Carlton MM
13533 Warrant Officer Charles H. Causton DCM
15768 Private Joseph Chapman
16401 Private Frederick William Charles
14427 Lance Corporal Thomas Edwin Circus
Private G. Clanty – no other information about this soldier currently available.
Lieutenant Ian Drummond Claughton
31955 Private Charles Arthur Coe
20473 Private James Cole
24872 Lance-Corporal John Richard Collen
13814 Private Albert Conquest
17266 Private Warren Ivan Cook
16412 Lance Corporal Herbert Edwin Webb Cornwell
13661 Private Ernest Cox
16641 Lance Corporal Edwin George Cracknell
3/10029 Regimental Serjeant Major Crissal DCM
Second Lieutenant W. Curtiss
15770 Lance Corporal Thomas Charles Custance
16343 Private Billy Daniels
Second Lieutenant Desmond John Darley
14430 Arthur Samuel Dawson
15474 Private Percy Dawson
15760 Private Alfred Arnold Day
14431 Private George Day
13652 Serjeant Jack Day
15092 Corporal Sidney James Day VC

20502 Private Walter Day
13791 Corporal Walter George Day
14436 Corporal Herbert Desborough
16404 Private Alan Dockerill
16374 Private Jonas Dodson
3/9492 Serjeant Percy Albert Dowe MM
18636 Private Gadsby Dring
16587 Private Alfred Driver
14432 Corporal George Percy Driver
14425 Private Herbert Webster Driver MM
Major General John Duncan CB CMG DSO
17360 Lance Corporal Arthur Josiah Elbourne
Lieutenant Paul Vychan Emrys-Evans
Major W.A. Farquhar
24224 Serjeant Alfred Grant Rule Few DCM
Second Lieutenant William Moulton Fiddian
Brigadier General Hugh Gregory Fitton
13670 Private William Flack
13738 Private George William Flood
16440 Private William Bertie Fox
20572 Private Ernest Thomas Freeman
23752 Private Gordon Cecil Freestone
13795 Private John Henry Fromant
17271 Lance Corporal Arthur Gauge
16357 Private Stanley Gawthorpe
Lieutenant W. George Gentle MC
17079 Private Archie Gilson
Lieutenant Robert Quilter Gilson
13675 Private Sidney James Goddard
13589 Private Harry Goody
Brigadier General Robert Clemens Gore
Second Lieutenant Hugh Stevenson Grand
15610 Private Leonard Hagger
Captain Wilfred Rodenhurst Hall MC
15578 Regimental Quartermaster Serjeant Bernard Hammond MSM
20445 Private Arthur Hancock
20444 Private Henry Hancock
23687 Private Elias Hankin
13565 Serjeant Alec Hard
13571 Serjeant Claude Reginald Hard
13572 Serjeant Theodore Hard
14435 Private Edward Harknett
14433 Serjeant Richard Harley MM
Captain John Norman Harmer

Captain Daniel William Harper
15759 Private Percy Victor Harper
Captain Wilfred Ernest Harrison MC
23672 Private Arthur James Hart
23971 Private James William Hepher
Colonel C.T. Heylock
Second Lieutenant F.M. Higen
43467 Signaller Fred Hills
43488 Private Herbert Hills
16338 Private Harry Hines
15758 Corporal Wilfred Hipwell
13743 Serjeant Harry Hobbs
15833 Serjeant William John Honeywood MM
16336 Lance Corporal Oliver Hopkin MM
17046 Private Harry Hopkins
51289 Private Frank Haydn Hornsey
43478 Private Howard Charles Howlett
16235 Private Ernest Oswald Howlett
16581 Private Joseph Howlett MM
17240 Private Charles Hubbard
15702 Private Walter William Huckle
13785 Lance-Corporal William Horace Humphreys
Second Lieutenant John William Reynolds Hunt
3/10030 Private Harry Hutt
13586 Private Reginald Charles Impey
Major General Ingouville-Williams
53500 Private Alfred Isaacson
16601 Lance Corporal Anthony Isaacson
14306 Private Ernest Isaacson
17353 Serjeant Simon Jacklin
15899 Corporal Walter Jackson
1623 Private Stanley Jacobs
Second Lieutenant C.O.F. Jenkin
Lieutenant D.B. Johnson MC
3/10192 Company Serjeant Major Thomas Jolly
Second Lieutenant Clement Percy Joscelyne
15353 Lance Corporal Charles Keep
Lieutenant Colonel Kendrick DSO
24808 Private Arthur Reginald Kidd
21893 Private George Kidman
17366 Corporal Herbert Harry Kitson
17358 Private Walter Lambert
50211 Private Sidney George Lawrence
16275 Private George Lee

41861 Private Reginald Edward Lee
14046 Serjeant Reginald Levitt
15663 Private Alfred Aaron Linford
14190 Lance Corporal Samuel Stephen Henry Ling
23635 Private Edmund Looker
43885 Private Claude Lynn
14423 Edwin Alfred Lyon
16600 Serjeant Clarence Thomas Mabbutt MM
Captain Isaac Alexander Mack
8594 Company Quartermaster Serjeant Harry Mann DCM MM
Private Jack Mansfield – service number not known
17633 Private Harry Martin
15616 Lance Corporal Arthur James Mason
16552 Corporal Joseph Mason
Second Lieutenant V.K. Mason
Lieutenant Maxwell-Lawford
15618 Company Serjeant Major Stanley William Mead DCM MM
16820 Private Alfred William Medcalf
23301 Private Albert Edward Miller
16183 Private Charles Frederick Miller MM
18367 Private Arthur Missen
44036 Private Robinson Mitham
9124 Private Ernest Mole
42657 Private Albert Edward Morfee
16588 Private William Morley
Second Lieutenant T.M. Myers
201799 Private Claude M. Newman
General Cecil Lothian Nicholson KCB CMG
15583 Private Harry George Norton
16383 Private William Henry Palmer
16620 Lance Corporal Victor K. Pamment DCM
23511 Serjeant Arthur Pammenter
16659 Private Frederick Papworth
Second Lieutenant Wilfred Henry Parker MC
16814 Private Charles Edward Patten
17610 Private Ernest Harry Walter Pearson
Captain Henry James Percival
12461 Private Joseph Perry
13606 Private Wilfred Charles Pettitt
13574 Private Ernest Phillips
15357 Private George William Pink
Second Lieutenant R.T. Poles
17165 Private Joseph Pope
8748 Serjeant Leonard Pottrell

13573 Serjeant Smith Stevens Poulter MM
15811 Lance-Corporal William Pratt DCM
13542 Private Ernest Edwin Pridham
16325 Private Frederick John Prime
16333 Private James William Prior
Second Lieutenant F. Puller
13811 Private William Cupit Rash
Captain L.H. Redwell MC
Lieutenant H.A. Reed MC
16327 Lance Corporal Basil Augustus Reeves
Captain George Frederick Reid MC
15585 Private William Renshaw
43517 Private Ernest Revell
17522 Private Alfred Reynolds
Lieutenant Colonel Morris Ernald Richardson DSO
20150 Private Henry George (Harry) Rider
16577 Private Sidney Rolls
12183 Private Fred Rose
8520 Corporal William Rose DCM MM
15890 Private Harold Thomas Royston
16960 Private James Sallis
15792 Private William Saxby
13767 Private Victor Sayer
Lieutenant K. Scott-Walker MC
Captain Arthur E. Seddon
17037 Private William John Senescall
15879 Private Sidney Sharp
Second Lieutenant Cyril Sheen
24766 Private Albert Shipp
Colonel Charles Wyndham Somerset CB CMG MVO
24738 Private Ernest Frederick South MM
16272 Private Ernie Spendelow
49521 Private Arthur Cyril Standen
29222 Private B.C. Stocking MM
15880 Private Fred Sulman
16893 Private Allen Tack
13580 Private Bert William Taylor
16604 Private William Taylor
Captain F.L. Tempest MC
13625 Drummer Benjamin Robert Thompson MM
16321 Private William Webster Toates
Lieutenant Colonel Gerald Louis Johnson Tuck DSO and Bar
Lieutenant George Turner MC
Captain Sydney Ward Turner MC and Bar

13631 Regimental Serjeant Major James Tyrrell
18367 Private Joseph Utteridge
13536 Private George Warren
Major G. West
3/10089 Serjeant F. White
13822 Serjeant Robert Marking White
13813 Lance Corporal George William Whittaker
15818 Private Albert Wilderspin
14417 Lance Corporal John Wilderspin
15901 Private William Joseph Wilderspin
15636 Private Harry Wilkins
Drummer Arthur Wilson – service number unknown
13649 Private Robert (Bob) Wilson
15657 Private Bertie Oliver Woodcock
Captain C.H. Woods
Captain John Wesley Wootton
15845 Private Arthur Thomas Worland
15633 Private Harry Worland
22162 Private Herbert Worland
49277 Corporal Henry Worley
Major Andrew B. Wright MC and Bar

# Index